Dr Pierre Dukan

with the invaluable help
of Rachel Levy

The Complete Dukan
Cookbook

HODDER &
STOUGHTON

Contents

Preface

When my publisher suggested that I should start work on a new book, the one you are holding now, I told her that I was fearful of seeing my readers tire at last of my writing talents and, what was more, that I had already written a recipe book for them. In reply, this wonderful woman explained to me that it was not her idea at all; it came from groups of bookshops and from their direct contact with customers. These bookshops are insatiable, I thought.

'You are mistaken, Monsieur Dukan, it's not the bookshops that want another book but your readers. Yes, they do already have your recipe book. They are glad to have these recipes and they use them, but they want more. They also found your first recipe book a little austere, so they would love the next recipes to be in colour because they need photos to make them dream.'

I could understand her reasoning, but I remained undecided because, however successful my method has been in my own country, in France, I am well aware that success and being too much in the public eye are likely to annoy and antagonize. The relationship I enjoy with my readers and public has become, alongside my work and family, one of my main reasons for living. I live two-thirds of my waking life with my patients, readers and internet subscribers and I am convinced that they feature too in many of my dreams at night. Whatever criticism my detractors might direct at me, this public forms a community that, through its trust, support and warm friendship, has always kept me going.

I had an opportunity recently to make this connection when Anses (the French Agency for Food, Environmental and Occupational Health & Safety) produced a study looking at the potential risks in all current diets. Anses tested these diets in a purely virtual and theoretical way and I have already made my thoughts known about its overcautious and peculiarly defeatist results. Microscopes and magnifying glasses were used to detect the tiniest deficiency in the slightest vitamin while all the misery and distress of 'fat people' and the devastating effects that weight problems and obesity inflict on them were completely overlooked. In the meantime IFOP, the French market research institute, published a large independent survey which put an end to this non-event. Yet at that time I heard my rivals and detractors, and some journalists, keen to stir up an audience, lay their criticism on thick. I was able to measure the full extent of the common sense shared by all those who had lost weight with my method, and even more importantly their affection, during those few weeks. For me, this relationship of trust and affection is so precious that I did not want to provide any further ammunition to those people whom my success annoys by bringing out another book.

And yet, I did write that book, since you are holding it now. I made up my mind after meeting two people. One evening during one of my consultations, seeing a few of my books out on my desk, a patient asked me when my next book was due to be published. I have been treating this patient personally for a long time, so she knows everything about my diet and has all my works. I asked her in what way another book could be of any help or interest to her. And she replied with these words, which took me greatly by surprise and also made me think long and hard:

'Doctor, I really like coming to our consultations and being supervised by you personally, and as far as that's concerned you help me a lot. But at the risk of disappointing you, what you write has an even deeper and more decisive impact on me than the treatment you give me in our face-to-face consultations. I can afford to come and see you while I am losing weight but I know a lot of other people who follow your method just by using your books and they lose weight as easily as me and sometimes even more easily. I have all your books, but in each one you have a different way of persuading and getting your message across and so I will definitely buy your next book.'

That was my first shock.

On another day I went into a local restaurant where the owner came up to me as he recognized my face from the television and he thanked me for helping him lose weight through my books. As he had had to feed himself using my 100 foods, following my recipes had been easy for him and at the same time he had improved upon them using his professional know-how. He showed me his 'Dukan menu', which he gave to customers following my diet. We were chatting away when he said to me:

'What's good about you is that you aren't selling us anything.'
I looked at him, somewhat amused, and I answered: *'Are you joking? I'm the doctor who sells the most books in France.'*
And do you know what he said in reply? *'Don't confuse things! It's not you who are selling, Doctor, it's us who are buying!'*

So I decided to 'get writing' because I felt I needed to. I could see a purpose and I also felt that I was not reneging on the promise I had made never to write a book or get involved in anything commercial that was not directly and exclusively connected with helping my patients or readers.

In this book you will find over 200 new recipes and others too, presented in a way that will appeal to your senses. Feasting your eyes on these recipes will help make your diet a success.

I want to take the opportunity here in this introduction to tell you about a discovery. As I have spent so long working with overweight people, with my end purpose focused on helping them lose weight, my mind has always been on the alert to understand what it means to be overweight. Being overweight is a new, complex medical condition that encompasses the whole individual – their body, their metabolism and their psyche as much as the society in which they live. Being overweight has become a global problem and to interpret it as it appears to us today we first need to realize that it is an **extremely recent phenomenon**, scarcely more than 50 years old. Before the Second World War, there were only a few isolated cases of overweight people, a few affluent *bon viveurs* and some other rarer cases of people who were overweight for strictly medical, hormonal or psychiatric reasons. It was only from the 1960s onwards, and especially in the 1970s, that we started to see weight problems in their true colours – as a disease of society and even of our civilization. It was around this time that I started working in nutrition and my career became caught up with the emergence, then the explosion, of weight problems in all the developed countries. So, for the past 35 years, I have been actively involved in fighting this illness as well as attentively observing the way it has spread and developed, and this has allowed me to analyze the situation as follows.

The emergence of nutrition as a discipline based around calories

In the aftermath of the Second World War, with all the food shortages, you needed to be a prophet to foresee how abundance would lead to a devastating weight-problem epidemic. Nutrition was decreed a science, and to deal with weight problems it naively opted for a mathematical, calorie-counting model, i.e. low-calorie dieting. The theory was: 'If too many calories make people put on weight, fewer calories must make them lose it.' The first nutritionists tore off in this direction and gradually turned this idea into a dogma which has never been abandoned. In the 60 years that followed, each passing year provided a little extra proof that man was not merely a simple combustion engine.

In the 1970s, the Atkins diet attempted to break this dogma. Realizing the blatant inadequacy of low-calorie diets, Dr Atkins raised the stakes by abandoning calorie-counting in favour of food categories – i.e. the three universal food groups: proteins, carbohydrates and lipids (fats) – based on the fact that not all calories have the same impact on weight. Unfortunately, his diet imposed no restriction on eating animal fats, which meant it failed, and so there was a return to the tyranny of low-calorie dieting. The establishment has obstinately imposed low-calorie dieting and counting the calories in everything we eat, and to my mind this is the main cause for the weight-problem epidemic that been allowed to spread across the world and become the prime factor in mortality. Let us first lift the veil of secrecy concealing the true toxicity that lies behind these weight problems. For most doctors and the general public, we die in two ways nowadays, either from cancer or from heart problems. In fact this is inaccurate; **being overweight is currently the principal killer disease**. You will never hear anyone say that a person 'has died from weight'; rather the death is due to cancer, diabetes, a heart attack, a stroke or uncontrolled high blood pressure. However, behind all these deaths, a common enemy is lurking in disguise and pulling the strings – obesity, and before the onset of obesity, being overweight. Almost 80 per cent of people with diabetes and high blood pressure who suffer from strokes and heart disease are overweight. And very many cancers, including the most common and the most feared, are directly linked to being overweight.

Since the Atkins diet, other diets have appeared and added to its vision, such as the Montignac, South Beach and Glycaemic Index diets. Compared to low-calorie dieting, all these diets were a step in the right direction. However, the supporters of official nutrition, the people who had created the low-calorie method in the 1950s and who then became the guardians of its dogma, could never agree to give it up. Wedded to their positions, doctors and scientists continued and still continue to uphold this theory despite it being blatantly obvious that it has failed and is only making the weight-problem epidemic worse. This refusal to see what was happening and to draw conclusions from such blatant failure, with its tragic repercussions on the health and survival of millions of human beings, is to my mind a scandal. Today, nobody can say just how many thousands and tens of thousands of deaths across the world can be attributed to this blindness. Throughout these decades, official nutrition rested on its laurels, all the while stifling new talent and new diets that at their time heralded significant progress.

The first protein diet in France

When I created the first French protein diet, I engaged in an open battle against the low-calorie theory. I then positioned myself using a food-group strategy and chose the one that I thought best suited to losing weight. Fats are extremely rich and open the door to cholesterol. Carbohydrates are addictive and open the door to diabetes and compulsions. Proteins do not lead to any pathology; the only precaution that needs to be taken is to avoid eating too much protein if you suffer from renal failure. With this in mind, my method favours proteins as its driving force. For the very few days of the initial Attack phase only proteins are eaten and then vegetables are added to the proteins in the Cruise phase. In Consolidation, the third phase, in addition to proteins and vegetables you can eat fruit, bread, cheese, starchy foods and two weekly celebration meals. During the final permanent Stabilization period, proteins are concentrated into a single day, protein Thursdays.

However, as I developed my method, I saw and understood that my method was not restricted to this single concept of proteins. Throughout my life I have treated so many overweight people, I have spent so much time talking to them and I have seen them live their lives and come to me usually when adversity was forcing them to give up and put on a little or a lot of weight. For some it would be a huge amount. Given the number of cases I have observed and treated, I could see a common element emerge, shared by almost all my patients, which is hardly ever mentioned in scientific or public debates on this subject.

The common element systematically at work here is that people who put on weight are failing to find fulfilment, either temporarily or permanently. They do not get enough pleasure out of their lives, and life's stresses, strains and problems pile up. All the time I have been working as a doctor, at first in my consultations and then with my readers and internet users from the global village, the men and women who have come to me for help have done so because they were haunted by a simple idea. For them it was about getting rid of a certain quantity of 'ordinary, yellow fat' as if it were the contents of your kitchen rubbish bin.

In actual fact, this excess weight is only a material marker, a gauge whose hidden meaning is being overlooked. This fat store always reveals a troubled relationship with food. We never eat badly or too much without there being a reason for it. If you place your hand on a hot stove you will remove it immediately without even thinking about it. I discovered that each overweight patient always had some suffering, some malaise, some emptiness or something missing. I know that some of my readers who are overweight will not swallow the idea that they are carrying this suffering around. Probably because the word suffering is not quite the word that fits them, but there is always, and yes, I am saying always, a 'hole', an obstacle or more precisely some lack of balance in their lives which needs to be put right, some dissatisfaction that needs to be eased, alleviated and smoothed away. I have in mind a patient who was a powerful, rich, highly esteemed and fat man. He refused to see how his privileged position was making him isolated and overworked and sought all sorts of other reasons to explain why he was obese to avoid facing up to what in his eyes would have been deemed a weakness. In fact this man was suffering because he was deriving all his pleasure from a single source, one that others could see and envy, but it was not enough to make him happy.

This configuration is common to so many overweight people, this underlying suffering that needs to be put right and which is vaguely searching for its antidote. To me it appeared that this suffering is what is really responsible for people becoming overweight, the underlying reason for it. And I believe that all life is governed by a process of getting biological parameters back into balance, so I include controlling pleasure and lack of pleasure in this reflex that ensures our survival. So when the pleasure scales swing towards lack of pleasure and the body sees this imbalance as a threat, as a priority it will channel all its efforts into creating some pleasure as quickly as possible. And for a large number of people, the simplest and most immediate way of obtaining some pleasure is to taste foods that are as pleasing as possible to the senses, i.e. rich foods full of fat, sugar and salt, foods that 'make you fat'.

At this stage in my career, my approach had really moved on. As soon as I entered the medical field, I had the opportunity of treating very overweight and obese patients and this made me see for myself just how pointless the low-calorie method was that was being used at the time. Having seen that it was totally at odds with the psychology of overweight people, I very quickly turned my back on this method. So I left the world of low-calorie dieting and moved on to food categories and the three universal food groups – proteins, fats and carbohydrates. I was struck by everything that one of these food groups, proteins, could offer. I very quickly realized how I could use proteins to fight weight problems. **Proteins are clearly the only vital food group**, the one that man cannot synthesize himself. Without proteins, man will die. Moreover, unlike lipids and carbohydrates (fats and sugars), proteins are not meant to be used as energy to fuel the body, but as a component that helps the body tissues and organs to grow and repair themselves. Furthermore, and we tend to forget this given that we now have such wide access to comfort foods, proteins are also the most human of foods, the food **richest in meaning and the most emotionally charged**. Because during the 80,000 years of our prehistory, man became human through hunting, which was the only way of getting those vital proteins.

The success of my method, my books and my website has opened up a new dimension for me as I can now reach large numbers of people. I went from seeing tens of people in my surgery to getting feedback from almost 20 million readers living in many different countries and cultures. From such a wide population of overweight people, I was able to detect that there are **core behaviour patterns shared by those men and women who have been most successful in losing weight.** This made me realize that, when fighting weight problems, anyone who did not naturally and instinctively use these enabling behaviour patterns was less well equipped than those who did, and that it was vital to list and record these invaluable behaviour patterns so that I could understand them and integrate them into my method and so boost its effectiveness.

I was in no doubt about proteins. Analyzing these large numbers had only served to confirm to me that proteins were indeed the biological and metabolic driving force behind my method, a tool that worked extremely well but which I could still further improve upon by combining proteins with this new range of behaviour patterns that promote weight loss. In this way I grew used to seeing weight problems as an enemy that had to be tackled and this menacing enemy appeared holding a concrete weapon in its hands, which is food with its calories, fats and carbs and its power to addict.

At this stage in my thinking I realized that up until then the fight against weight problems had always been concentrated on calories or food categories; in other words, against the weapon and not the 'hidden hand' that was carrying and wielding this weapon. I discovered this hidden hand and analyzed how it operated by studying extensive populations of overweight people. This showed how weight problems are able to overwhelm anyone who is not protected by their '**enabling behaviour patterns**'. For a long time I had thought that such vulnerability was a result of being overweight. In actual fact it was the cause. The people who were losing the fight were those very people who did not have or did not use their enabling behaviour patterns. For me this marked a real discovery.

11 ways to achieve lasting weight loss through behaviour
How could those people who were not using their enabling behaviour patterns start using them again? I revised my whole method and built into it a series of pointers, catchy ideas, alternating sequences and ways of encouraging decisions to induce these behaviour patterns to resist weight gain. As it happens, these behaviour patterns all tend to strengthen overall motivation greatly either by lessening frustration or by generating

gratification. This strategy activates behaviour that creates the most pleasure, satisfaction, pride, confidence, self-esteem, well-being and joy in looking normal and looking after one's health. And, at the same time, it shapes and presents the method in such a way that following the diet creates the least deprivation, frustration, suffering and failure and with the least possible lack of pleasure. With the power of these enabling behaviour patterns working alongside the power of proteins, not only is it possible for people to lose weight more easily and quickly but at last they stand a real chance of not putting back on what they manage to lose. So what did I weave into my method to stimulate behaviour conducive to weight loss?

1. THE POWER OF SIMPLICITY
Simplicity underlies every aspect of my method and its diet. All complex methods have foundered. The first of them, low-calorie dieting based on calorie-counting, was theoretical, difficult and unreliable and it ran completely counter to the 'fat' person's psychology. First, it requires you to know the calories in each separate food item and to come up with a calculation for a meal with many different foods and ingredients that may be obvious or hidden, such as the fats in dressings. Other equally complex methods, such as the Montignac, advocate calculating carbohydrates, and the Glycaemic Index adds an extra level of complexity. The Atkins diet does not avoid complexity altogether either as it suggests you work out yourself how much carbohydrate you can have and still lose weight, which for ordinary mortals is quite impossible.

With my method I give you 100 foods, 72 high-protein foods and 28 vegetables. You are allowed everything on the list of 100 foods and any food that does not appear on it is not permitted. This clear, simple and concrete distinction does away with any difficulty and anyone using it can grasp the distinction in an instant.

2. AS MUCH AS YOU WANT – THE ANTIDOTE TO FRUSTRATION

You are allowed these 100 foods without any restriction on quantity, timing or combination. They are presented as comprising a buffet where you can help yourself to as much as you want and where you can help yourself again at whatever time of the day. But anything that is not out there on this buffet cannot be eaten. This is a way of offsetting what the diet may lack in quality by what it can offer in quantity, which means opting for a behaviour pattern conducive to increasing pleasure and reducing lack of pleasure.

3. THE FIRST ATTACK-PHASE DAYS PRODUCE GREAT RESULTS

The initial phase works with a range of low-fat, high-protein foods only. That the Attack phase works so quickly produces happiness and very real pleasure as it opens the door to hope, offering tangible success and confidence in a method that keeps its promises, and this tends to boost the dieter's motivation.

4. A TIGHT, PRECISE STRUCTURE AND FRAMEWORK

This is one of the method's strongest points for promoting behaviour patterns conducive to losing weight. The method is made up of two parts, one for losing weight and one for stabilizing the weight you get down to. Each part includes two phases and the four phases follow on from each other, starting with the strictest and ending with the most open. From the very first day of the Attack phase, the person using the method is looked after and is never, ever left on their own. The programme is presented as a complete and precise road map that leaves little room for choices and uncertainty. All the user has to do is settle into the little four-compartment train and let themselves be driven along, following a well-signposted route that reduces any temptation to stray away from it. Each phase has its own pattern, purpose, speed and results – you just have to let yourself be guided.

5. AN ALTERNATING PATTERN TO FIGHT MONOTONY

Weight is mostly lost in the Cruise phase. Cruise advances at an average pace of a couple of pounds lost per week; it is the most difficult phase because it is during this period that moments of stagnation are likely to occur. Alternating daily between the pure proteins diet and the proteins + vegetables diet works like a two-stroke engine. A very intense time followed by a gentler time will keep your metabolism on its toes, so that it does not have a chance to get used to dieting and resist it. Furthermore, following this alternating sequence means that you avoid sinking into a uniform, boring routine which you will want to escape.

6. THE IDEA OF TRUE WEIGHT

I devised this concept as I had come across too many people, especially women, who had failed to lose weight because they were unaware of the notion and consequently had set off on an adventure without knowing where they were heading. This True Weight is the weight you can attain and at the same time stabilize while achieving the best results as far as your health, beauty and well-being are concerned. The medical profession uses the international standard of body mass index, the BMI, to measure whether a weight is normal or not. Although this index is very useful for pinpointing variations across a population it is of far less use for the individual as it takes only weight and height into account and nothing else, not even age or gender.

I created True Weight as part of my drive to promote behaviour conducive to losing weight. True Weight is a scientific weight and at the same time a talisman that protects you from aimlessness and unobtainable goals. As well as weight and height, to calculate it I included 11 elements that are as personal as your age and gender. I took into account the background to your weight, everything that is hard-wired into your body's memory – the number of diets you have tried, the most and least you have ever weighed and the gap between them, which I term as your weight range. The greater your range, the more difficult it will be for you to get back down to the lower level. I have also included your cruise weight, the weight that you have stayed at for the longest time in your life, while also allowing for the weight you carry around with you in your head, your dream weight, which can be taken into account but without letting it dominate. Also, to calculate your True Weight, your family history has to be considered and whether there is any tendency to put on weight, and if you are a woman how many children you have had. Finally, it is important that your bone structure is also included, as a large skeleton is heavy. You cannot calculate this True Weight on your own as the algorithms required are too complex. So to know what your True Weight is, go to my coaching website www.dukandiet.co.uk and in 11 clicks you can enter your 11 parameters and find out what is the right and proper weight that you should be targeting to make your dieting a success.

7. FOR EVERY POUND LOST, 5 DAYS IN THE CONSOLIDATION PHASE

Once you have attained your True Weight how do you then land gently without crashing? This is the whole thinking behind my Consolidation phase and why it has been made simple, effective and accessible to everybody. It is a transitional phase between 'all-out dieting' and not dieting. It starts the day you see your True Weight show up on your scales. It is built around the base of proteins and vegetables eaten together, which I consider to be the cornerstone of man's food heritage. I give you *carte blanche* to eat these foods for the rest of your life and most especially to eat as much as you want of them, because the more proteins and vegetables you eat, the less you will consume of other foods that are always going to be less natural and by definition more fattening.

To this proteins + vegetables base, you add per day two portions of fruit along with two slices of wholemeal bread and a daily portion of any type of hard-rind cheese; and per week two generous portions of starchy foods and two celebration meals. This is all placed under the protection of your protein Thursdays. To help with behaviour, this phase has the advantage of being easy to work out: it lasts 5 days for every pound lost, so if you lose 10 pounds that makes 50 days, 20 pounds means 100 days and so on.

A further advantage is that once you have introduced all the foods in this phase you will then have what I term a 'normal' diet for a 'normal' person – a perfectly nutritional diet for an ordinary individual whose life is sufficiently rewarding that they do not have to use food to offset any damage caused by the strictures of our consumer society. The foods allowed in the Consolidation phase enable someone who has just lost weight to cope with a standard diet that is a little frugal by current consumer standards but which is normal and healthy and will guarantee good health and well-being.

Learning how to eat through eating. This transition phase lasts long enough to give the person going through it sufficient time to absorb it directly and learn about nutrition with reference to their own body, which is far more effective than learning about it from a book. By following this phase, a person will discover the comparative value of different food types based on when they are introduced. So, starting off with proteins only in the Attack phase, you understand the **vital** role they play since man cannot synthesize them and without proteins we would die. By adding vegetables next, you intuitively grasp their **essential** role. Then you have fruit which is **necessary**, bread which is **useful**, cheese which is **important** and now combines calcium, proteins, calories and pleasure, starchy foods which are **energy-giving** and, lastly, celebration meals which are about **pleasure from eating and conviviality**. As you move up the seven steps of this stairway, Vital, Essential, Necessary, Useful, Important, Energy-giving and Pleasure

food, the progression becomes hard-wired through conditioning and positive reinforcement, forming behaviour patterns that will protect and control your weight thereafter.

8. STABILIZATION IN 3 SIMPLE MEASURES, BUT FOR LIFE

This phase is my method's central pillar because if it does not hold up, all the rest will collapse. So I have built Stabilization around a whole array of behaviour patterns for success. Someone who has attained their True Weight and finished their Consolidation phase has proved that they are serious about being 'cured' of their weight problems. Having successfully negotiated the zone where the greatest immediate risks lie, their body is calmed and has lost its violent desire to exact revenge. However, this person will now discover a different perspective, namely endurance, as the journey no longer requires you to be just a sprinter; now you need to be a long-distance runner too. Yet the past history of someone who has been repeatedly overweight clearly shows that this is not what they are cut out for. This is why I have built them a framework and helpful behaviour patterns on which to lean. Using as a base what they have learnt in Consolidation about eating a normal diet, they can now eat freely without following a restrictive or imposed diet while still remembering everything learnt during Consolidation.

Since the person following the diet was once a 'fat' person and the period I am talking about here is none other than … the rest of their life, it is obvious that the edifice will not stand up unless there is a certain number of rules, guidelines and rituals.

However, to be able to keep to them over such a long time, these rules have to be reasonable. Three measures have the job of shoring up your

True Weight. These measures are concrete, simple, extremely effective, not-too-frustrating but non-negotiable. The first is **Protein Thursdays**, one day per week that is laid down to avoid repeated procrastination and then abandoning the idea altogether. This is a single day that marks a boundary which it is difficult to transgress, a day that ritualizes behaviour patterns so that you stick with the method. The second measure is **giving up lifts and escalators as well as walking 20 minutes every day. Eating three tablespoons of oat bran** daily is the third measure. The public has shown its support for oat bran as a foodstuff. In the space of a few years, after becoming part of my diet, it has turned into one of the best ways of promoting weight-control behaviour patterns, since the majority of people who use it when they lose weight continue using it for the rest of their lives.

A large independent survey carried out by IFOP on 1,525 people studied these three measures for permanent stabilization. It showed that 78 per cent of respondents had maintained their weight for nine months after attaining their True Weight and that they found it easy to keep to these three measures over the long term.

9. WALKING PRESCRIBED AS MEDICATION

For a long time, I made the classic mistake common at the time in the field of nutrition which was to 'recommend' exercise on top of dieting. I say 'mistake' because vague recommendations have no impact whatsoever on the person receiving them. In fact, there is no consensus on how useful exercise is for losing weight. From my own personal experience, I think that people who want to lose weight are interested only in the diet and scarcely believe that exercise can be effective. So when I ask them about exercise they skate over the subject and give answers

that are vague and difficult to quantify. 'Yes, I'm quite active' or 'I use public transport' or 'Doctor, you know when you've got kids you're always on the go.'

However, for the past three years I have become aware that exercise is not some add-on in the fight against weight problems. Lots of tremendously useful surveys carried out in North America have proved that not only does regular exercise burn up calories, which has long been known, but that it also stimulates the brain to secrete two vital transmitter substances: serotonin and dopamine.

Serotonin is the transmitter substance that controls our mood. It determines whether we experience life as pleasant and it positively colours our mood. Serotonin allows us to manage the balance between pleasure and lack of pleasure. Modern-day antidepressants are based on serotonin; they slow down its destruction and increase the quantity circulating in the bloodstream. If you look at the patient leaflet in a pack of such medication you will see that the antidepressant is called an SRI, a serotonin reuptake inhibitor. And it has been scientifically proved that taking exercise can produce just as much serotonin as an antidepressant, but without the downsides.

Dopamine is an essential transmitter substance, responsible for nothing less than giving you the motivation to live. This substance is capable of getting you up and going. It gets you out of bed in the morning, ready to enjoy life to the full, and it provides you with that vital energy that depressed people so sadly lack. Once you reach a turning point and make the decision to go all out to lose weight, it is this energy that triggers your decision.

Mindful of how vitally important these two brain transmitter substances are in prompting 'rewarding'

been prescribing walking just as I would medication, my patients have been walking. This is a very enlightening example that shows us how behaviour patterns can be acted upon. I am not advocating walking as the only exercise possible but I chose it because it is by far our most simple and natural physical activity. It can be prescribed to absolutely anybody, even the very seriously obese. You can go walking anywhere, at any time of the day or night, wearing whatever you want. And, most importantly, walking is the form of exercise you can most easily stick with over time, once you have made it part of your routine.

10. 1,200 RECIPES TO HELP YOU FORGET YOU ARE DIETING

If you have read my books you will know how much importance I attach to managing pleasure and lack of pleasure in our primitive brain. Man was not parachuted on to this earth as a clean slate and without any pedigree. He emerged from the animal world with two-thirds of his brain dedicated to managing his survival automatically. He shares the first third of his brain, the most primitive part, with that of all reptiles and it is the centre of his instincts. He shares the second third with that of the first mammals. Here is the centre for memory, conditioning, emotions and feelings. It is controlled by a decisive tool, pleasure or lack of pleasure, the carrot or the stick: 'You can have pleasure and be content if you do this, but if you do not, you will suffer.' Of course there is still the upper third, the brain of reason, logic, consciousness, speech and writing. This third is responsible for progress, science and technology, and for a long time now it has enabled the individual to achieve results through action. It is this part of the brain that mastered fire and invented the wheel and arrow. But as learning and science progressed, this brain switched allegiance and abandoned the individual to team up instead with society. It is this

behaviour patterns that really help people to lose weight, I decided to stop simply recommending exercise and started to prescribe it instead. It so happened that one morning, while treating a patient who was hedging my questions about what exercise she actually took, I grabbed a prescription and wrote out on the Japanese vellum paper as neatly as I could: 'You must walk 20 minutes a day during the four days of your Attack phase. During the Cruise phase increase this to 30 minutes, and if during this phase your weight should stagnate for more than six days, increase your walking to 60 minutes per day for four days to 'break through' the stagnation plateau. In the Consolidation phase walk for 25 minutes and in permanent Stabilization walk 20 minutes every day for the rest of your life.' And from that day on, since I have brain that has produced knowledge as well as an economic model for the world that no longer takes the individual's happiness into account.

The weight of happiness. You do not need to be a philosopher or sociologist to realize that it is becoming increasingly difficult to find fulfilment in our society, which operates like a huge anthill. One of the most reliable indicators of this divorce between the individual and society is the spread of weight problems in the West. However, we have not heard the last of the individual. Indeed, it is as if evolution had foreseen this divorce. Two-thirds of our reason for living and our decisions are controlled by that part of our brain that protects us automatically since it has no consciousness. Happily, this means that when I feel thirsty I drink and when I am about to run my heart starts beating faster without me having to ask it to do so. In practice, this all gets controlled automatically but 'without my consent'. What is less well known, but even more important, is that what holds true for the body and our main instincts also holds true for our emotions, feelings and our pleasure. You have no influence at all on when your emotions will burst forth and no power whatsoever to create pleasure at will. Pleasure and its opposite number, lack of pleasure, are there to manoeuvre you so that you act in ways that promote your survival and distance you from anything that might threaten it. Without such precaution it is likely that mankind would not even be here now, since our pride leads us to believe that we are masters of our destiny and that we decide it of our own free will. Individually, it is our animal brain that 'decide us'; our conscious human brain is present, smoothing the edges and pretending to make decisions, but it cannot take the helm or drive the engine. The engine and the energy it produces are in the hypothalamus; the helm is in the limbic system where steering the course between pleasure and no pleasure takes place.

To come back to our problem of being overweight. I have not been digressing, but I did want to lay the theoretical foundation that you need so you can grasp what is going on inside your brain and then draw upon this knowledge to lose weight more effectively.

I will once again remind you that if you have put on weight it is because some discomfort or suffering has led you to eat too much or to eat badly in order to produce pleasure as an antidote to what caused you to suffer in the first place. This all take places without you making any decision about it, and very often without you even realizing it, and just as often it will trigger in you very strong feelings of guilt.

Since you are reading this book, you probably at present want to lose some weight. A path lies before you that branches out in two directions. One way leads to dieting, and the frustration and lack of pleasure usually associated with it. The other leads you to the growing pleasure of rediscovering your well-being, of regaining your beauty and with it your attractiveness, and of knowing that you are looking after your health. Down this path too is the immense pleasure you get from success, from exerting self-control and from regaining self-confidence and self-esteem. The only problem is that we experience the 'pleasurelessness' of dieting in the here and now, whereas the pleasures we get from losing weight are conferred at some point in the future. And losing sight of the wood for the trees, your primitive brain is more easily tempted by immediate gain. This is animal logic, the logic of survival. And this logic does not reason, which once again proves that reason has no say when it comes to choices about life. This takes us back to our topic, this tenth way of helping us adopt behaviour that will encourage weight loss. How can we shift the cursor away from no pleasure and towards pleasure so that we lose weight more effectively and without draining all our motivation by the time we reach the crucial point of Stabilization?

My method offers 1,200 simple, easy, varied and tasty recipes whose role is precisely that, to tone down the frugality of the diet when it is followed without imagination or much thought. Ever since a public and then a community took to my diet, I have been receiving messages every day, mostly from women either wanting to share a new recipe they have devised or their way of adapting one of mine. If, with Japan, France is the country that has the slimmest and lightest women, this is because we are the nation that has most keenly resisted ready-made food and losing our structure around mealtimes. Most French people do not eat in the street while talking on a mobile phone. We still hold the record for taking the longest lunch break in Europe. These are all protective behaviour patterns that have disappeared from the American way of life, which partly explains the heavy toll of weight problems in that country. **In France there are still people who cook** and it is a huge advantage to be able to provide people who want to slim with recipes based on pure proteins and proteins + vegetables. Around 1,200 recipes provide a great source of pleasure and having such a wide range of dishes softens the restrictions that come with any dieting. What is more, once you realize that in just a few minutes you can make yourself an oat bran muffin, pizza base or some gingerbread and that even on pure protein days you can tuck into a delicious pudding, custard flan or mousse, these recipes become a real weapon of choice while losing weight.

And again, after you have lost weight, these recipes will help you stabilize the new weight you have achieved. Because once you have learnt how to find pleasure while shedding the pounds you will not forget the recipes you used when it was the dieting that was spurring you on. Finally, when a mother knows how to use tasty recipes to lose weight, her children are more likely to learn from them than children whose mothers are unaware of such ideas and rely all too often on processed, ready-made food. There was not enough space in this book to include the 1,200 recipes that comprise my method's culinary legacy but here you have over 360 of them, beautifully presented with wonderful colour photos, since presentation also has its role to play. *Bon appétit*!

11. DAILY, PERSONALIZED, INTERACTIVE COACHING – THE WAY FORWARD IN FIGHTING WEIGHT PROBLEMS

I know that the great majority of the ten and a half million French readers of my books have followed my method as a solo race with the road map I give as their only guide. That a small, simple paperback book could create such enthusiasm and produce such results is to my mind a miracle. After a decade, my publisher is surprised to see that there are always more people buying my books year on year. The method's great merit is that it is clear, simple and easy to grasp. The foods you are allowed are clearly identified and all others are ruled out in exchange for the freedom to eat as much as you want of what you are allowed, at whatever time and in whatever combination. Lastly, the method is a series of phases, starting with the strictest and ending with the most open as you go back to eating normally with three simple, concrete and logical rules to protect all you have achieved.

With this simple, effective road map in front of them, and surrounded by friends, family and colleagues who swear by the method's results, a majority of the people who read my books, feeling they are safe, decide to go for it and start dieting. I have never denied that losing weight is no easy task since we live in a world where consumption has turned us into spoilt children, a rich and highly stimulating world but one which is cruel and creates anxiety and little opportunity for self-fulfilment. People who have put on weight have done so to compensate for some suffering. Giving up comfort food means abandoning your shelter and becoming even more exposed, and to do this requires firm belief and being able to draw on vital energy. Not everyone who starts on my diet has such deeply rooted inner conviction or energy. And it is only once they have set out on the journey that vulnerabilities and intolerance to difficulties become apparent, and in particular the persistent problem of 'becoming bogged down' when weight persistently stagnates and will not give way even though the diet is being followed to the letter. The more weight you have to lose, the more time goes by, the longer these stagnation plateaux last and the danger of throwing it all in becomes greater.

Easy cases and difficult cases
Most people who set out on their journey resist these difficulties and manage to attain their initial goal, their True Weight. They then sail away from the calm coastline, out on to the open seas where a wide horizon awaits them. Keeping on course will mostly depend on whether emotional calm or turbulence lies ahead of them and whether or not they can negotiate life's difficulties.

Under pressure from stress, loneliness and emotional suffering, there are others who grow weary; they run out of steam and give up. With the accumulation of adversities and worries, worn down by stress and with life failing to offer enough pleasure and happiness, their certainties start to fade away. Food worms its way in and then takes over, making a mockery of any resolutions. Fighting on all fronts is difficult.

Each morning I receive lots of letters from satisfied readers, happy with their new weight which seems settled despite the passing of time with its ups and downs. They are my pride and my joy, so if you are one of them, please write and tell me because it recharges me with the energy I devote to you. And I need this energy because other countries with far greater weight problems are fascinated by what is happening in France, the country with the slimmest women, so now I have to travel widely to explain, win people over and cure them.

However, there are other letters in my morning post from people asking for help and also unfortunately some from people who have f ailed. For anyone who feels on the verge of sinking and sends me an SOS, I will say 'keep going', as I still manage to uphold the promise I made myself which was to answer anyone who asked me for help. These people include those who have given up before reaching their goal as well as those who have managed to reach it but could not hold on to it. It has to be acknowledged that they have been unable to make the journey on their own, and however structured my method may be, they need extra supervision and help. They need a hand to grab hold of and a voice they can hear and follow.

These vulnerable cases, these people who falter, I know them well because they are the ones who ask me for help and need personal supervision. With them we get to the very crux of the problem of being overweight – where the desire to lose weight and the pleasure losing weight affords are not enough reason to throw away the crutch that food can offer. The forces are equally balanced and can tip one way or the other. With this sort of conflict of opposing forces, being supervised, monitored and looked after competently and purposefully will make all the difference. I've spent 35 years working away at this, bringing all my help and empathy to weigh on the right side of the scales. However, what can be achieved in a one-to-one consultation cannot be extended to hundreds of thousands, even millions, of people.

So, for them, I created my daily, personalized, interactive coaching. Please take note! On the internet you often see all sorts of sites claiming to provide a service of this sort; a service that calls itself personalized and guarantees supervision. Let us take a closer look at any one of these larger sites but not the smaller ones as they do not have the financial backing. Even better, go on to the main American sites, some of which are entire industries and are listed on the stock market. Sign up with your partner or with a friend who is a different gender and whose age is as far apart from yours as possible. Sign up on the same day and as long as you remain members you will receive the same instructions and the same general advice. That's not all: the people sending you these instructions, meal and exercise suggestions have absolutely no way of knowing what you do with their advice for the simple reason that they never ask you, so you cannot tell them. To avoid your next set of instructions sounding ridiculous, they have to be kept as neutral and as wide-ranging as possible.

A service where nobody knows who you are, or what you do with the suggestions you are given, cannot be called coaching. Because I saw that there was this huge gap, I tried to create a truly personalized and interactive website. Thirty-two doctors worked alongside me, with a team of IT experts in artificial intelligence. It took four years to get what I wanted. When you subscribe to the coaching service we have set up, you have to answer 80 questions. They allow me to know who you are, how and why you put on weight, and therefore how you can lose it and stand the very best chance of not putting it back on.

With this innovative service you get an email **every morning** with eating advice – three menus for lunchtime and three for the evening. Your meals are carefully designed around your work, your tastes and eating preferences, where you eat, how much you need to eat at mealtimes and whether you need to snack in between and so on. You will also receive exercise instructions; one section is compulsory and the other optional, and they take account of how active you are and your age. And the third section of the email offers you motivational support based on your level of motivation, the difficulties you are encountering and any frustration you are feeling. This set of instructions is personalized; you need only to read it to understand this. These instructions will support and protect you.

However, I still do not know what you will do with these instructions – will you follow them or will you ignore them?

There is only one way to find out – you will have to **tell me**, by reporting back. So I make this possible for you: **every evening**, with seven clicks, you can – no, you must – send me back your weight for that day, with any eating lapses graded according to whether they were minor, average, major or binges (I keep a record as you are quite likely to forget). I also need to assess your motivation level, as well as your level of frustration, both on a scale of 1–5, and to know whether you have followed your exercise instructions, both compulsory and optional. Finally, you tell me which food you have most craved for during the day, because I can produce a wild card to put paid to these hankerings.

And when your report reaches me, I then have all the information I need to adapt **the instructions that I will send you the following day**. This way, I can congratulate you on your success and for keeping up the pace, or I can gently chide you and try to get you back on track again. You are right in thinking that if you have not followed your diet or not followed it properly, or have not taken any exercise, your next instructions will be stricter to make up for time lost. I will need to make you more active, inspire you to keep working at your diet, and if you are not managing to do this I will ask you to come and talk to me in person during a live chat session. Day after day, you will make progress, helped along by the dieticians on the site and the other members of the forum. Almost 95 per cent of subscribers who receive this monitoring manage to attain their True Weight. However, once it is attained the coaching does not stop; quite the opposite, it stays with you right throughout Consolidation. And if you complete this crucial phase it will be there to support you over the long term, throughout the Stabilization phase with its protein Thursdays, daily 20-minute walk and 3 tablespoons of oat bran.

With this kind of support, the path that leads to your True Weight becomes a valley that gets ever deeper and whose banks carry instructions, empathy, support and praise, and at times admonition to act as a safeguard so you do not wander off route. The real revolution, in behaviour patterns, is now possible because this sort of monitoring can be used to support very large numbers of members, daily and over a very long period. I am convinced that managing behaviour like this is the way forward since there are so many overweight people waiting for a solution. This is the solution I have devised for you on **www.dukandiet.co.uk**. The personalization and the to-and-fro monitoring are two features of the site that you will not find on any other.

In these few introductory pages I have told you the story of my work as a nutritionist and my continous, unrelenting search for a solution to weight problems. Now you know why I turned away from the calorie-counting strategy that was failing and instead chose one based on food groups. There are only three food groups on earth – proteins, lipids (fats) and carbohydrates. Of these three universal food groups I chose proteins as the guiding principle behind my method. Why? Because proteins are the only food group whose job is not to provide energy. In fact, not only are proteins a poor source of calories, they also are a poor fuel and I would like you to grasp fully the significance of what I have just written. This is a really important piece of information and it upsets those who have clung on to the calorie-counting dogma and who, in the 21st century, still persist in stating that, regardless of what food group they happen to belong to, all calories have the same value! Should any health professional ever tell you this, remember that:

- When you eat fats and sugars, you extract energy and therefore calories from these foods that you use to live and which you will store away if you have consumed more than you need. It requires little effort for the body to digest and absorb sugar; only 5 calories are needed per 100 calories of sugars consumed and processed. Slow-release sugars such as provided by pasta or lentils require a few more calories, but for white sugar, white bread and honey the number is almost negligible, and it is hardly any more for fats. If you eat 100 calories of butter or oil, your body will have to burn 9 calories for the other 91 calories to get into your bloodstream. But with proteins it is quite a different story. To dismantle 100 calories of these long chains whose links are firmly welded together, your body will have to burn 32 calories, and this is what happens every time you eat white fish, steak, prawns, egg white or low-fat yoghurt.

- When your diet is varied and provides you with a balanced combination of the three food groups, your body burns up the carbohydrates first, using either fast-release sugars to get instantly available energy or slow-release sugars for more sustained work. As regards fats, which are full of calories, once its sugar reserves are exhausted the body uses fats to top up any requirements. So what are proteins used for? Your body makes eager use of them to maintain your muscles, replenish your red blood cells and skin, make your nails and hair grow, heal any cuts and wounds and to ensure that your memories get imprinted on to protein molecules. However, as soon as your body has taken care of these vital functions, some part of the remaining proteins is converted into energy, but with considerable losses, and then the rest is eliminated.

You will now understand why I have given proteins such special status. I know that I can tell you to eat proteins without counting the calories because your body will extract very few calories from them, which means that you can lose weight quickly. The behaviour patterns that will best help you stabilize the weight you slim down to are the traces left in your subconscious and the habits learnt through the part these proteins play in your weight loss. You will not just understand or learn, you will truly experience with your own flesh and body the role that proteins play in your dieting adventure. When you go back to your normal life, from my diet you will retain a connection with and an appreciation of high-protein foods. The more they feature in what you eat in the future, the closer your metabolism will be to that of a person who tends not to put on weight, when once it was that of an overweight person. And it will be easier and simpler for you to stabilize your True Weight.

For me, this is how proteins and their particular characteristics have worked as a driving force. And then on to this nutritional and metabolic basis, in an intuitive and experimental way, I built and structured a method and in doing so I opened another door that led to behaviour patterns. What I realized was that my patients were neither robots nor combustion engines. They were human beings made of flesh and blood, emotions, feelings, habits, urges and instincts, magnetically attracted to pleasure and with an aversion to lack of pleasure. These patients, these human beings, touched me because more so than other people they seemed programmed to seek their comfort in food. The fact of belonging to the human race, being born into a specific family, into a particular culture at a certain time in our civilization, each time creates a unique brain that is different from all others. But this difference that, dear reader, makes you a unique individual is based on a universal and common foundation that also makes you a recognizable human being. This distinction is crucial, not only for understanding about losing weight but also for setting about losing it. The individual inside you has its very own relationship with food. This relationship may mean that you prefer savoury to sweet foods, or vice versa, it may make you snack, or not, outside mealtimes, make you want to eat more at midday than in the evening or the other way round, and you may or may not need to eat copiously to feel full up and at peace. All these differences can point to whether you have a propensity for putting on weight.

But over and beyond these differences, there is inside you a human being with characteristics that are common to all other humans, a restricted choice of characteristics but each one of them has absolute and inescapable power. This was how I came across these 'archetypes' in our relationship with food. These archetypes, these constants in our human nature, are in head-on conflict with our modern lifestyle which explains our current propensity for becoming fat and why we have a weight-problem epidemic. With my method, I have taken a stand and I have gone back to these fundamental human behaviour patterns as a way of helping to resolve the crisis. This is why I have shown you my 11 ways for impacting on behaviour, because they add a new dimension to my method. This new approach, which combines hunter-gatherer proteins and vegetables with 'enabling' behaviour patterns, will not only help you lose weight more easily, more quickly and without suffering from hunger, but it will also alter the way you use the different food groups subsequently and thereby increase your chances of not putting weight back on once you have lost it.

Among these ways of modifying behaviour, the 10th one on my list is simply about making use of one of life's mainstays, enjoyed by all animals and especially man, which is the pleasure we get from eating, and channelling this pleasure into losing weight. For as long as food was scarce and precious, up until the 1940s, seeking pleasure from food was associated with another mainstay in human life, our need to create something of beauty, which were both expressed in the art of cooking. Conviviality and a magical and religious element found expression through the gift of working with foods, flavours and textures and creating from them culinary works of art that thrill the taste buds. This has fascinated man since he gave up eating raw food and started cooking.

Conversely, in our collective subconscious dieting has always been associated with being punished and being forced to leave all these culinary delights behind. Over the past 35 years, through the friendship shared with so many creative, ingenious men and women, and from a desire to tone down the diet's dietetic approach, many recipes have been created. Today, I stand in awe at all that can be produced from using just 72 protein foods, 28 vegetables, oat bran, some herbs, spices, flavourings and sweeteners.

I offer this book and its treasures to you, my readers, my friends, to the millions of men and women I know only intuitively and not in person but to whom I feel deeply connected. Do not let yourself be put off by the wonderful photos; each and every one of you can make all these recipes. And, most importantly, please use this book; I can assure you that you will lose weight more easily, more quickly and without giving up hope. And if you wish to play your part in getting things moving and add your stone to the edifice as we fight to tackle weight problems, let your children taste these recipes too – and, even better still, teach your children how to make them!

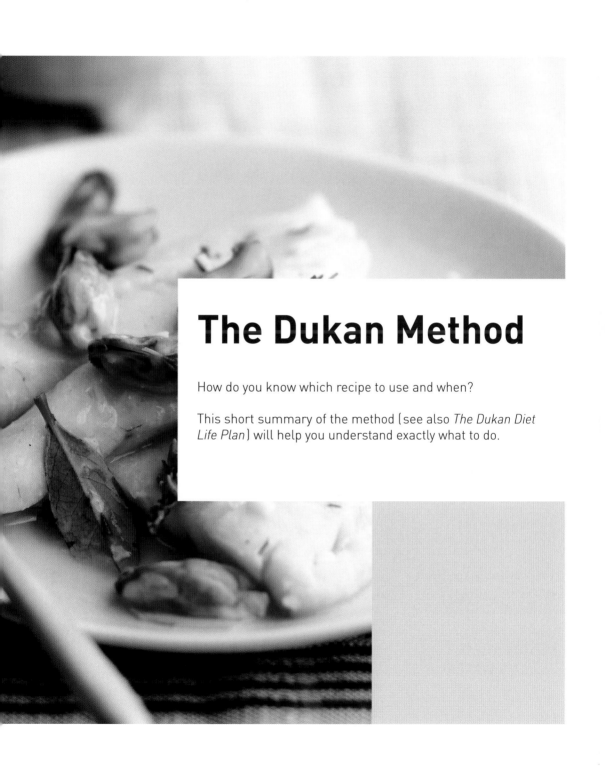

The Dukan Method

How do you know which recipe to use and when?

This short summary of the method (see also *The Dukan Diet Life Plan*) will help you understand exactly what to do.

True Weight

By definition this is a personal weight. To be relevant and workable, it must take age and gender into account. It must be able to differentiate between male and female morphotypes (body size and ratio) and in particular between the differing amounts of weight men and women need to lose. Similarly with regard to age, we know that, with each extra decade, a healthy weight for women increases by 800g (1lb 12oz) and by 1.2kg (2lb 11oz) for men. What is more, the need to achieve a target weight and the possibilities of doing so obviously differ depending on whether you are 20 or 50.

I recommend you to go to the websites **www.dukandiet.co.uk** and **www.myweightbook.com** (section: My future weight). On both sites you will find a free questionnaire with 11 questions. Fill in this questionnaire and straightaway you will have your very own True Weight.

The main principles

This tried-and-tested method is based on a certain number of key principles.

4 phases to achieve rapid and lasting weight loss

• **Phase 1 – Attack (pure proteins, PP)**

Only natural, pure proteins are eaten in this phase of your diet. Attack gets going with lightning speed and your weight loss will be very quick.

• **Phase 2 – Cruise**
(alternating between pure proteins, PP and proteins + vegetables, PV)

After the Attack period, when you started to wage war on your surplus pounds, comes a Cruise period, during which you follow a diet of alternating proteins. Your meals will consist of proteins one day, then vegetables and proteins the next. This way you will reach your target weight.

• **Phase 3 – Consolidation**

Consolidation is when you gradually reintroduce foods that have so far been banned. Once you have got down to the weight you want, it is important to avoid the rebound phenomenon; after any rapid weight loss the body tends to pile back on the lost pounds extremely quickly. So this is an especially tricky period and your diet is by no means at an end. For every pound you lose, you will need to remain five days in the Consolidation phase.

• **Phase 4 – Stabilization**

The permanent Stabilization period is just as crucial since it is decisive in determining the success of your diet. So that you do not regain any of the weight you have lost, you will need to apply three simple measures throughout your life. In particular, one day a week you will have to follow a pure protein day, preferably every Thursday. These protein Thursdays will protect you from regaining weight.

For zero frustration, 100 'as much as you want' foods

There is absolutely no need to weigh any food with this method. You can eat as much as you want of all the foods that are allowed. The

Attack phase, when you are allowed 72 proteins only, does not last very long. You will very quickly move into the Cruise phase with its 28 vegetables, when you are allowed 100 foods.

Oat bran

This is my method's star food and to my mind oat bran is the healthiest foodstuff there is. Oat bran aids digestion; it makes you feel full and satisfied; it reduces your cholesterol level and helps to protect you from diabetes and cancer of the colon. You will eat oat bran throughout the diet in varying quantities.

Regular exercise

You don't have to join a gym to follow this diet. All you need to do is include a minimum amount of exercise in your daily routine – a 20–30-minute walk every day and walking up the stairs instead of taking the lift or escalator.

How much oat bran should I have each day?

As you follow the method, eating oat bran will always help you with your weight loss and with your digestion too.

Phase 1 – Attack
1½ tablespoons per day
Phase 2 – Cruise
2 tablespoons per day
Phase 3 – Consolidation
2½ tablespoons per day
Phase 4 – Stabilization
3 tablespoons per day

Keep to a mealtime pattern

With your meals, it is important that you stick to a routine otherwise you will end up feeling frustrated after a few days. Sitting down to eat and sharing a nice hot dish is always a comforting and convivial moment. Of course, for the time being, your meal will consist of protein foods only. However, with the recipes that follow, you will discover how it is possible to come up with really tasty menus using just proteins. As you put your menus together according to what you enjoy eating, do try always to include a starter, a main dish and a pudding.

Phase 1 – Attack
(pure proteins, PP)

The pure proteins phase is lightning quick. By following it you will be in control of a mighty bulldozer that crushes all resistance in its path. So get on board!

As much PP as you want
Of all the foodstuffs we eat, only egg white is made up of virtually pure proteins. However, there is a certain number of foods that come close to the perfection we are seeking. The following list includes foods that are extremely high in pure proteins, which are allowed during this first phase:
• beef (but not rib steak, rib or any cuts for stewing)
• veal
• poultry (except duck and goose)
• cooked ham slices (no fat or rind)
• fish
• crustaceans and shellfish
• eggs
• vegetable proteins
• fat-free dairy products

You can eat as much as you want of all these foods.

A short phase to achieve spectacular weight loss
This Attack phase is a real psychological turning point and surprise for your metabolism. It should enable you to shed quickly and effectively the maximum amount of weight your body is capable of losing during this brief time span. You will be surprised yourself by it.

How long it lasts will depend on how much weight you have to lose and how many diets you have previously tried. Here are a few pointers to help you set yourself a clear goal and stick to it:

Target weight loss	Phase 1 lasts
≤ 5kg (11lb)	1 day
≤ 10kg (22lb)	5 days
10–20kg (22–44lb)	5 days
≥ 20kg (44lb)	7 days (after seeking medical advice)

Drink lots

To make sure you eliminate waste products efficiently, it is absolutely essential that you drink at least 1.5 litres – about 2½ pints – of water per day, especially at mealtimes. Don't forget to include any tea or coffee that you drink as well as herbal teas or infusions. Also remember to use water and any of the drinks you are allowed as a way of suppressing your appetite, because drinking helps to make you feel full.

Walk

Go walking for at least 20 minutes every day.

Proteins, a vital nutrient

As part of a diet, it is not dangerous to eat only proteins; in fact, quite the opposite is true, as proteins form the only group of nutrients that your body cannot synthesize on its own. By drawing upon its reserves, your body will find the carbohydrates and lipids (fats) it needs for energy. However, it is incapable of making proteins itself, which is why a diet lacking in proteins may be dangerous. Faced with a shortage, the body will take the proteins it requires for its survival from the muscles, skin and even bones. A diet must always provide at least 1 gram of protein per day for every kilo – 2lb – of body weight, and the proteins should be evenly distributed over the day's three meals.

What can you eat in Attack?

On the right you'll find a list of the foods you are allowed.

> Remember to use seasonings and spices to enhance the flavour of the foods you are allowed.

> Indulge yourself with fat-free dairy products so that you fill up on soft, creamy foods.

> Don't forget to use gelling agents (gelatine, agar-agar, etc.) to give your dishes more texture.

> And try out flavourings too (see page 41) so that you can concoct some tasty puddings for yourself.

> Take a look at the **pure protein** recipe section starting on page 74 – there are plenty of ideas and they will help avoid any monotony.

Offal

Calf's liver
Chicken liver
Tongue (calf's and
  lamb's)
Veal kidney

Cooked/cured meats

Bresaola (air-dried/
  wind-dried beef)
Cooked chicken/turkey
  slices (without any
  fat or rind)
Cooked ham slices
  (without any fat
  or rind)

Meat

Beef steak
Fillet of beef
Minced steak
  (max. 5% fat content)
Rabbit
Roast beef
Roast veal
Rump steak
Sirloin steak
Veal chop (trimmed
  of any fat)
Veal escalope
Venison

Poultry

Chicken (without
the skin)
Guinea fowl
Ostrich steak
Partridge
Pheasant
Pigeon
Poussin
Quail
Turkey

Fish

Cod (fresh)/Ling
Dab/Lemon sole
Dover sole
Fish roe (cod, salmon,
herring, mullet)
Grey mullet
Haddock
Hake
Halibut
Herring
Mackerel
Monkfish
Plaice
Pollock/Coley
Rainbow trout/
Salmon trout
Red mullet
Salmon/Smoked
salmon (and smoked
trout, haddock
and eel)
Sardines
Sea bass
Sea bream
Seafood sticks (surimi)
Skate
Swordfish
Tuna (and tinned tuna
in water or brine)
Turbot
Whiting

Seafood

Calamari/Squid
Clams
Cockles
Crab
Crayfish
Dublin Bay prawns
Lobster
Mussels
Oysters
Prawns/Shrimps
Scallops
Whelks

Eggs

Hen's eggs
Quail's eggs

Dairy products

Fat-free fromage frais
Fat-free Greek yoghurt
Fat-free natural yoghurt
(plain or flavoured
with sweetener)
Skimmed milk (fresh
or powdered)
Virtually fat-free cottage
cheese
Virtually fat-free quark

Vegetable proteins

Konjac
Oat bran
Seitan
Tofu

Phase 2 – Cruise
(alternating between PP and PV)

Those eagerly awaited vegetables are back on the menu again; you eat them on alternate days along with the pure proteins until you get down to your True Weight.

Weight loss over the long term

When you are in the alternating phase you will no doubt notice your weight loss slow down. This is quite normal as your body has to adjust to this new phase in order to take the diet in its stride over the long term.

Whereas your weight loss has so far been spectacular, all of a sudden your scales seem to be stuck. As soon as vegetables are reintroduced, so too is the water that a protein-only diet has artificially flushed out. The alternating phases are by definition less water-repellent than the pure protein phases. However, take heart. As your fat disappears, the weight you are losing is real enough; and, although it may be somewhat camouflaged by fluid gain, it is still going on without any problem.

Of course, on pure protein days you'll be delighted to see your scales point in the right direction again. As you get into your diet, you'll find it's like going down a flight of stairs – stagnation as you pause on a step, then suddenly you drop down to the next step, and so on.

How long should this phase last? That all depends on how many pounds you want to lose. It will last until you reach your target weight.

Alternating pure proteins (PP) and proteins + vegetables (PV)

There are different ways of alternating but the one that works best and with least frustration is the 1 day/1 day rhythm.

• 5 PP days/5 PV days

This is a strong rhythm, often too strong, and it requires unswerving motivation. Going for five days without any vegetables may seem long. I recommend it for the very severely obese.

• **1 PP day/1 PV day**
This is the most comfortable way of alternating and the one that creates the least frustration.

• **2 PP days/7 PV days**
This way of alternating is suitable for people who are fragile, elderly or who have little weight to lose. Weight is lost gently over a period of time.

• **2 PP days followed by a normal diet for 5 days**
This pace best suits women with a gynoid body shape, who have a slim upper body but saddlebag thighs.

100 'as much as you want' foods

You can continue eating as much as you want of the proteins you are allowed.

Now you will add certain vegetables to your menu: tomatoes, cucumber, radish, spinach, asparagus, leeks, French beans, cabbage, mushrooms, celery, fennel, all sorts of salad leaves, chicory, chard, aubergines, courgettes, peppers and even carrots and beetroot as long as you don't eat them at every meal.

You can eat as much as you want of these vegetables with no restriction on quantity but without overdoing it.

However, stay well clear of salad dressings as oils are not allowed.

Walk

Your 'prescription' walk should now be extended to 30 minutes per day.

You can also eat vegetables as much as you want

Provided you choose from the list on page 33, you are allowed all these vegetables, raw or cooked, with no limit on quantity. You can eat them whenever you fancy. However, do take care to follow the instructions about how to prepare them so that you avoid increasing your intake of fats, which must be cut out as entirely as possible.

What can you eat in Cruise?

Alternate between pure proteins (PP) and proteins + vegetables (PV), eating as much as you want from the list on the right.

> You are allowed 'tolerated' foods (see the list on page 43).

> For your **pure protein (PP)** days refer to the list of foods allowed in Attack (pages 28–9) and the recipe section starting on page 74.

> For **proteins + vegetables (PV) days**, take a look at the recipe section starting on page 214.

> Don't forget to use spices and seasonings to bring out the flavour of the foods you are allowed.

> Also remember to use gelatine, agar-agar and food flavourings to make yourself some scrumptious desserts.

Offal

Calf's liver
Chicken liver
Tongue (calf's
  and lamb's)
Veal kidney

Cooked/cured meats

Bresaola (air-dried/
  wind-dried beef)
Cooked chicken/turkey
  slices (without any
  fat or rind)
Cooked ham slices
  (without any fat
  or rind)

Meat

Beef steak
Fillet of beef
Minced steak (max.
  5% fat content)
Rabbit
Roast beef
Roast veal
Rump steak
Sirloin steak
Veal chop (trimmed
  of any fat)
Veal escalope
Venison

Poultry

Chicken (without
  the skin)
Guinea fowl
Ostrich steak
Partridge
Pheasant
Pigeon
Poussin
Quail
Turkey

Fish

Cod (fresh)/Ling
Dab/Lemon sole
Dover sole
Fish roe (cod, salmon,
  herring, mullet)
Grey mullet
Haddock
Hake
Halibut
Herring
Mackerel
Monkfish
Plaice
Pollock/Coley
Rainbow trout/Salmon
  trout
Red mullet
Salmon/Smoked
  salmon (and smoked
  trout, haddock and
  eel)
Sardines
Sea bass
Sea bream
Seafood sticks (surimi)
Skate
Swordfish
Tuna (and tinned tuna
  in water or brine)
Turbot
Whiting

Seafood

Calamari/Squid
Clams
Cockles
Crab
Crayfish
Dublin Bay prawns
Lobster
Mussels
Oysters
Prawns/Shrimps
Scallops
Whelks

Eggs

Hen's eggs
Quail's eggs

Dairy products

Fat-free fromage frais
Fat-free Greek yoghurt
Fat-free natural yoghurt
  (plain or flavoured
  with sweetener)
Skimmed milk (fresh
  or powdered)
Virtually fat-free cottage
  cheese
Virtually fat-free quark

Vegetable proteins

Konjac
Oat bran
Seitan
Tofu

Vegetables

Artichoke (globe)
Asparagus
Aubergine
Beetroot
Broccoli/Purple
  sprouting broccoli
Brussels sprouts
Cabbage (red,
  white and green)
Carrot
Cauliflower
Celery/Celeriac
Chicory
Courgette
Cucumber
Fennel

Why reintroduce wholemeal bread and not white bread?

White bread is not a natural food because it uses flour that is made by artificially separating the wheat from its husk, the bran. It is a food that is too easily absorbed. White bread is quickly digested, so it does not provide you with all the goodness you get from wholemeal bread.

Wholemeal or wholewheat bread contains a natural proportion of bran and the wheat germ is also intact. Bran helps to protect you from bowel cancer, excess cholesterol, diabetes, constipation and, what interests us here, it also looks after your figure: once it reaches the small intestine, the bran becomes sticky and traps some calories, which eventually get eliminated along with the stools without your body absorbing them. As wholemeal bread also takes much longer to digest, it helps to make you feel full.

Phase 3 – Consolidation

Once you have reached your True Weight, you must go through the Consolidation phase so that you don't put any weight back on.

For every pound lost, you spend 5 days in consolidation

The Consolidation phase is divided into two periods of equal length. If you have lost 10lb you will have to stay in Consolidation 1 for 25 days, then 25 days in Consolidation 2. If you have lost 60lb, you will have to stick with Consolidation 1 for 150 days and then the same again in Consolidation 2. But don't worry: even if Consolidation is a tricky period, you can eat foods again that up until now were not allowed. So your menus will be more varied and there will plenty for you to enjoy.

Reintroducing foods that were not allowed, but in limited quantities

As well as the protein foods and vegetables from the Cruise phase, certain foods are at last permitted again. However, you will have to follow a set of instructions that are specific enough to prevent you from losing control in any way.

• **1 portion of fruit per day (except grapes, bananas, cherries and dried fruit) in Consolidation 1, and 2 portions in Consolidation 2**
= 1 apple, pear, orange, grapefruit, peach, nectarine, etc.
= 1 dish of small fruit (e.g. strawberries, raspberries)
= ½ of much larger fruit (e.g. melon).
= 2 medium-sized fruit (e.g. apricots, plums)

• **2 slices of wholemeal bread per day (50g/1¾oz)**
You can eat them at any time of the day – for breakfast, as a lunchtime sandwich with cold meat or ham, or even in the evening with your portion of cheese.

• **40g (1½oz) mature cheese per day**
You are allowed to eat all hard-rind cheeses such as Cheddar, Gouda, Comté or Tomme de Savoie, etc.
>>For now, avoid fermented cheeses such as blue cheese, Camembert and goat's cheese.
>>Take care to eat this portion in a single go, so that you avoid making mistakes with quantities and nibbling at extra cheese.

• 1 × 225g (8oz) serving of starchy foods per week in Consolidation 1, and 2 servings in Consolidation 2

= Pasta (preferably wholemeal)

= Couscous, polenta, bulgur wheat

= Brown or wild rice

= Lentils

>> Avoid white rice and potatoes

• 1 portion of leg of lamb or roast pork fillet per week

One or two celebration meals per week

Once a week in Consolidation 1, and twice a week in Consolidation 2, you will be able to enjoy a meal when you can eat whatever you like without worrying about whether the foods are allowed or not. Please note that this means two meals a week and not two days a week. My patients often mix this up. But take note! You are not allowed second helpings of the same dish – for everything you will eat and drink, one 'unit' only. Make sure that you space these meals out to give your body time to recover.

One day of pure proteins (PP) per week

This day of pure proteins will guarantee that you do not put any weight back on. So you will be allowed only the Attack phase proteins (see the list on pages 28–9), with no limit on quantity. Make this little effort, because it is the only restriction in the Consolidation phase. As far as you possibly can, keep Thursdays as your pure protein day and avoid all 'tolerated foods' (see the list on page 43).

Walk

Make sure you walk at least 25 minutes per day.

Can I eat low-fat cheeses?

Most low-fat cheeses are of no interest whatsoever to the taste buds and you will be tempted to eat more than you should. However, Tomme de Savoie (a hard French cheese from the Alps) is a naturally low-fat cheese. It used to be made from semi-skimmed milk and, given the boom in low-fat products, some manufacturers have gone back to the original recipe, much to our great delight. This surprising cheese is a genuinely flavoursome, mellow variety with plenty of texture but without a rubbery taste. Tomme de Savoie is low on calories and saturated fatty acids, and we all know how harmful these are for the heart and blood vessels. You won't find it easily in supermarkets but try specialist cheesemongers. You can eat a little more of it – up to 60g (2¼oz) a day – without feeling guilty!

What can you eat in Consolidation?

At last the range of foods you are allowed is much greater. On the right you'll find a list of all the foods you are permitted, except when it's your protein Thursday.

> For your protein Thursdays refer back to the Attack phase list on pages 28–9 and to the pure protein recipe section starting on page 74.

> To get inspiration for some mouth-watering ideas take a look at the protein + vegetable recipes (page 214) and the Consolidation recipes (page 402).

> You are allowed 'tolerated' foods – see page 43.

> You can have foods that are still 'not allowed' for your celebration meals.

Offal

Calf's liver
Chicken liver
Tongue (calf's and
  lamb's)
Veal kidney

Cooked/cured meats

Bresaola (air-dried/
  wind-dried beef)
Cooked chicken/turkey
  slices (without any fat
  or rind)
Cooked ham slices
  (without any fat or rind)

Poultry

Chicken (without
  the skin)
Guinea fowl
Ostrich steak
Partridge
Pheasant
Pigeon
Poussin
Quail
Turkey

Meat

Beef steak
Fillet of beef
Leg of lamb
Minced steak (max.
  5% fat content)
Rabbit
Roast beef
Roast pork fillet
Roast veal
Rump steak
Sirloin steak
Veal chop (trimmed
  of any fat)
Veal escalope
Venison

Starchy foods
(1– 2 servings per week)

Bulgur wheat
Couscous
Dried peas
Flageolet beans
Garden peas
Haricot beans
Kidney beans
Lentils
Pasta (preferably
  wholemeal)
Polenta
Rice (preferably brown
  or wild)
Split peas

Eggs

Hen's eggs
Quail's eggs

Dairy products

Fat-free fromage frais
Fat-free Greek yoghurt
Fat-free natural yoghurt
(plain or flavoured
with sweetener)
Skimmed milk (fresh or
powdered)
Virtually fat-free cottage
cheese
Virtually fat-free quark

Bread
(2 slices per day)

Brown bread
Wholemeal bread

Cheese
(1 portion per day)

Beaufort
Comté
Edam
Emmental
Gouda
Mimolette
Tomme de Savoie

Fish

Cod (fresh)/Ling
Dab/Lemon sole
Dover sole
Fish roe (cod, salmon,
herring, mullet)
Grey mullet
Haddock
Hake
Halibut
Herring
Mackerel
Monkfish
Plaice
Pollock/Coley
Rainbow trout/Salmon
trout
Red mullet
Salmon/Smoked
salmon (and smoked
trout, haddock and
eel)
Sardines
Sea bass
Sea bream
Seafood sticks (surimi))
Skate
Swordfish
Tuna (and tinned tuna
in water or brine)
Turbot
Whiting

Vegetable proteins

Konjac
Oat bran
Seitan
Tofu

Seafood

Calamari/Squid
Clams
Cockles
Crab
Crayfish
Dublin Bay prawns
Lobster
Mussels
Oysters
Prawns/Shrimps
Scallops
Whelks

Fruit
(1–2 portions per day)

ALL EXCEPT:
Bananas
Cherries
Dried fruit and nuts
Grapes

Vegetables

Artichoke (globe)
Asparagus
Aubergine
Beetroot
Broccoli/Purple
sprouting broccoli
Brussels sprouts
Cabbage (red, white
and green)
Carrot
Cauliflower
Celery/Celeriac
Chicory
Courgette
Cucumber
Fennel
French beans/String
beans/Mangetout
Kohlrabi
Leek
Mushrooms
Onion
Palm hearts
Peppers
Pumpkin/Marrow/
Squash
Radish
Rhubarb
Salad leaves (curly
endive, lamb's
lettuce, etc.)
Soya beans
Spinach/Swiss chard
Tomato

Phase 4 – Stabilization

Congratulations: you have achieved and consolidated your True Weight and you can look forward to a new life and to eating more freely. Remember, though, that you will be able to protect this True Weight more easily if you stick as closely as possible to the eating habits you acquired during Consolidation. Stabilization comes with three simple, concrete but non-negotiable measures.

A protein Thursday every week

From now on you are free to eat normally six days out of seven, but this final permanent instruction will be all there is to protect you from your tendency to put weight back on. On this day, you will select the purest possible proteins. You may also on occasion use powdered proteins (but not just any old powder) if this can help you. As with the Consolidation phase, this instruction is of course non-negotiable – you must persevere with the habit you acquired during your diet.

3 tablespoon of oat bran per day

Eating oat bran every day is beneficial for your health and will help to ensure that your newly rediscovered figure is there for good.

A major contract – you agree to give up lifts and escalators

If you are not sporty, give up taking lifts and escalators and avoid using your car for very short journeys: in other words, get yourself moving! To motivate yourself, you can buy a pedometer to count the number of steps you take each day. You don't have to turn into a top-level athlete, but part of your daily routine is to get your legs working. You will be looking after the planet as well as your health!

Walk

Walk for at least 20 minutes every day.

What can you eat in Stabilization?

Except for one day a week, anything you want!

> Thursdays are strictly protein-only. Use the purest possible protein foods (see the Attack list on pages 28–9) and the **pure protein** recipe section starting on page 74.

> On your protein Thursdays, you are not allowed 'tolerated' foods (please refer to the list on page 43).

> Every other day, you can choose whatever you fancy from all the recipes that follow.

How to cook the Dukan way
Where can I find oat bran, flavourings, etc.?

Key ingredients

Oat bran

Be careful which oat bran you buy as the different sorts available are not all of equal merit. For oat bran to be medicinal rather than just for cooking purposes, it must be produced by grinding and separating the grain from the bran in a particular way, i.e. with specific milling and sifting. Working with Finnish agricultural engineers, I determined that this was M2bis milling and B6 sifting. Oat bran is available in all health-food shops, but the medicinal type is only to be found in some pharmacies and health-food stores and on the internet at: www.mydukandietshop.co.uk.

Wheat bran

There are few other foods that contain as much insoluble fibre as wheat bran and it is widely used to prevent constipation. Its texture and hardness can give some recipes density and consistency. It is available in health-food stores, in some pharmacies and on the internet at **www.mydukandietshop.co.uk**.

Sweeteners

I have selected different types of sweetener according to whether they taste best for the recipe or can withstand cooking. These sweeteners have all been subjected to extensive scientific research to ensure that they are completely safe to eat. With regard to aspartame, thousands of studies have shown that is harmless. A person weighing 60kg (9½ stone) would have to take 282 tablets or 169 tablespoon to exceed the recommended daily dose.

The sweeteners in this book are:
• Canderel and Canderel vanilla sticks (aspartame)
• crystallized stevia (a plant with a high sweetening power), which is ideal for all cold desserts or those that are slightly warmed. Stevia

goes particularly well with fruit recipes and is available in supermarkets, health-food stores and on the internet at **www.mydukandietshop. co.uk**

- liquid Hermesetas (cyclamate and saccharin) for any intense cooking
- Splenda (sucralose), which is perfect for desserts

Food flavourings

I have been working long and hard to find ways of getting the taste of certain foods without the calories that come with them. In the fight against weight problems, this extraordinary concept has a great future ahead of it.

Unfortunately these flavourings (there are about 30) are not widely available but can be found at **www.mydukandietshop.co.uk**.

Gelatine

This is a product of animal origin that generally comes in leaf form but you can also buy powder. The leaves need to be rehydrated first in cold water before being wrung out and added to hot, but not boiling, liquid. Once dissolved, the liquid is left to cool down, when it turns to gel. To eat Kosher or Halal, you can use gelatine made from fish by-products.

Agar-agar

This seaweed-based gelling agent has recently become available and is even easier to use than gelatine. To make custards, jellies and so on, you just mix a 2g sachet of agar-agar powder into 500ml (18fl oz) liquid, heat the mixture until it boils and then leave it to cool. The less liquid you use, the firmer the texture will be. Agar-agar is available on the internet at **www.mydukandietshop.co.uk**, or in health-food shops or those selling organic food.

Cornflour (tolerated)

Cornflour is a 'tolerated' food, which means you must not eat more than 1 tablespoonl per day. I gave cornflour this status as it is extremely useful for binding sauces and making desserts and light cakes. Cornflour does not contain any gluten.

Sugar-free, fat-reduced cocoa powder (tolerated)

This is the very essence of chocolate but without any of the fat or sugar. It allows you to produce wonderful, light cakes and biscuits without depriving yourself of the taste of chocolate. However, it is still

a 'tolerated' food, which means you must not exceed a daily ration of 1 teaspoon.

Not very widely available in supermarkets, it can be found on the internet at **www.mydukandietshop.co.uk** and in certain pharmacies and health-food stores. There are sugar-free cocoas such as the fabulous Van Houten, but as they are not fat-reduced they do not fit the bill.

Really useful utensils

Whenever possible, use silicone moulds. These new products have revolutionized traditional cooking methods, enabling you to cook, bake and mould your dishes without using any fat.

For healthy, tasty food you also need to use non-stick sheets for baking and cooking, non-stck frying pans, and a plancha (griddle). You can find silicone moulds and non-stick sheets at **www.mydukan-dietshop.co.uk**.

TOLERATED FOODS

From Phase 2 – Cruise, there is a certain number of basic foodstuffs and cooking aids that are deemed 'tolerated'.
• Do not exceed 2 portions per day.
• In Stabilization and Consolidation, they are not allowed on your protein days.

Chicken sausages max.10% fat (100g/3½oz)
Cooking wine, for cooking without a lid
   (3 tablespoons or 30g/1oz)
Cornflour (1 tablespoon or 20g/¾oz)
Crème fraîche 3% fat (1 tablespoon or 30g /1oz)
Fat-free cordials (20ml/¾fl oz)
Extra-light cream cheese 7% fat (40g/1½oz)
Fat-free fruit yoghurt (1 x 125g)
Fat-reduced, sugar-free cocoa powder 11% fat
   (1 teaspoon or 7g)
Goji berries (1–3 tablespoons, depending on the
   phase)
Low-fat grated cheese 7% fat (30g/1oz)
Merguez sausages, well pricked and well cooked
   (50g/1¾oz)
Oil (3 drops or 3g)
Original fat-free Actimel (1 x 100g)
Plain soy yoghurt (1 x 125g)
Ready-to-use gazpacho (1 glass or 150ml/5fl oz)
Ricore chicory coffee (1 teaspoon or 7g)
Soy flour (1 tablespoon or 20g/¾oz)
Soya milk (1 glass or 150ml/5fl oz)
Sweetened soy sauce (1 teaspoon or 5ml)
Tempeh (50g/1¾oz)

The essentials

Dukan bread, oat bran galettes, Dukan sauces, must-eat puddings, all the Dukan specialities that have made the diet a success!

Bread and galettes p. 46   **Sauces** p. 58   **Puddings** p. 70

1 serving
Preparation time
5 minutes
Cooking time
5–10 minutes
Ingredients
1 egg
15g (½oz) fat-free fromage frais
15g (½oz) virtually fat-free quark
1 tablespoon cornflour
1 teaspoon instant dried yeast
Dried herbs and spices of your
    choice
(Be careful not to add any salt!)

*Contains 1 tolerated food portion
per person*

Dukan bread (without bread maker)

Pain Dukan sans machine

■ **CRUISE**
■ **CONSOLIDATION EXCEPT FOR PP THURSDAYS**
■ **STABILIZATION EXCEPT FOR PP THURSDAYS**

Mix together all the ingredients and pour them into a rectangular tin measuring 15 x 20cm (6 x 8in). The dough must be at least 5mm (¼in) thick; if not, use a smaller tin.

Preheat the oven to 200°C/400°F/Gas 6, or you can bake your bread in a microwave. If using the microwave, cover the tin with clingfilm and cook on maximum for 5 minutes. Once it is cooked, remove the clingfilm straightaway and turn the bread out so that it does not sink back into the tin.

If using the oven, bake the bread for at least 10 minutes.

Oat bran bread (with bread maker)

Pain au son d'avoine en machine à pain

Makes 1 × 500g (1lb 2oz) loaf
Preparation time
10 minutes
Cooking time
30 minutes (depending on the machine)
Ingredients
200ml (7fl oz) skimmed milk
2 eggs, beaten
6 tablespoons fat-free fromage frais
8g instant dried yeast
240g (8½oz) oat bran
60g (2¼oz) wheat bran
½ teaspoon table salt

■ ATTACK   ■ CONSOLIDATION
■ CRUISE   ■ STABILIZATION

Set your bread machine on the 'quick wholemeal bread' programme.

Combine all the ingredients in the bread machine pan, place in the machine and start the programme.

Once the programme has finished, turn out the loaf and leave it to cool on a wire rack.

Using an electric knife or a knife with a very thin blade, cut the loaf into 12 slices or servings so that you get your daily portion of oat bran.

Store in a cool place and toast your slice each day.

Oat bran sandwich loaf

Pain de mie au son d'avoine

4 servings
Preparation time
10 minutes
Cooking time
4 minutes
Ingredients
4 eggs
4 tablespoons fat-free fromage frais
12 tablespoons oat bran
4 teaspoons instant dried yeast
Flavourings and herbs of your choice
(Be careful not to add any salt!)

■ ATTACK   ■ CONSOLIDATION
■ CRUISE   ■ STABILIZATION

Mix all the ingredients together.

Pour the dough into a microwavable container and bake the loaf for 4 minutes on maximum.

Turn the loaf out of the mould and leave to cool down. Cut the loaf into slices, which can be toasted if you prefer your bread to be crispier.

Bran and soya bread

Pain aux sons et au soja

Makes 1x 500g (1lb 2oz) loaf
Preparation time
10 minutes
Cooking time
35 minutes
Ingredients
200ml (7fl oz) soya milk
1 × 8g sachet baking powder
2 eggs, beaten
75g (2¾oz) plain soya yoghurt
200g (7oz) oat bran
100g (3½oz) wheat bran
1 teaspoon salt

Contains 2 tolerated food portions
per person

■ CRUISE
■ CONSOLIDATION EXCEPT FOR PP THURSDAYS
■ STABILIZATION EXCEPT FOR PP THURSDAYS

Preheat the oven to 200°C/400°F/Gas 6 and line a loaf tin with greaseproof paper.

Combine all the ingredients and pour the mixture into the cake tin. Bake in the oven for about 35 minutes.

Once the loaf is cooked, remove it from the oven and leave it to cool down.

You can also make this loaf using a bread maker – set your machine on the 'quick wholemeal bread' programme.

Oat bran blinis

Blinis de son d'avoine

4 servings
Preparation time
5 minutes
Cooking time
10 minutes
Ingredients
4 egg whites
12 tablespoons oat bran
8 tablespoons fat-free fromage frais

■ ATTACK   ■ CONSOLIDATION
■ CRUISE   ■ STABILIZATION

Beat the egg whites until stiff.

Combine the oat bran and fromage frais until you get a smooth paste, then gently fold in the egg whites.

Warm a non-stick frying pan over a medium heat and pour in a quarter of the mixture per blini. Cook for about 5 minutes then, using a spatula, turn the blini over and cook for a further 5 minutes.

To make a gourmet blini, add a few toasted linseeds or sesame seeds. You can also ring the changes by adding mixed dried herbs, some rosemary, a drizzle of lemon juice or even some nori seaweed.

1 serving
Preparation time
10 minutes
Cooking time
15 minutes
Ingredients
2 tablespoons oat bran
1 tablespoon wheat bran
1 tablespoon fat-free fromage frais
50g (1¾oz) virtually fat-free quark
3 eggs, separated, whites stiffly
   beaten
A few herbs (optional)
Salt and black pepper
Ingredients to choose from:
185g (6¼oz) tuna, flaked
Or 200g (7oz) smoked salmon,
   chopped
Or 150g (5½oz) ham (without fat or
   rind), chopped
Or 150g (5½oz) extra-lean beef (5%
   fat) chopped, cooked

Savoury galette

Galette salée

■ ATTACK   ▨ CONSOLIDATION
■ CRUISE   ■ STABILIZATION

Combine all the ingredients for the base (except the egg whites) and mix until smooth. Add herbs to taste and season with salt and pepper.

Finally, add the other ingredients of your choice, along with the stiffly beaten egg whites.

Warm a non-stick frying pan, pour the mixture in and cook over a medium heat for about 8 minutes. Use a spatula to turn the galette over
and then cook for a further 7 minutes.

Sweet galette

Galette sucrée

■ ATTACK   ▨ CONSOLIDATION

▨ CRUISE   ■ STABILIZATION

1 serving

Preparation time

10 minutes

Cooking time

15 minutes

Ingredients

2 tablespoons oat bran

1 tablespoon fat-free fromage frais

50g (1¾oz) virtually fat-free quark

1 tablespoon Hermesetas liquid
   sweetener

3 eggs, separated, whites stiffly
   beaten

Flavours to choose from:

2 tablespoons bitter almond
   flavouring

Or 2 tablespoons orange
   flower water

Or 1 teaspoon sugar-free, fat-
   reduced cocoa powder (not
   allowed in Attack or on protein
   Thursdays) plus 1 egg yolk

Combine all the ingredients for the base (except the egg whites) and mix until smooth.

Then add your flavouring of choice, along with the stiffly beaten egg whites.

Warm a non-stick frying pan, pour the mixture in and cook over a medium heat for about 8 minutes. Use a spatula to turn the galette over and cook for a further 7 minutes.

2 servings
Preparation time
20 minutes
Cooking time
40 minutes
Ingredients
5 eggs
250ml (9fl oz) skimmed milk
250g (9oz) pure protein powder*
A few basil leaves, chopped
Salt and black pepper
250g (9oz) fat-free fromage frais
½ × 8g sachet instant dried yeast
Ingredients to choose from:
A few cornichons
100g (3½oz) ham (without fat
   or rind)
1 bunch chives, chopped

Available in health-food stores

Fromage frais galette

Galette au fromage blanc

■ **ATTACK**   ■ **CONSOLIDATION**
■ **CRUISE**   ■ **STABILIZATION**

Preheat the oven to 200°C/400°F/Gas 6.

Whisk the eggs in a large bowl to make up an omelette. Gradually stir in the milk, the protein powder and basil leaves, and season with salt and pepper. Mix everything together vigorously with a spatula, so that the mixture is smooth.

Using the spatula, gradually work in the fromage frais and lastly the yeast. Then add one or more of the extra ingredients: cornichons and/or ham and/or chives. Pour into a flan dish and bake in the oven for 40 minutes.

Allow to cool a little and turn out while the dish is still warm. This fromage frais galette can be eaten either warm or cold, with an aperitif.

1 serving
Preparation time
25 minutes
Cooking time
45 minutes
Ingredients
2 tablespoons oat bran
1 tablespoon wheat bran
1 tablespoon fat-free fromage frais
50g (1¾oz) virtually fat-free quark
3 eggs
Salt and black pepper
5–6 slices bresaola
1 tablespoon extra-light cream
   cheese

Contains ½ tolerated food portion
per person

Bresaola galette

Galette à la viande des Grisons

■ **CRUISE**
■ **CONSOLIDATION EXCEPT FOR PP THURSDAYS**
■ **STABILIZATION EXCEPT FOR PP THURSDAYS**

Make the galette by mixing together the oat and wheat brans, fromage frais, quark and eggs. Season with salt and black pepper.

Warm a non-stick frying pan over a medium heat, pour in the galette mixture and cook for about 8 minutes. Using a spatula, turn the galette over and cook for a further 7 minutes.

Once the galette is cooked, spread the bresaola slices and extra-light cream cheese on top. To finish the galette, place under the grill for 5 minutes. Serve straightaway.

Makes 10 portions
Preparation time
10 minutes
Cooking time
10 minutes
Ingredients
12 small shallots
8 tablespoons wine vinegar
200ml (7fl oz) skimmed milk
1 egg yolk, beaten
Salt and black pepper

Shallot sauce

Sauce à l'échalote

■ ATTACK   ▨ CONSOLIDATION
▨ CRUISE   ■ STABILIZATION

Peel and chop the shallots and place in a saucepan with the vinegar. Boil for 10 minutes.

Remove from the heat and add the milk and egg yolk, stirring vigorously. Season with salt and pepper to taste.

Serve immediately.

Makes 5 portions
Preparation time
10 minutes
Cooking time
15 minutes
Ingredients
2 tablespoons tomato purée
4 tablespoons skimmed milk
7 small cornichons, chopped
12 capers
Salt and black pepper

Caper sauce

Sauce aux câpres

■ ATTACK   ▨ CONSOLIDATION
▨ CRUISE   ■ STABILIZATION

Mix together the tomato purée and milk. Add 100ml (3½fl oz) water and the cornichons.

Boil for 15 minutes and then add the capers, salt and pepper.

Serve straight away.

Makes 2 portions
Preparation time
5 minutes
Refrigeration time
15 minutes
Ingredients
100g (3½oz) fat-free fromage frais
Juice of ½ lemon
Salt and black pepper
2 small onions (or parsley), finely
   chopped
½ fennel bulb, finely chopped
1 teaspoon finely chopped basil

Fromage frais and fennel sauce

Sauce au fromage blanc

■ **ATTACK**   ■ **CONSOLIDATION**
■ **CRUISE**   ■ **STABILIZATION**

Mix together the fromage frais and lemon juice. Season with salt and pepper.

Add the onions (or parsley), fennel and basil.

Mix everything together thoroughly and place in the fridge for at least 15 minutes, until ready to serve.

Makes 4 portions
Preparation time
10 minutes
Cooking time
1 minute
Ingredients
100g (3½oz) spinach
Salt
2 tablespoons fat-free yoghurt
200ml (7fl oz) low-salt chicken stock
Pinch of grated nutmeg

Spinach sauce
Sauce aux épinards

■ **CRUISE PV**
■ **CONSOLIDATION EXCEPT FOR PP THURSDAYS**
■ **STABILIZATION EXCEPT FOR PP THURSDAYS**

Wash the spinach and quickly blanch it in salted boiling water. Drain well and then blend it in a food processor, or chop finely.

Add the yoghurt, then gradually stir in the chicken stock. Cook for 1 minute over a high heat.

Add the pinch of nutmeg and salt to taste.

Makes 4 portions
Preparation time
6 minutes
Cooking time
4–5 minutes
Ingredients
2 tablespoons cornflour
500ml (18fl oz) skimmed milk
Pinch of grated nutmeg
Salt and black pepper

Contains ½ tolerated food portion per person

Dukan béchamel sauce

Sauce béchamel Dukan

■ CRUISE
■ CONSOLIDATION EXCEPT FOR PP THURSDAYS
■ STABILIZATION EXCEPT FOR PP THURSDAYS

In a saucepan, gradually whisk the cornflour into the cold milk until the mixture is smooth.

Heat the milk over a low heat until the sauce thickens, stirring all the time with a wooden spoon.

Add nutmeg, salt and pepper to taste.

White sauce
Sauce blanche

Makes 3 portions
Preparation time
15 minutes
Cooking time
3 minutes
Ingredients
250ml (9fl oz) low-salt chicken stock
2 tablespoons skimmed milk
1 tablespoon cornflour
Salt and black pepper
Pinch of grated nutmeg

*Contains 1/3 tolerated food portion
per person*

■ CRUISE
■ CONSOLIDATION EXCEPT FOR PP THURSDAYS
■ STABILIZATION EXCEPT FOR PP THURSDAYS

In a saucepan mix together the cold stock and milk, then gradually blend in the cornflour.

Warm the mixture over a gentle heat until it starts to thicken, stirring gently with a wooden spoon. Then remove the pan from the heat and season with salt and black pepper.

Add the grated nutmeg.

Lemon and chive sauce
Sauce citron

Makes 4 portions
Preparation time
10 minutes
Ingredients
1 lemon
300g (10½oz) fat-free yoghurt
1 bunch chives
Salt and black pepper

■ ATTACK   ■ CONSOLIDATION
■ CRUISE   ■ STABILIZATION

Squeeze the lemon and stir the juice into the yoghurt.

Finely chop the chives and add them to the sauce.

Season with salt and pepper.

Mustard sauce

Sauce moutarde

Makes 8 portions
Preparation time
10 minutes
Cooking time
5 minutes
Ingredients
2 teaspoons cornflour
1 hard-boiled egg yolk
2 teaspoons cider vinegar
2 teaspoons mustard
A few herbs of your choice,
    chopped
Salt and black pepper

■ **ATTACK**   ▨ **CONSOLIDATION**
■ **CRUISE**   ■ **STABILIZATION**

Mix the cornflour with 1 tablespoon cold water, then whisk this paste into 200ml (7fl oz) water and bring to the boil in a small saucepan. Simmer briefly, then remove from the heat and leave to cool.

Blend the egg yolk with the vinegar and mustard and work this into the diluted cornflour. Finally add the herbs and some salt and pepper.

If the sauce does not seem runny enough, add a little more vinegar.

Gribiche sauce

Sauce gribiche

Makes 8 portions
Preparation time
10 minutes
Ingredients
1 teaspoon mustard
1 tablespoon cider vinegar
Salt and black pepper
2 tablespoons tarragon-flavoured oil
250g (9oz) fat-free fromage frais
2 hard-boiled eggs, chopped
1 shallot, chopped
3 cornichons, finely diced
Leaves from few sprigs of tarragon,
    chopped

■ **ATTACK**   ▨ **CONSOLIDATION**
■ **CRUISE**   ■ **STABILIZATION**

Put the mustard, vinegar, salt and pepper in a bowl and emulsify by slowly adding the oil.

Gradually add the fromage frais, then mix in the chopped hard-boiled eggs, shallot, cornichons and tarragon.

Adjust the seasoning to taste.

Hollandaise sauce

Sauce hollandaise

Makes 2 portions
Preparation time
15 minutes
Cooking time
5 minutes
Ingredients
1 egg
1 teaspoon mustard
1 tablespoon skimmed milk
1 teaspoon lemon juice
Salt and black pepper

■ **ATTACK**   ■ **CONSOLIDATION**
■ **CRUISE**   ■ **STABILIZATION**

Separate the egg white from the yolk.

Put the egg yolk, mustard and milk in a bowl in a bain-marie and whisk vigorously until the sauce thickens without curdling. Remove from the heat while continuing to beat the sauce and add the lemon juice and some salt and black pepper.

Beat the egg white until stiff and carefully fold into the sauce. Adjust the seasoning.

Maya's sauce

Sauce Maya

Makes 6 portions
Preparation time
5 minutes
Ingredients
1 tablespoon mustard
5 tablespoons balsamic vinegar
1 teaspoon vegetable oil
1 garlic clove, crushed
7 basil leaves, chopped
Salt and black pepper

■ **ATTACK**   ■ **CONSOLIDATION**
■ **CRUISE**   ■ **STABILIZATION**

Take a small glass jar with a lid and put all the ingredients into it. Add 1 tablespoonful water.

Close the lid and shake vigorously.

Store in the fridge to use as needed.

 Maya is my daughter and she and her brother, Sacha, are my life's greatest achievements. This sauce had to be named after Maya simply because, following my advice, she was the one who created it and for years we've been enjoying it every day. Which tells you, dear readers, how happy I am to share this sauce recipe with you now.

Makes 10 portions
Preparation time
15 minutes
Cooking time
50 minutes
Ingredients
1 small onion, finely chopped
1 garlic clove, finely chopped
1 small tin tomato purée
2 tablespoons diet tomato ketchup
1 tin diet cola
1 tablespoon mustard
1 tablespoon Worcestershire sauce
3 tablespoons cider vinegar
1 teaspoon paprika
Grated zest of ¼ unwaxed orange
A few cloves
Salt and black pepper

Papa-U barbecue sauce

Sauce Papa-U barbecue

■ **ATTACK**   ■ **CONSOLIDATION**
■ **CRUISE**   ■ **STABILIZATION**

Fry the onion for 3–5 minutes in a high-sided non-stick frying pan. Add the garlic and cook for a further 1–2 minutes.

Meanwhile, mix the rest of the ingredients together in a bowl along with half a glass of water.

Pour this mixture into the frying pan. Stir everything together and leave to simmer over a gentle heat for 45 minutes until all the flavours have had time to develop and the sauce has reduced.

Makes 4 portions
Preparation time
10 minutes
Ingredients
3 egg yolks, at room temperature
3 tablespoon Dijon mustard
Salt and black pepper
Pinch of chopped parsley or chives
   (optional)
9 tablespoons fat-free fromage frais
   or quark

Dukan mayonnaise

Mayonnaise Dukan

■ **ATTACK**   ■ **CONSOLIDATION**
■ **CRUISE**   ■ **STABILIZATION**

Place the egg yolks, in a small bowl and combine with the mustard.
Season with salt and pepper and add the herbs, if using. Gradually
mix in the fromage frais or quark, stirring continuously. Store in the
fridge until needed.

American-style oil-free mayonnaise

Mayonnaise sans huile à l'américaine

■ **ATTACK**   ■ CONSOLIDATION
■ **CRUISE**   ■ **STABILIZATION**

Makes 1 portion
Preparation time
5 minutes
Cooking time
12 minutes
Ingredients
1 egg
4 tablespoons fat-free fromage frais
½ tablespoon Dijon mustard
Salt and black pepper

Hard-boil the egg by placing it in a small pan of cold water over a high heat. Once the water starts boiling, cook the egg for 12 minutes.

Remove from the heat and run under cold water so that all the hot water in the pan is replaced by cold. Shell the egg.

Remove the yolk and crush it very thoroughly with a fork. Mix in the fromage frais, mustard, salt and black pepper.

Taste and adjust the seasoning if necessary.

Tomato sauce

Coulis de tomates

■ **ATTACK**   ■ CONSOLIDATION
■ **CRUISE**   ■ **STABILIZATION**

Makes 2 portions
Preparation time
5 minutes
Cooking time
20 minutes
Ingredients
70g (2½ oz) finely chopped onion
6-8 fresh tomatoes, peeled and
    seeds removed (or 1 x 410g
    (14½oz) can peeled tomatoes)
½ teaspoon dried basil
½ teaspoon dried mint
½ teaspoon dried tarragon
Salt and black pepper

Put all the ingredients in a non-stick saucepan, including salt and pepper to taste. Cover and simmer over a low heat for 20 minutes.

4 servings
Preparation time
5 minutes
Refrigeration time
30 minutes
Ingredients
600g (1lb 5oz) fat-free natural
   yoghurt
500ml (18fl oz) skimmed milk
Pinch of salt
¼ teaspoon crushed green
   cardamom
3 drops rose water

Salted lassi

Lassi salé

■ ATTACK   ■ CONSOLIDATION
■ CRUISE   ■ STABILIZATION

Mix all the ingredients together and beat with a whisk.
Pour the lassi into attractive glasses and chill for 30 minutes before serving. Store in the fridge.

Lassis are an Indian speciality and can be drunk either throughout or at the end of a meal.

Rhubarb compote

Compote à la rhubarbe

4 servings
Preparation time
25 minutes
Cooking time
30 minutes
Ingredients
800g (1lb 12oz) rhubarb, fresh
   or frozen
6 teaspoons crystallized stevia
   (or more according to taste)
Vanilla essence

■ **CRUISE PV**
■ **CONSOLIDATION EXCEPT FOR PP THURSDAYS**
■ **STABILIZATION EXCEPT FOR PP THURSDAYS**

Rinse the rhubarb and, without peeling it, chop it into 1–2cm-(½ – ¾in)-thick chunks.

Put the rhubarb chunks in a saucepan and sprinkle over the sweetener. Let the rhubarb release its juice for 10–15 minutes, before you start cooking.

Cook the rhubarb over a gentle heat in its own liquid, taking care to stir at regular intervals. Add the vanilla essence and leave to simmer for about 30 minutes, until you have the consistency you want.

 From the Cruise phase onwards, rhubarb is the only fruit/vegetable allowed and it can be eaten as a dessert or as a condiment by those who like a sweet-savoury taste.

Muffins

4 servings
Preparation time
10 minutes
Cooking time
30 minutes
Ingredients
4 eggs
Pinch of salt
4 tablespoons wheat bran
8 tablespoons oat bran
4 tablespoons fat-free fromage frais
½ teaspoon Hermesetas liquid
  sweetener
Choice of flavouring: grated lemon
  zest, ground cinnamon, or coffee
  (instant coffee made with water),
  to taste

■ **ATTACK** ■ **CONSOLIDATION**
■ **CRUISE** ■ **STABILIZATION**

Preheat the oven to 180°C/350°F/Gas 4.

Separate the egg yolks from the whites. Add a pinch of salt to the whites and beat until stiff.

In a bowl, mix together all the other ingredients, then gently fold in the stiffly beaten egg whites.

Pour the mixture into a silicone muffin tin and bake in the oven for 20–30 minutes.

Pure proteins (PP)

Pure proteins are the only foods allowed in **Phase 1 – Attack**. They will follow you into **Phase 2 – Cruise**,, when you will eat them on your PP days, then once a week on your protein day. In the pages that follow, you will find plenty of ideas to give your taste buds a treat.

Starters p. 76   **Main courses** p. 124   **Desserts** p. 186

6 servings
Preparation time
25 minutes
Cooking time
3-4 minutes
Refrigeration time
20 minutes
Ingredients
Appetizer 1
2 slices cooked chicken
50g (1¾oz) virtually fat-free quark
1 teaspoon curry powder
Salt and black pepper
Appetizer 2
2 hard-boiled eggs
50g (1¾oz) virtually fat-free quark
1 teaspoon cumin seeds
Salt and black pepper
Appetizer 3
3 chicken livers
1 teaspoon dried onion powder
50g (1¾oz) virtually fat-free quark
Salt and black pepper

A trio of appetizers

Cuillerées apéritives en farandole

■ **ATTACK**   ■ **CONSOLIDATION**
■ **CRUISE**   ■ **STABILIZATION**

Appetizer 1: Crumble the cooked chicken into a food-processor bowl and add the quark, curry powder, salt and black pepper. Blend until smooth and keep in the fridge until ready to serve.

Appetizer 2: Shell the hard-boiled eggs and roughly chop them up. Put them in a food-processor bowl along with the quark, cumin seeds, salt and black pepper. Blend until smooth and keep in the fridge until ready to serve.

Appetizer 3: Gently fry the chicken livers in a non-stick frying pan while sprinkling the onion powder over them. Once they have cooked through, leave them to cool for about 10 minutes. Next put the chicken livers in a food-processor bowl with the quark, salt and black pepper. Blend until smooth and keep in the fridge until ready to serve.

Shape the mixtures into small spoonfuls and serve them as appetizers on individual porcelain spoons.

8 servings
Preparation time
10 minutes
Cooking time
15 minutes
Ingredients
2 garlic cloves, crushed
Fresh herbs, finely chopped
200g (7oz) virtually fat-free quark
2 eggs, lightly beaten
2 sprigs flat-leaf parsley

Little quark pots

Petits cannelés apéritifs aux carrés frais

■ ATTACK   ▨ CONSOLIDATION
■ CRUISE   ■ STABILIZATION

Preheat the oven to 180°C/350°F/Gas 4.

Stir the garlic and herbs into the quark, then work in the eggs without overbeating the mixture.

Wash and dry the flat-leaf parsley before chopping it up roughly and adding it to the quark mixture.

Divide the mixture between individual moulds and place them on a baking tray. Bake in the oven for 15 minutes.

Remove the tray from the oven and leave the moulds to cool down for a few minutes before turning out the quark savouries. They can be served as either an appetizer or a starter.

4 servings
Preparation time
20 minutes
Refrigeration time
1 hour minimum
Ingredients
300g (10½oz) fresh salmon
(without the skin)
1 sachet court-bouillon or stock
(approx 500g)
4 slices smoked trout
50g (1¾oz) virtually fat-free quark
Juice of ½ lemon
4 tablespoons fat-free fromage frais
1 × 100g jar red lumpfish roe

Salmon and trout starters

Verrines de saumon et truite

■ **ATTACK**   ▨ **CONSOLIDATION**
■ **CRUISE**   ■ **STABILIZATION**

Poach the salmon in the court-bouillon for 5–10 minutes. Drain carefully, then transfer the salmon to a dish and break it into pieces.

Very finely dice 2 of the smoked trout slices and add to the crumbled salmon along with the quark, lemon juice, fromage frais and half of the lumpfish roe.

Line four glass dishes with the remaining smoked trout, then fill them with the salmon mixture.

Chill in the fridge for at least 1 hour.

When you are ready to serve, garnish with a little of the remaining lumpfish roe scattered over the top of each dish.

4 servings
Preparation time
10 minutes
Refrigeration time
1 hour
Ingredients
300g (10½oz) virtually fat-free quark
400g (14oz) seafood sticks, grated
4 tablespoons lemon juice
Salt and black pepper
1 bunch chives, finely chopped

Seafood-stick and chive bites

Boulettes surimi-ciboulette

■ **ATTACK**   ■ **CONSOLIDATION**
■ **CRUISE**   ■ **STABILIZATION**

Break up the quark with a fork and mix in the grated seafood sticks and lemon juice. Season with salt and black pepper.

Place in the fridge for 1 hour, so that the mixture becomes firm.

When you are ready to serve, use a teaspoon to shape the mixture into small balls, then roll them in the finely chopped chives until they are well covered. Arrange them on a dish with some wooden cocktail sticks and serve with your aperitif drinks.

Chicken-liver terrine

Terrine de foies de volaille

4 servings
Make a day in advance
Preparation time
15 minutes
Cooking time
5 minutes
Refrigeration time
24 hours
Ingredients
300g (10½oz) chicken livers
3 tablespoons raspberry vinegar
Salt and black pepper
1 bunch tarragon
150g (5½oz) fat-free fromage frais

■ ATTACK   ■ CONSOLIDATION
■ CRUISE   ■ STABILIZATION

Cook the chicken livers over a high heat in a non-stick frying pan, and then deglaze with the raspberry vinegar. Season with salt and black pepper.

Remove all the tarragon leaves from the stems (discard the stems) and place in a blender along with the chicken livers and fromage frais.

Blend to a purée and pour the mixture into a terrine dish.

Refrigerate for 24 hours. Serve well chilled.

6 servings
Preparation time
20 minutes
Cooking time
40 minutes
Ingredients
300g (10½oz) chicken breasts
5 eggs
200g (7oz) virtually fat-free quark
200ml (7fl oz) skimmed milk
Salt and black pepper

Chicken and quark quiche

Quiche au poulet et aux carrés frais

■ **ATTACK**   ▪ CONSOLIDATION
■ **CRUISE**   ■ **STABILIZATION**

Cut the chicken into thin strips and lightly fry, without any fat, for 6–7 minutes in a non-stick frying pan. Remove from the heat and keep to one side.

Preheat the oven to 160°C/325°F/Gas 3.

Beat the eggs together in a bowl. Then work in the quark and add the skimmed milk. Season with salt and black pepper.

Pour the egg mixture into a non-stick quiche mould (or a flexible silicone mould), then arrange the strips of chicken evenly over the top. Bake in the oven for about 35 minutes.

Leave the quiche to cool a little before turning it out on to a plate and cutting it into slices. Serve warm or cold.

You will need to wait until you are in the PV Cruise phase before adding the rocket leaves shown in the photo.

2 servings
Preparation time
10 minutes
Cooking time
30 minutes
Ingredients
4 eggs
500g (1lb 2oz) fat-free fromage
frais
300g (10½oz) cooked and shelled
prawns
Salt and black pepper

Prawn bake

Gâteau de crevettes

■ **ATTACK**　　■ **CONSOLIDATION**
■ **CRUISE**　　■ **STABILIZATION**

Preheat the oven to 200°C/400°F/Gas 6.

Break the eggs into a bowl and whisk them together.

Stir in the fromage frais, mixing it in very thoroughly. Chop the prawns into pieces and add them to the fromage frais mixture. Season with salt and black pepper.

Pour the mixture into an ovenproof dish or tin, and bake in the oven for 30 minutes. Serve warm

Prawn tartare

Tartare de crevettes

2 servings
Preparation time
10 minutes
Ingredients
5 sprigs dill
6 tablespoons Dukan mayonnaise
  (see page 68)
250g (9oz) cooked and shelled
  prawns
2 pinches of paprika
Black pepper

■ **ATTACK** ▨ **CONSOLIDATION**
■ **CRUISE** ■ **STABILIZATION**

Wash the dill and chop it very finely. Stir the chopped dill into the mayonnaise.

Roughly chop the prawns and add them to the mayonnaise.

Sprinkle over the paprika and stir the mixture once again.

Season with black pepper and serve well chilled.

4 servings
Preparation time
20 minutes
Cooking time
10 minutes
Refrigeration time
2 hours
Ingredients
4 x 240g (9oz) salmon steaks
2 low-salt fish stock cubes
8 gelatine leaves
4 sprigs dill
50g (1¾oz) salmon roe
1 slice smoked salmon, cut into
    small strips

You will need a steamer

Three-salmon timbale

Timbale aux trois saumons

■ **ATTACK**   ■ **CONSOLIDATION**
■ **CRUISE**   ■ **STABILIZATION**

Place four good-sized individual moulds in the freezer.

Steam the salmon steaks for 5 minutes. Remove the skin and any bones and leave to cool.

Bring 250ml (9fl oz) water to the boil with the fish stock cubes and reduce over a high heat for 5 minutes. Remove from the heat and add the gelatine, which has been softened beforehand in some cold water.

Take the moulds out of the freezer and pour a little of the cooled gelatine mixture into the bottom of each. Then add a sprig of dill, most of the salmon roe (reserve a little for the garnish), the cooked salmon steaks and strips of smoked salmon. Pour in the rest of the gelatine mixture and refrigerate for 2 hours.

Turn the salmon timbales out on to serving plates and scatter over the remaining salmon roe.

Fish agar-agar

Agar-agar de poisson

2 servings
Preparation time
15 minutes
Cooking time
10 minutes
Refrigeration time
2 hours minimum
Ingredients
150ml (5fl oz) low-fat court-bouillon
  or stock
Salt and black pepper
1 × 2g sachet agar-agar powder
3 x 120g (4½oz) white fish fillets,
  cut into pieces
Juice of ½ lemon

■ **ATTACK**   ■ **CONSOLIDATION**
■ **CRUISE**   ■ **STABILIZATION**

Over a gentle heat, warm 250ml (9fl oz) water in a pan with the court-bouillon, salt, black pepper and agar-agar.

After 5 minutes, add the fish fillets and continue cooking, covered, for a further 4 minutes.

Blend the mixture in a food processor and stir in the lemon juice before pouring it into a loaf tin.

Leave to cool and then refrigerate for at least 2 hours.

In the Cruise phase, you can serve this dish with a warm tomato coulis.

4 servings
Preparation time
5 minutes
Refrigeration time
1 hour
Ingredients
½ lemon
3 Russian-style gherkins (malossol)
500g (1lb 2oz) fat-free fromage
frais
30g (1oz) virtually fat-free quark
1 tablespoon paprika, plus extra to
garnish
Salt and black pepper

Hungarian-style paprika fromage frais

Fromage blanc au paprika
à la hongroise

■ **ATTACK**　　■ **CONSOLIDATION**
■ **CRUISE**　　■ **STABILIZATION**

Squeeze the half-lemon into a small bowl. Finely dice the gherkins.

In a larger bowl, mix together the fromage frais, quark, diced gherkins, paprika and 1 tablespoon of the lemon juice. Season with salt and black pepper and mix everything together thoroughly. Refrigerate for 1 hour and serve well chilled.

To garnish, sprinkle a light dusting of paprika over the fromage frais mixture.

Thai chicken broth

Bouillon de poulet à la thaie

4 servings
Preparation time
15 minutes
Cooking time
2–3 hours
Ingredients
2 chicken carcasses
1 onion, quartered
1 bunch coriander stalks, roughly
   chopped
2 fresh lemongrass stalks (white part
   only), crushed
2 kaffir lime leaves, chopped
1 tablespoon chopped galangal root
   (or fresh ginger)
Salt and black pepper

■ **ATTACK**   ▨ **CONSOLIDATION**
■ **CRUISE**   ■ **STABILIZATION**

Put the chicken carcasses into a large pan containing 2 litres (3½ pints) cold water. Bring to the boil and skim off any froth.

Turn down the heat and add the onion, coriander, lemongrass stalks, kaffir lime leaves and galangal or ginger. Leave to simmer gently for 2–3 hours, taking care not to overheat because this will make the broth go cloudy. Strain the broth before serving.

The kaffir lime leaves and lemongrass will give a lovely lemony flavour.

4 servings
Preparation time
15 minutes
Cooking time
5–6 minutes
Refrigeration time
2 hours minimum
Ingredients
4 eggs
400ml (14fl oz) vegetable stock
1 teaspoon agar-agar
100g (3½oz) virtually fat-free quark,
   with garlic and fresh herbs
   crumbled
1 small bunch dill, finely chopped

Soft-boiled eggs and quark in aspic

Aspics d'oeufs mollets aux carrés frais

■ ATTACK   ▨ CONSOLIDATION
■ CRUISE   ■ STABILIZATION

Place the eggs in a pan of simmering water and leave them to cook for exactly 5 minutes (6 minutes for large eggs).

Remove the soft-boiled eggs from the water with a slotted spoon, put them under cold running water to cool, then shell them.

In the meantime, bring the vegetable stock to the boil, sprinkle in the agar-agar and leave to simmer for 2 minutes.

Arrange an egg in the centre of each of four ramekin dishes and then add a quarter of the quark and some dill to each. Pour some agar-agar stock into the ramekins and leave to cool to room temperature before refrigerating for at least 2 hours.

When ready to serve, ease the jellied eggs carefully out of the ramekins.

4 servings
Preparation time
15 minutes
Cooking time
15 minutes
Ingredients
8 scallops
200g (7oz) fat-free fromage frais
2 eggs, separated
Salt and black pepper

You will need a steamer

Scallop mousse

Mousse de Saint-Jacques

■ **ATTACK**   ■ **CONSOLIDATION**
■ **CRUISE**   ■ **STABILIZATION**

Chop the scallops intoo small pieces. Blend the scallops with the fromage frais.

Add the egg yolks to the scallop mixture and season to taste with salt and black pepper.

Beat the egg whites until stiff, then gently fold them into the mixture.

Pour the mixture into four ramekins and steam for 15 minutes in a steamer.

Turn out the mousses and serve hot with Lemon and chive sauce (see page 62).

5 servings
Preparation time
10 minutes
Cooking time
45 minutes
Ingredients
200g (7oz) smoked salmon
1 tablespoon cornflour
350ml (12fl oz) skimmed milk
2 eggs
120g (4¼oz) tinned crab meat
(drained weight)
Salt and black pepper
Pinch of fish stock powder

Little crab and salmon flans

Petits flans au crabe et au saumon

■ ATTACK   ■ CONSOLIDATION
■ CRUISE   ■ STABILIZATION

Preheat the oven to 180°C/350°F/Gas 4.

Cut the smoked salmon into small cubes and divide between five ovenproof ramekin dishes.

Add the cornflour to the skimmed milk. Whisk the eggs into the cornflour mixture and then add the drained crab meat. Season with salt and black pepper and carefully stir in the fish stock powder.

Pour the mixture over the chopped smoked salmon.

Place the ramekins in a bain-marie and bake in the oven for 45 minutes.

2 servings
Preparation time
15 minutes
Cooking time
20 minutes
Ingredients
2 slices extra-lean cooked turkey
   or chicken
3 eggs
6 tablespoons fat-free fromage frais
½ onion, finely chopped
Pinch of grated nutmeg
Salt and black pepper

No-pastry quiche

Quiche sans pâte

■ **ATTACK**　　■ **CONSOLIDATION**
■ **CRUISE**　　■ **STABILIZATION**

Preheat the oven to 240°C/475°F/Gas 9.

Cut the cooked turkey or chicken slices into small pieces.

In a bowl, whisk the eggs and then gently fold in the fromage frais, cooked meat pieces, onion and nutmeg. Season with salt and black pepper.

Pour the mixture into a non-stick flan dish and bake in the oven for 20 minutes.

Serve the quiche warm from the oven.

You will need to wait until you are in the PV Cruise phase before adding the rocket leaves shown in the photo.

Eggs cocotte with salmon

Oeufs cocotte au saumon

6 servings
Preparation time
10 minutes
Cooking time
5 minutes
Ingredients
12 teaspoons fat-free fromage frais
2 large slices smoked salmon
6 eggs
1 small bunch tarragon or chervil,
    finely chopped
Salt and black pepper

■ **ATTACK**　　■ **CONSOLIDATION**
■ **CRUISE**　　■ **STABILIZATION**

Put 2 teaspoons of the fromage frais into each of six ovenproof ramekin dishes.

To each ramekin add a third of a slice of smoked salmon, cut into very thin strips, and then break an egg over the top.

Place the ramekins in a high-sided saucepan filled with boiling water, like a bain-marie. Cover and cook for 3–5 minutes over a medium heat. Scatter over the chopped tarragon or chervil and serve.

Instead of smoked salmon you may use ham, bresaola or any other protein that suits your taste.

4 servings
Preparation time
20 minutes
Ingredients
4 tablespoons soy sauce
5–6 tablespoons balsamic vinegar
15 drops of orange flavouring
1 red onion
250g (9oz) roast beef, sliced
    very thinly

Orange-marinated sliced roast beef

Fines tranches de rosbif froid mariné à l'orange

■ **ATTACK**   ■ **CONSOLIDATION**
■ **CRUISE**   ■ **STABILIZATION**

Make the marinade by combining the soy sauce, balsamic vinegar and orange flavouring.

Use a mandolin vegetable slicer to slice the red onion very thinly. Place the slices in iced water and leave for 10 minutes. Then drain them and pat dry on kitchen paper.

When you are ready to serve, use a pastry brush to coat the roast beef slices with the marinade and arrange them on four plates with the slices of red onion on top. Season to taste any remaining marinade.

4 servings
Make a day in advance
Preparation time
30 minutes
Cooking time
3 hours
Refrigeration time
8 hours
Ingredients
2 veal trotters, cut into three
2 garlic cloves, finely chopped
1 teaspoon dried thyme
1 teaspoon ground bay leaf
Salt and black pepper
½ bunch parsley
White wine vinegar

Polish-style jellied veal trotters

Pieds de veau en gelée,
façon polonaise

■ ATTACK   □ CONSOLIDATION
■ CRUISE   ■ STABILIZATION

Place the veal trotter pieces in a large pan with the garlic, thyme and bay leaf. Season with salt and black pepper and add approximately 2 litres (3½ pints) cold water. Cover the pan and leave to simmer over a gentle heat for 3 hours.

Rinse and finely chop the parsley. Drain the veal trotters and keep the stock to one side.

Remove and discard the bones from the veal trotters. Use a blender to chop up the veal meat and transfer to a dish. Add the reserved veal stock and the chopped parsley. Leave to cool.

Once the stock has cooled down, place the dish in the fridge overnight for the mixture to set. The following day, cut the jellied veal into large cubes and serve with some vinegar as an accompaniment.

Chicken flan with bran

Tarte au poulet aux sons

■ ATTACK   ▨ CONSOLIDATION
■ CRUISE   ■ STABILIZATION

4 servings
Preparation time
10 minutes
Cooking time
30 minutes
Ingredients
4 tablespoons oat bran
2 tablespoons wheat bran
100g (3½oz) silken tofu, crumbled
6 tablespoons fat-free fromage frais
100g (3½oz) virtually fat-free quark
2 eggs
3 x 100g (4oz) cooked chicken breasts
A little curry powder
Salt and black pepper

Preheat the oven to 180°C/350°F/Gas 4.

Put the brans, silken tofu, fromage frais, quark and eggs in a bowl and whisk them together.

Cut the chicken into small pieces and add to the bran mixture. Sprinkle in the curry powder, and season with salt and black pepper.

Pour the mixture into a non-stick flan mould and bake in the oven for about 30 minutes.

This flan tastes equally good hot or cold.

Dukan-style chicken nuggets

Nuggets de poulet façon Dukan

■ ATTACK   ▨ CONSOLIDATION
■ CRUISE   ■ STABILIZATION

4 servings
Preparation time
15 minutes
Cooking time
15 minutes
Ingredients
4 x 120g (4½oz) chicken breasts
2 eggs
Salt and black pepper
4 tablespoons oat bran

Cut the chicken into nugget-size pieces.

Whisk the eggs together in a bowl and season with salt and black pepper.

Dip the chicken pieces in the beaten egg mixture and then roll them in the bran until they are well coated. Gently fry the nuggets in a non-stick frying pan without any fat until they turn golden brown and the chicken cooked through. Serve hot.

4 servings
Preparation time
25 minutes
Marinating time
2 hours
Ingredients
1kg (2lb 4oz) fresh salmon
Juice of 4 lemons
Salt and black pepper
1 small bunch dill, finely
chopped
8 tablespoons fat-free fromage
frais
Herbs and seasoning of your choice
(garlic, shallots, dill, chives, etc.),
finely chopped

Salmon carpaccio with fromage frais sauce

Carpaccio de saumon sauce au fromage blanc

■ **ATTACK**   ■ **CONSOLIDATION**
■ **CRUISE**   ■ **STABILIZATION**

Slice the salmon very thinly and put to one side.

Squeeze the lemons into a dish.

Place the salmon slices in the lemon juice and season with salt and black pepper. Add the finely chopped dill.

Place the salmon in the fridge and leave to marinate and 'cook' for about 2 hours.

To make the sauce, mix together the fromage frais with the herbs and seasoning of your choice.

Serve the salmon carpaccio with the sauce on the side.

Thai-style seafood soup

Soupe marine à la thaïe

■ **ATTACK** ■ **CONSOLIDATION**
■ **CRUISE** ■ **STABILIZATION**

4 servings
Preparation time
15 minutes
Cooking time
25 minutes
Ingredients
200g (7oz) salmon fillet
12 large headless raw prawns
1 unwaxed lime
1 bird's-eye chilli
2 fresh lemongrass stalks
50g (1¾oz) fresh ginger
Salt and black pepper
2 tablespoons finely chopped chives
A few drops of soy sauce

Cut the salmon into small cubes and shell the prawns.

Rinse the lime and chilli and cut into very thin slices. Remove any hard bits from the lemongrass stalks and chop them up very finely. Peel the ginger and cut into very thin sticks. Pour 1l (18fl oz) water into a large pan and add the lime, chilli, lemongrass and ginger. Bring to the boil, then simmer for 15 minutes.

Add the salmon and prawns and bring back to the boil. Cook for a further 10 minutes over a very gentle heat. Season with salt and black pepper to taste.

Divide the soup between four warmed bowls. Scatter over the finely chopped chives and add a few drops of soy sauce. Serve piping hot.

4 servings
Make a day in advance
Preparation time
20 minutes
Refrigeration time
12 hours
Ingredients
320g (11¼oz) extra-lean cooked
   ham (without fat or rind)
300g (10½oz) fat-free fromage frais
Salt and black pepper
1 small bunch parsley, chopped
4 egg whites
2½ gelatine leaves

Ham mousse

Mousse au jambon

■ ATTACK   ■ CONSOLIDATION
■ CRUISE   ■ STABILIZATION

Cut the ham into small pieces, then blend with the fromage frais. Season with salt and black pepper and add the chopped parsley.

Whisk the egg whites until stiff and gently fold them into the ham mixture.

Soften the gelatine in a little cold water and then dissolve it in 20ml (¾fl oz) boiling water. Stir the gelatine into the ham mousse and pour the mousse mixture into a charlotte mould. Leave to set in the fridge for 12 hours.

Serve well chilled.

8 servings
Make a day in advance
Preparation time
25 minutes
Cooking time
55 minutes
Refrigeration time
6 hours minimum
Ingredients
1kg (2lb 4oz) monkfish fillet
Juice of 2 lemons
5 eggs
250g (9oz) virtually fat-free quark
3 teaspoons tomato purée
White pepper
150g (5½oz) fat-free natural yoghurt
Sprigs of dill or lumpfish roe, to
   garnish

You will need a steamer

Monkfish and quark loaf
Pain de lotte aux carrés frais

■ **ATTACK**   ■ **CONSOLIDATION**
■ **CRUISE**   ■ **STABILIZATION**

Cut the monkfish fillet into cubes, sprinkle over half the lemon juice and place in a steamer. Steam for 8 minutes, then leave to cool.

Preheat the oven to 150°C/300°F/Gas 2.

In a bowl, whisk the eggs together until they are nice and frothy. Gently fold in 150g (5½oz) of the quark with the tomato purée and add some white pepper.

Pour a thin layer of this mixture into a non-stick loaf tin. Add some of the monkfish cubes and cover them with some of the quark mixture. Keep adding alternate layers until the loaf tin is full. Place the loaf tin in a bain-marie and bake in the oven for about 45 minutes.

Remove the loaf from the oven and leave it to cool to room temperature before refrigerating for at least 6 hours.

Cut the monkfish loaf into generous slices and serve with a sauce made by blending the remaining quark with the natural yoghurt and the remaining lemon juice. Serve garnished with sprigs of dill or lumpfish roe.

4 servings
Preparation time
15 minutes
Cooking time
15 minutes
Ingredients
2 tablespoons finely chopped chives
4 eggs plus 4 egg whites
8 tablespoons fat-free fromage frais
8 tablespoons oat bran
4 tablespoons wheat bran
Salt and black pepper
4 slices smoked salmon, cut into
   pieces

Mini galettes, scrambled eggs and smoked salmon

Petites galettes, scramble eggs au saumon fumé

■ **ATTACK**   ▦ **CONSOLIDATION**
▦ **CRUISE**   ■ **STABILIZATION**

In a bowl, stir together the chives, egg whites and half the fromage frais. Add 2 tablespoons water and mix until you have a smooth paste. Stir in the brans.

Warm a large non-stick frying pan over a gentle heat. Drop tablespoonfuls of the galette mixture into the hot frying pan, spreading them out slightly to form small rounds. Cook the galettes, keeping them warm as you go, until all the mixture is used up.

In a bowl, whisk together the 4 whole eggs and add the remaining fromage frais.

Heat a second non-stick frying pan over a gentle heat and cook the eggs, stirring continuously with a spatula. Add a little salt and season with black pepper according to taste.

Arrange the mini galettes on a serving dish, with some scrambled eggs on top. Finally, add the smoked salmon pieces when you are ready to serve.

4 servings
Preparation time
12 minutes
Cooking time
10 minutes
Refrigeration time
20 minutes
Ingredients
10 eggs
200g (7oz) virtually fat-free quark,
   with garlic and herbs
3 slices extra-lean cooked ham
   (without fat or rind)
White pepper

Ham and quark omelette roulade

Omelette roulée aux carrés frais et au jambon

■ **ATTACK**   ▨ **CONSOLIDATION**
▨ **CRUISE**   ■ **STABILIZATION**

Whisk the eggs together with 50g (1¾oz) of the quark until smooth and creamy. Cut the ham into thin strips.

Heat a 30cm- (12in)- diameter non-stick frying pan over a high heat. Pour the egg mixture into the pan and fry for 1 minute. Turn down the heat, cover the pan and cook for a further 4–5 minutes. Flip the omelette over and cook the other side for 3–4 minutes. Turn off the heat, leave to cool and then transfer the omelette to a large plate.

Spread the remaining quark over the omelette and scatter the ham on top. Add some white pepper.

Roll the omelette up like a Swiss roll, wrap it in clingfilm to protect it and refrigerate.

When you are ready to serve, remove the clingfilm and cut the omelette roulade into generous slices.

3 servings
Preparation time
10 minutes
Cooking time
12 minutes
Refrigeration time
3 hours
Ingredients
3 eggs
3 teaspoons cornflour
250g (9oz) fat-free fromage frais
2 tablespoons finely chopped chives
1 tablespoon chopped fresh ginger
100g (3½oz) smoked salmon
Black pepper
A few sprigs parsley, to garnish

*Contains 1 tolerated food portion
per person*

Smoked salmon rolls

Roulés au saumon fumé

■ **CRUISE**
■ **CONSOLIDATION EXCEPT FOR PP THURSDAYS**
■ **STABILIZATION EXCEPT FOR PP THURSDAYS**

Combine the eggs with 3 tablespoons water and the cornflour.

Warm a small non-stick frying pan and cook the mixture in batches so that you end up with three small, thin omelettes.

Carefully spread some fromage frais over each omelette and sprinkle over the finely chopped chives and ginger. Cut the smoked salmon into small pieces and divide among the omelettes. Season with black pepper.

Roll each omelette up, nice and tightly, and wrap in clingfilm. Leave the rolls in the fridge for 3 hours.

To serve, remove the clingfilm and, using a very sharp knife, cut the rolls into slices. Garnish with parsley.

Indian-style eggs cocotte

Oeufs cocotte à l'indienne

2 servings
Preparation time
10 minutes
Cooking time
10 minutes
Ingredients
1 teaspoon tandoori spice powder
4 tablespoons fat-free fromage frais
2 eggs
2 tablespoons low-fat crème fraîche
(3% fat)
1 small bunch chives, finely
chopped

*Contains 1 tolerated food portion
per person*

■ **CRUISE**
■ **CONSOLIDATION EXCEPT FOR PP THURSDAYS**
■ **STABILIZATION EXCEPT FOR PP THURSDAYS**

Preheat the oven to 180°C/350°F/Gas 4.

Stir the tandoori spice into the fromage frais.

Put a tablespoon of the fromage frais mixture into each of two small ovenproof ramekin dishes, then break in an egg and add a second tablespoon of the mixture. Finish off with a tablespoon of crème fraîche. Bake in the oven for about 10 minutes, keeping an eye on the ramekins to check when they are cooked.

When you remove the ramekins from the oven, scatter over the chives and serve immediately.

2 servings
Preparation time
10 minutes
Cooking time
45 minutes
Ingredients
150ml (5fl oz) skimmed milk
2 tablespoons cornflour
4 eggs, separated
300g (12oz) fat-free fromage frais
200g (7oz) extra-lean cooked ham
  (without fat or rind)
Salt and black pepper
A little grated nutmeg

*Contains 1 tolerated food portion
per person*

Ham soufflé

Soufflé au jambon

■ **CRUISE**
■ **CONSOLIDATION EXCEPT FOR PP THURSDAYS**
■ **STABILIZATION EXCEPT FOR PP THURSDAYS**

Preheat the oven to 200°C/400°F/Gas 6.

Combine the skimmed milk and cornflour.

Stir the egg yolks into the fromage frais. Add the milk, stirring continuously with a wooden spoon.

Cut the ham into small, thin strips and add to the fromage frais mixture. Season with salt and black pepper and add a little nutmeg.

Whisk the egg whites with a pinch of salt until very stiff. Gently fold them into the fromage frais mixture.

Pour the mixture into a non-stick soufflé mould and bake in the oven for 45 minutes.

When you remove the soufflé from the oven, you may find that the fromage frais has produced a little water, so drain this away before serving.

4 servings
Preparation time
15 minutes
Cooking time
30 minutes
Ingredients
4 turkey (or chicken) escalopes
1 large onion, finely chopped
2 tablespoons mixed herbs and
　spices
(cumin seeds, basil, herbes
de Provence, black pepper, salt,
　paprika, ground ginger)
6 eggs, beaten
2 tablespoons cornflour

*Contains ½ tolerated food portion
per person*

Baked turkey loaf

Cake à la dinde

■ **CRUISE**
■ **CONSOLIDATION EXCEPT FOR PP THURSDAYS**
■ **STABILIZATION EXCEPT FOR PP THURSDAYS**

Preheat the oven to 180°C/350°F/Gas 4.

Blend the uncooked meat with the onion in a food processor. Add the herbs and spices and gently fold in the eggs and cornflour.

Pour the mixture into a non-stick loaf tin and bake in the oven, in a bain-marie, for 20–30 minutes.

Serve warm or cold, cut into slices.

2 servings
Preparation time
10 minutes
Cooking time
45 minutes
Ingredients
150ml (5fl oz) skimmed milk
2 tablespoons cornflour
4 eggs, separated
100g (3½oz) fat-free fromage frais
300g (10½oz) tinned crab meat,
    flaked
Salt and black pepper

Crab soufflé

Soufflé de crabe

■ CRUISE
■ CONSOLIDATION EXCEPT FOR PP THURSDAYS
■ STABILIZATION EXCEPT FOR PP THURSDAYS

Preheat the oven to 200°C/400°F/Gas 6.

Combine the skimmed milk and cornflour.

Stir the egg yolks into the fromage frais. Pour in the milk and, using a wooden spoon, stir the ingredients thoroughly. Add the crab meat and season with salt and black pepper.

Whisk the egg whites until very stiff, adding a pinch of salt. Gently fold the egg whites into the crab mixture.

Pour the mixture into a non-stick soufflé mould and bake in the oven for 45 minutes. Serve immediately.

4 servings
Preparation time
10 minutes
Cooking time
15 minutes
Ingredients
4 tablespoons fat-free fromage frais
Salt and black pepper
200g (7oz) tinned crab meat
4 eggs
4 tablespoons low-fat crème fraîche
(3% fat)
4 chives, chopped

Contains 1 tolerated food portion per person

Eggs cocotte with crab

Oeufs cocotte au crabe

- **CRUISE**
- **CONSOLIDATION EXCEPT FOR PP THURSDAYS**
- **STABILIZATION EXCEPT FOR PP THURSDAYS**

Preheat the oven to 180°C/350°F/Gas 4.

Put a tablespoon of fromage frais into each of four ovenproof ramekin dishes and season with salt and black pepper.

Divide the crab meat between the ramekins, then break an egg into each. Bake the eggs cocotte in a bain-marie in the oven for 15 minutes.

Five minutes before the cocottes are ready, warm the crème fraîche in a small pan over a gentle heat and add the chives.

Take the ramekins out of the oven, pour over the chive sauce and serve immediately.

4 servings
Preparation time
10 minutes
Cooking time
10 minutes
Ingredients
8 eggs
Salt and black pepper
½ teaspoon mild paprika
250g (9oz) cooked and shelled
    prawns
8 tablespoons low-fat cream
    (3% fat)
2 sprigs dill, chopped

*Contains 2 tolerated food portions
per person*

Egg ramekins
with prawns

Ramequins d'oeufs aux crevettes

■ **CRUISE**
■ **CONSOLIDATION EXCEPT FOR PP THURSDAYS**
■ **STABILIZATION EXCEPT FOR PP THURSDAYS**

Preheat the oven to 200°C/400°F/Gas 6.

Whisk the eggs very thoroughly in a bowl, season with salt and black pepper and add the paprika. Chop up the prawns and gently fold them into the egg mixture along with the cream.

Divide the egg mixture between four ovenproof ramekin dishes. Place the ramekins in a bain-marie and bake in the oven for 10 minutes.

Remove the ramekins from the oven, scatter over the chopped dill and serve straightaway.

2 servings
Preparation time
10 minutes
Cooking time
10 minutes
Marinating time
30 minutes
Ingredients
400g (14oz) fillet steak
2 tablespoons soy sauce
1 tablespoon oyster sauce
1 large piece fresh ginger, grated
Black pepper
4 garlic cloves
A few coriander leaves

Vietnamese shaking beef
Boeuf Luc Lac

- ■ **ATTACK**   ■ **CONSOLIDATION**
- ■ **CRUISE**   ■ **STABILIZATION**

Cut the beef into 1cm (½in) cubes. Mix with the soy sauce, oyster sauce, ginger and a little black pepper. Leave to marinate for at least 30 minutes.

Just before serving, brown the garlic in a non-stick frying pan. As soon as it starts to brown and smell good, add the meat and cook over a very high heat.

Stir the pan quickly for 10–15 seconds. The meat should not be overcooked and should still be a little rare.

Garnish with a few coriander leaves and serve straightaway.

4 servings
Preparation time
20 minutes
Cooking time
1 hour
Ingredients
1 x 1.5kg (3lb 4oz) chicken, or 6
    chicken pieces
2 large onions, finely chopped
3 garlic cloves, finely chopped
A few cloves
1 x 5cm (2in) piece fresh ginger,
    grated
Salt and black pepper

Ginger chicken
Poulet au gingembre

■ **ATTACK**   ▪ **CONSOLIDATION**
■ **CRUISE**   ■ **STABILIZATION**

If using a whole chicken, cut it into 6 portion-sized pieces.

Brown the onions and garlic in a large non-stick frying pan.

Stick the cloves into the chicken pieces and add them to the frying pan. Cover with water.

Add the ginger and season with salt and black pepper.

Cook over a medium heat until all the water has evaporated, about an hour. Serve hot.

4 servings
Preparation time
15 minutes
Cooking time
50 minutes
Ingredients
2 x 100g (4oz) thin turkey
   escalopes
2 x 300g (10½oz) saddles of rabbit
Mixed herbs (thyme, bay leaves,
   savory, marjoram, rosemary)
Salt and black pepper

Rabbit and turkey herb parcels

Lapin en papillotte

■ ATTACK   ▨ CONSOLIDATION
■ CRUISE   ■ STABILIZATION

Preheat the oven to 220°C/425°F/Gas 7.

Cut the turkey escalopes in half. In a non-stick frying pan, quickly cook them over a very high heat.

Cut each rabbit saddle in two and place half a turkey escalope around each piece.

Place each saddle on to a sheet of aluminium foil or greaseproof paper and add the herbs. Season to taste with salt and black pepper.

Fold into parcels, place on a baking sheet and bake in the oven for 50 minutes. Serve piping hot.

3 servings
Preparation time
20 minutes
Cooking time
15 minutes
Ingredients
1 medium onion, chopped
750g (1lb 10oz) minced beef
   (5% fat)
2 garlic cloves, crushed
1 egg, lightly beaten
2 tablespoons soy sauce
1 tablespoon Worcestershire sauce
2 tablespoons finely chopped
   rosemary
1–2 tablespoons finely chopped
   mint (or basil)
Salt and black pepper

Meatballs with rosemary and mint

Boulettes de viande aux herbes

■ **ATTACK**   ■ **CONSOLIDATION**
■ **CRUISE**   ■ **STABILIZATION**

Mix together all the ingredients and season with salt and black pepper. Shape the mixture into walnut-sized balls. Cook the meatballs a few at a time, in a high-sided non-stick frying pan over a medium heat for around 5 minutes until they are golden brown all over.

Before serving, drain off any fat on some kitchen paper. In the Cruise phase the meatballs may be served with tomato sauce (see page 69).

2 servings
Preparation time
5 minutes
Cooking time
10–14 minutes
Ingredients
400g (14oz) minced beef (5% fat)
2 tablespoons wheat bran
1 tablespoon oat bran
1 onion, finely chopped
1 egg, beaten
¼ teaspoon salt
Black pepper

Minced-beef hamburgers
Steak hachés façon hamburgers

■ ATTACK   ■ CONSOLIDATION
■ CRUISE   ■ STABILIZATION

Combine all the ingredients in a bowl.

Divide the mixture in half so as to make 2 nice thick burgers, about 2cm (¾in) thick.

Using some kitchen paper, lightly oil a non-stick grill pan and warm it over a medium heat. As soon as the pan is hot, grill the hamburgers for 5–7 minutes on each side. Serve piping hot.

4 servings
Preparation time
20 minutes
Refrigeration time
3–4 hours
Cooking time
10 minutes
Ingredients
6 tablespoons Dijon or wholegrain
  mustard
4 tablespoons balsamic vinegar
2 garlic cloves, crushed
1 tablespoon black pepper
2 teaspoons fennel seeds
480g (1lb 1oz) fillet steak

Fillet steak in a mustard crust

Filet de bœuf en croûte de moutarde

■ **ATTACK**   ▨ **CONSOLIDATION**
■ **CRUISE**   ■ **STABILIZATION**

Mix together the mustard, balsamic vinegar, garlic, black pepper and fennel seeds in a small bowl. Stir very thoroughly.

Cut the fillet steak into 4 pieces. Spread the mustard mixture over both sides of all the steak pieces, keeping a little in reserve to pour over the meat once it is cooked.

Cover the meat with clingfilm and leave to marinate in the fridge for 3–4 hours.

Remove the steak pieces from the fridge and grill them over a medium heat for about 5 minutes on each side.

Pour over the remaining marinade and leave the meat to rest in a warm place for 5 minutes before serving.

4 servings
Preparation time
30 minutes
Refrigeration time
10 minutes
Ingredients
4 spring onions
1 × 5cm (2in) piece fresh ginger
600g (1lb 5oz) very fresh fillet
    of veal
2 unwaxed limes
1 teaspoon Tabasco
1 tablespoon balsamic vinegar
Fleur de sel (coarse sea salt)
Black pepper
6 chives, chopped

Veal tartare

Tartare de veau de lait

- ■ ATTACK
- ■ CRUISE
- ■ CONSOLIDATION
- ■ STABILIZATION

Finely chop the spring onions, including about 3cm (1¼in) of the green stalks. Peel and grate the ginger. Grate the zest from the limes.

Put a small bowl inside a larger one filled with ice cubes. Using a very sharp knife, so that contact with the meat is minimal, cut the fillet of veal as quickly as possible into very small cubes. Put the cubes into the smaller bowl so that they remain well chilled.

Add the chopped spring onions, both white and green parts, ginger, lime zest, Tabasco, balsamic vinegar, salt and black pepper. Use a fork to combine all the ingredients very thoroughly. Cover the bowl with clingfilm and refrigerate.

When you are ready to serve, take a biscuit cutter about 6–8cm (2½–3¼in) in diameter and 3cm (1¼in) high to make four individual tartares. Alternatively you can use small ramekin dishes. Scatter over some chopped chives and serve.

2 servings
Preparation time
20 minutes
Ingredients
400g (14oz) sea bass fillets
2 shallots, finely chopped
A few chives, finely chopped
Salt and black pepper
4 unwaxed limes, sliced
125g (4½oz) fat-free fromage frais
Juice of ½ lemon

Sea bass tartare with lime

Tartare de loup au citron vert

■ **ATTACK**   ▨ **CONSOLIDATION**
■ **CRUISE**   ■ **STABILIZATION**

Use a knife to cut the bass up roughly into small pieces. Combine the fish with the shallots and chives and season to taste with salt and black pepper.

Arrange the tartare on plates garnished with the lime slices.

Lightly whisk the fromage frais, season and add the lemon juice. Serve the tartare cold with the fromage frais sauce.

2 servings
Preparation time
5 minutes
Cooking time
5–10 minutes
Ingredients
4 rashers fat-reduced bacon
4 eggs, beaten
100ml (3½fl oz) skimmed milk
1 garlic clove, chopped
¼ bunch parsley, finely chopped
Black pepper

Light bacon omelette

Omelette légère au bacon

■ **ATTACK**   ▨ **CONSOLIDATION**
■ **CRUISE**   ■ **STABILIZATION**

Cut the bacon into thin strips.

Combine all the ingredients in a bowl and season with black pepper.

Heat a non-stick frying pan. Pour the mixture into the pan and cook until the omelette has the desired texture. Serve immediately.

4 servings
Preparation time
5 minutes
Cooking time
12 minutes
Ingredients
4 veal chops
Herbes de Provence
Salt and black pepper

Veal chops with herbs

Côtes de veau aux herbes

■ **ATTACK**   ■ **CONSOLIDATION**
■ **CRUISE**   ■ **STABILIZATION**

Heat a non-stick frying pan without adding any fat.

Sear the veal chops on both sides over a high heat and then turn down the heat, sprinkle over the herbs and season with salt and black pepper. Cook the chops for 5 minutes on each side.

Before serving the chops, remove any fat from the meat.

Tandoori chicken

Poulet tandoori

4 servings
Make a day in advance
Preparation time
25 minutes
Cooking time
30 minutes
Refrigeration time
9 hours
Ingredients
4 chicken thighs
Salt and black pepper
Juice of 1 lime
150g (5½oz) fat-free natural yoghurt
4 garlic cloves, crushed
1 × 3cm (1¼in) piece fresh ginger,
   finely chopped
4 tablespoons tandoori spice powder

■ ATTACK   ■ CONSOLIDATION
■ CRUISE   ■ STABILIZATION

Cut each chicken thigh into two pieces and remove the skin. Use a very sharp knife to make incisions in the chicken.

Place the chicken pieces in a bowl, season with salt and black pepper and pour over the lime juice. Turn the chicken pieces over so they are well covered with the juice and then leave to marinate in the fridge for 1 hour.

Combine the yoghurt, garlic, ginger and tandoori spice powder. Add this mixture to the chicken pieces and stir together very thoroughly. Leave to marinate in the fridge overnight.

The following day, preheat the oven to 200°C/400°F/Gas 6.

Place the chicken pieces on a baking tray and cook in the oven for 10–15 minutes on each side, until they are cooked through. Keep an eye on the chicken as it cooks and baste with more marinade if necessary. Serve hot.

4 servings
Preparation time
30 minutes
Cooking time
10–12 minutes
Ingredients
1 litre (1¾ pints) small mussels
3 shallots, finely chopped
50ml (2fl oz) dry white wine
Sea salt
½ bunch flat-leaf parsley, finely
    chopped
150g (5½oz) virtually fat-free quark
    with garlic and herbs

Baked mussels with herbs and quark

Moules gratinées en persillade de carrés frais

■ **ATTACK**   ■ **CONSOLIDATION**
■ **CRUISE**   ■ **STABILIZATION**

Scrub the mussels, discarding any that are broken or open.

Warm a large stew pot over a high heat, throw in the mussels and shallots, then pour over the dry white wine. Cover and leave to bubble away for 5 minutes. Turn off the heat and remove the mussels using a slotted spoon, discarding any that have refused to open.

You can strain the cooking liquid and keep it for another recipe as it will freeze perfectly.

Once the mussels have cooled, remove from their shells, and put 20 large shells to one side. Arrange these shells on a baking sheet, firmly wedging them in a layer of sea salt. Divide the mussels between the shells, with 4–5 mussels per shell.

Preheat the oven to 180°C/350°F/Gas 4.

In a bowl, stir the parsley into the quark. Divide this mixture between the filled mussel shells, putting 2 small teaspoons on top of each one. Bake the mussels in the oven for 5–6 minutes, just long enough for the quark to crisp up. Serve straightaway.

Herb-stuffed baked salmon

Saumon farci

6 servings
Preparation time
30 minutes
Refrigeration time
3 hours minimum
Cooking time
40 minutes

Ingredients

1 bunch flat-leaf parsley, finely chopped
1 bunch coriander, finely chopped
½ chilli, finely chopped
5 lemongrass stalks, finely chopped
2 bunches spring onions, finely chopped
4 garlic cloves, finely chopped
1 unwaxed lemon, cut into thin slices
2 eggs, beaten
1 teaspoon ground cumin
1 teaspoon grated fresh ginger
50ml (2fl oz) white wine
1 × 1.5kg (3lb 5oz) salmon (cleaned and with central bone removed)
Salt and black pepper

Contains ½ tolerated food portion per person

■ CRUISE
■ CONSOLIDATION EXCEPT FOR PP THURSDAYS
■ STABILIZATION EXCEPT FOR PP THURSDAYS

Mix the herbs, lemongrass, spring onions, garlic and lemon slices together in bowl. Add the eggs, cumin and ginger. Bind the mixture with the white wine and leave to marinate for a few hours in the fridge.

Preheat the oven to 180°C/350°F/Gas 4 and line a baking tray with greaseproof paper.

Open up the salmon, season with salt and black pepper and stuff with the herb mixture.

Place the fish on the baking tray and cook in the oven for 40 minutes. Serve immediately.

2 servings
Preparation time
5 minutes
Cooking time
5–10 minutes
Ingredients
4 seafood sticks
4 eggs, beaten
100ml (3½fl oz) skimmed milk
1 garlic clove, chopped
¼ bunch parsley, chopped
Salt and black pepper

Seafood-stick omelette

Omelette au surimi

■ ATTACK   ■ CONSOLIDATION
■ CRUISE   ■ STABILIZATION

In a blender, whizz the seafood sticks into tiny pieces.

In a small bowl, stir together all the ingredients, season to taste and whisk thoroughly.

Warm a non-stick frying pan and pour in the mixture. Cook for as long as it takes to get the texture you like for your omelettes, then serve.

Grilled tuna steaks with quark mousse

Pavés de tuna grillés, mousse de carrés frais

4 servings
Preparation time
10 minutes
Refrigeration time
30 minutes minimum
Cooking time
5 minutes
Ingredients
150g (5½oz) virtually fat-free quark
with garlic and herbs
2 egg whites
Juice of 1 lemon
4 x 100g (4oz) fresh tuna steaks
A little paprika

■ ATTACK   ▨ CONSOLIDATION
■ CRUISE   ■ STABILIZATION

Put the quark in a bowl and stir with a spatula until smooth.

Whisk the egg whites with the lemon juice until very firm and then fold into the quark. Refrigerate for at least 30 minutes.

Five minutes before you are ready to serve, warm a non-stick grill pan (or frying pan) over a high heat.

Place the tuna steaks in the pan and sear them for 30 seconds on each side. Reduce the heat to medium and cook the steaks for a further 2–4 minutes, depending on how well done you like them; turn half-way through the cooking time.

Serve the tuna steaks immediately, with a nice portion of the quark mousse alongside. Sprinkle a dusting of paprika on top.

4 servings
Make a day in advance
Preparation time
20 minutes
Refrigeration time
8 hours
Cooking time
30 minutes
Ingredients
1 onion, finely chopped
200g (7oz) virtually fat-free quark
1 tablespoon mustard
150g (5½oz) fat-free natural
   yoghurt
1 teaspoon garam masala
600g (1lb 5oz) chicken breasts
Lemon juice and fresh coriander,
   to serve

Chicken korma with quark

Poulet korma aux carrés frais

■ **ATTACK**　　■ **CONSOLIDATION**
■ **CRUISE**　　■ **STABILIZATION**

Put the onion, quark and mustard in a bowl and stir together until you get a smooth paste. Gently fold in the yoghurt and garam masala.

Cut the chicken breasts into cubes or strips and add to the bowl, stirring them into the marinade so that they are completely coated. Cover with clingfilm and leave to marinate in the fridge overnight.

Preheat the oven to 200°C/400°F/Gas 6.

Put the chicken and marinade into an ovenproof dish and bake in the oven for 30 minutes. Stir the chicken pieces in the marinade several times during cooking so that they do not get burnt.

Serve piping hot, drizzled with a little lemon juice and garnished with some fresh coriander leaves on top.

Thyme chicken with a herb sauce

Poulet au thym

4 servings
Preparation time
25 minutes
Cooking time
30–35 minutes
Ingredients
1 x 1.5kg (3lb 4oz) chicken, cut into
  pieces
Salt and black pepper
1 bunch fresh thyme
2 shallots, finely chopped
450g (1lb) fat-free natural yoghurt
Juice of ½ lemon
1 bunch parsley, finely chopped
A few mint leaves, finely chopped
1 garlic clove, finely chopped

You will need a steamer

■ **ATTACK**　　■ **CONSOLIDATION**
■ **CRUISE**　　■ **STABILIZATION**

Season the chicken pieces with salt and black pepper.

Pour a good quantity of water into the bottom part of a steamer, add salt and bring to the boil.

In the upper part of the steamer, spread out half the thyme and place the chicken pieces on top. Cover the chicken with the rest of the thyme and the shallots.

Put the lid on and, as soon as the steam starts to escape, cook for 30–35 minutes.

In the meantime, make the sauce for the chicken. Pour the yoghurt into a bowl and add the lemon juice, parsley, mint and garlic. Season with salt and black pepper, then mix all the ingredients together thoroughly and keep cool until you are ready to serve.

When the chicken is cooked, serve it with the herb sauce on the side.

4 servings
Preparation time
15 minutes
Cooking time
30 minutes
Ingredients
400g (14oz) turkey escalopes
4 tablespoons mustard
4 slices bresaola
Herbes de Provence
Salt and black pepper

Turkey rolls with bresaola

Roulés de dinde à la viande des Grisons

■ ATTACK   ■ CONSOLIDATION
■ CRUISE   ■ STABILIZATION

Preheat the oven to 180°C/350°F/Gas 4.

If necessary, trim any fat from the turkey escalopes, then arrange each one on a sheet of aluminium foil or greaseproof paper.

Coat the escalopes with a tablespoon of mustard and wrap each one around a slice of bresaola. Scatter over the herbes de Provence and season with salt and black pepper.

Sprinkle over a little water, seal up the parcels and place them on a baking sheet. Bake in the oven for 30 minutes. Serve immediately.

4 servings
Preparation time
20 minutes
Cooking time
1½ hours
Ingredients
1 vanilla pod
1 cinnamon stick
½ teaspoon ground cumin
1 tablespoon honey flavouring
Salt and black pepper
1 x 1.5kg (3lb 4oz) chicken
1 unwaxed lemon
4 red onions, quartered

Mildly spiced roast chicken

Poulet rôti aux épices douces

■ **ATTACK**　　■ **CONSOLIDATION**
■ **CRUISE**　　■ **STABILIZATION**

Using a sharp knife, split the vanilla pod lengthways and remove the seeds. Break the cinnamon stick into small pieces and put in a large bowl with the vanilla seeds, cumin, honey flavouring, 4 tablespoons water, some salt and black pepper.

Rinse the chicken, pat it dry with kitchen paper and then roll it in the spice mixture until well coated. Place the chicken in an ovenproof dish.

Preheat the oven to 180°C/350°F/Gas 4.

Using a vegetable peeler, remove the zest from the lemon. Arrange the onion quarters around the chicken. Add the lemon zest and mix it in with any spice mixture at the bottom of the oven dish. Cook the chicken in the oven for 1½ hours, turning the onions from time to time so that they do not burn.

Serve the chicken and onions piping hot.

4 servings
Preparation time
15 minutes
Cooking time
25 minutes
Ingredients
600g (1lb 5oz) chicken breasts
1 small bunch flat-leaf parsley
150g (5½oz) virtually fat-free quark
2 tablespoons wholegrain mustard
White pepper

Oven-baked chicken parcels with mustard and quark

Papillottes de poulet à la moutarde et aux carrés frais

■ **ATTACK**　■ **CONSOLIDATION**
■ **CRUISE**　■ **STABILIZATION**

Cut the chicken breasts into strips and place them in a bowl. Roughly chop the parsley and add to the chicken strips along with the quark and mustard. Add some white pepper and stir all the ingredients together thoroughly so that the chicken strips are well coated.

Preheat the oven to 180°C/350°F/Gas 4.

Cut out four 20 × 20cm (8 × 8in) squares of aluminium foil or greaseproof paper. Divide the chicken mixture between the squares, placing some in the centre of each, then fold up into parcels.

Place the parcels on a baking sheet and bake in the oven for 25 minutes. Serve hot from the oven.

Cockle omelette

Omelette aux coques

2 servings
Preparation time
40 minutes
Cooking time
10 minutes
Ingredients
500g (1lb 2oz) cockles
100ml (3½fl oz) dry white wine
Salt and black pepper
2 shallots, finely chopped
1 onion, finely chopped
¼ bunch parsley, finely chopped
4 eggs
2 tablespoons low-fat cream
   (3% fat)

Contains 2 tolerated food portions
per person

■ CRUISE
■ CONSOLIDATION EXCEPT FOR PP THURSDAYS
■ STABILIZATION EXCEPT FOR PP THURSDAYS

Fill a large bowl with salted water and soak the cockles for
30 minutes. Quickly drain the cockles and transfer to a large pan.
Add the white wine, some salt and black pepper.

Heat the cockles for 5 minutes over a high heat to open them up
(discard any that stay closed). Remove from the heat and, once the
cockles have cooled down, take them out of their shells.

Put the shallots, onion and parsley in a bowl and stir in the cockles.
Season with salt and black pepper.

In another bowl,beat the eggs with the cream and season to taste.
Heat a non-stick frying pan over a medium heat and pour in the
egg mixture. When the omelette is starting to set, scatter the cockle
mixture on top. Finish cooking the omelette to your desired firmness
and serve straightaway.

4 servings
Preparation time
10 minutes
Cooking time
10 minutes
Ingredients
100g (3½oz) smoked salmon
8 eggs
Salt and black pepper
80ml (2¾fl oz) skimmed milk
1 tablespoon fat-free fromage frais
4 chives, to garnish

Scrambled eggs with smoked salmon

Brouillade au saumon fumé

■ **ATTACK**　　■ **CONSOLIDATION**
■ **CRUISE**　　■ **STABILIZATION**

Cut the smoked salmon into thin strips.

In a bowl, whisk the eggs together and add a small pinch of salt and some black pepper.

Warm the skimmed milk in a saucepan. Pour in the beaten eggs and cook over a gentle heat, stirring continuously with a spatula.

Remove the pan from the heat and gently stir in the smoked salmon and fromage frais. Serve straightaway, garnished with the chives.

4 servings
Preparation time
10 minutes
Cooking time
7–10 minutes
Ingredients
12 large spring onions or young
    garlic shoots
8 eggs
200ml (7fl oz) skimmed milk
2 tablespoons low-fat crème fraîche
    (3% fat)
A little grated nutmeg
Salt and black pepper
3 drops butter flavouring (optional)

*Contains ½ tolerated food portion
per person*

Spring onion omelette

Omelette du Sud-Ouest aux aillets

■ **CRUISE**
▨ **CONSOLIDATION EXCEPT FOR PP THURSDAYS**
■ **STABILIZATION EXCEPT FOR PP THURSDAYS**

Peel the spring onions or garlic shoots and keep only the round part. Slice very thinly and fry in a non-stick frying pan until golden brown.

In the meantime, whisk together the eggs, milk, crème fraîche and nutmeg. Season with salt and black pepper and add the butter flavouring (if using).

Pour the egg mixture into the frying pan and cook the omelette over a high heat until you get the texture you like. Halfway through, turn the omelette over and cook the other side. Serve immediately.

2 servings
Preparation time
30 minutes
Cooking time
15 minutes
Ingredients
4 hard-boiled eggs
4 slices extra-lean cooked ham
    (without fat or rind)
30g (1oz) grated low-fat Gruyère
    cheese
For the Dukan béchamel
1 tablespoon cornflour
250ml (9fl oz) skimmed milk
A little grated nutmeg
Salt and black pepper

*Contains 1 tolerated food portion
per person*

Egg gratin Savoyard

Gratin d'oeufs Savoyard

■ **CRUISE**
▨ **CONSOLIDATION EXCEPT FOR PP THURSDAYS**
■ **STABILIZATION EXCEPT FOR PP THURSDAYS**

Preheat the oven to 180°C/350°F/Gas 4.

Make a Dukan béchamel sauce following the recipe on page 61. Pour half of the sauce into a gratin dish.

Shell and halve the hard-boiled eggs and arrange on top of the béchamel sauce. Cut the ham into strips and place on top of the eggs. Cover the ham and eggs with the rest of the sauce. Scatter over the grated cheese.

Bake in the oven for about 15 minutes. Keep an eye on the gratin as it cooks. It is done once it has turned golden brown on top. Serve hot from the oven.

Oat-bran-crusted chicken

Poulet en croûte de son d'avoine

4 servings
Preparation time
5 minutes
Cooking time
40 minutes
Ingredients
1 egg
8 tablespoons oat bran
1 tablespoon chopped fresh
   rosemary, plus a few whole leaves
   to garnish
4 x 150g (5oz) chicken breasts
Salt and black pepper

■ **ATTACK**   ▨ **CONSOLIDATION**
■ **CRUISE**   ■ **STABILIZATION**

Preheat the oven to 200°C/400°F/Gas 6.

Whisk the egg in a bowl. Mix the oat bran and chopped rosemary together in another dish.

Dip the chicken breasts in the beaten egg and then into the oat bran and rosemary mixture so that they are well coated.

Season the chicken to taste and place in a shallow ovenproof dish. Bake in the oven for 30–40 minutes, keeping an eye on the chicken as it cooks.

Salmon burger

Hamburger de saumon

1 serving
Preparation time
10 minutes
Cooking time
4 minutes
Ingredients
2 tablespoons oat bran
1 egg
2 tablespoons fat-free fromage frais
1 teaspoon baking powder
1 teaspoon mustard
30g (1oz) virtually fat-free quark
A few sprigs of dill, finely chopped
1 slice smoked salmon

■ **ATTACK**　　■ **CONSOLIDATION**
■ **CRUISE**　　■ **STABILIZATION**

In a small bowl, combine the oat bran, egg, fromage frais and baking powder. Pour the dough into a round mould and bake for 4 minutes in a microwave oven.

Remove the bread from its mould and slice it in two horizontally. If you prefer a crispier burger bun, lightly toast the bread slices.

Spread the mustard over one slice, then spread the quark over the mustard, scatter over the chopped dill and place the smoked salmon on top. Finally, use the other bread half to complete the burger before serving.

4 servings
Preparation time
25 minutes
Cooking time
30 minutes
Ingredients
2 onions, chopped
3 tablespoons low-fat cream (3% fat)
1 tablespoon finely chopped dill
1 teaspoon finely chopped parsley
1 teaspoon olive flavouring
Salt and black pepper
600g (1lb 5oz) fillet of salmon
1 tablespoon balsamic vinegar
For the crumble topping
8 tablespoons oat bran
2 tablespoons fat-free fromage frais
1 tablespoon cornflour

Contains 1 tolerated food portion per person

Finnish-style salmon crumble

Crumble de saumon à la finlandaise

■ **CRUISE**
■ **CONSOLIDATION EXCEPT FOR PP THURSDAYS**
■ **STABILIZATION EXCEPT FOR PP THURSDAYS**

Preheat the oven to 180°C/350°F/Gas 4.

Put the onions in a frying pan with 3 tablespoons water. Fry over a high heat for 3 minutes until they turn golden brown. Keep to one side.

In a bowl, combine the cream, dill, parsley and olive flavouring, and season with salt and black pepper. Cut the salmon into 1–2cm (½–¾in) cubes.

To make the crumble topping, mix all the ingredients together.

Pour the balsamic vinegar into a gratin or crumble dish, and make sure it covers the bottom of the dish. Add the onions, spreading them out evenly, and then the salmon cubes, spreading them over the onions. Pour over the herb cream and crumble the topping on the top.

Bake in the oven for about 25 minutes and serve hot.

2 servings
Preparation time
10 minutes
Cooking time
20 minutes
Refrigeration time
2–3 hours
Ingredients
6 chicken wings
50ml (2fl oz) soy sauce
1 garlic clove, crushed
1 tablespoon liquid sweetener
4 teaspoons 5-spice powder (star
   anise, cloves, pepper, cinnamon,
   fennel)
1 teaspoon chopped fresh ginger

Crispy chicken wings

Ailes de poulet croustillantes

■ ATTACK   ■ CONSOLIDATION
■ CRUISE   ■ STABILIZATION

Place the chicken wings in a bowl.

In another bowl, mix together the remaining ingredients. Pour over the chicken and leave the wings to marinate in the fridge for 2–3 hours, turning them over once or twice.

Preheat the grill to medium.

Place the chicken wings in a roasting tin and cook under the grill. When the wings start to hiss and crackle, after 5–10 minutes, turn them over and cook them for a further 5–10 minutes.

4 servings
Preparation time
25 minutes
Cooking time
45–60 minutes
Ingredients
1 large chicken
1 onion
2 garlic heads
200g (7oz) virtually fat-free quark
    or extra-light cream cheese, with
    garlic and herbs
6 chives
2 sprigs thyme
1 bay leaf
Salt and black pepper

Garlic-stuffed chicken with herbs

Poulet confit ail et fines herbes

■ **ATTACK**   ▨ **CONSOLIDATION**
■ **CRUISE**   ■ **STABILIZATION**

Preheat the oven to 180°C/350°F/Gas 4.

Peel the onion and cut it into quaters. Peel the garlic cloves, taking care to leave the final layer of skin on half of them.

In a small bowl and using a garlic press, crush all the cloves that have been completely peeled and stir into the quark. Stuff the chicken with the quark and garlic mixture.

Chop the chives into 2cm (¾in) lengths. Place the chicken in a large ovenproof dish and put the thyme, bay leaf, chopped chives, onion and partially peeled garlic cloves around it. Season with salt and black pepper and pour a glass of water into the bottom of the dish.

Depending on the size of the chicken, it will need to cook for at least 60 minutes. To check whether it is done, pierce the thicker part of the thigh with a metal skewer; if the juices run clear with no blood, the bird is ready. Halfway through, baste the bird with the cooking juices and, if necessary, add another glass of water to the bottom of the dish.

Serve the chicken carved into portions.

Meatballs with quark

Boulettes de boeuf aux carrés frais

4 servings
Preparation time
15 minutes
Cooking time
10–12 minutes
Ingredients
600g (1lb 5oz) minced beef (5% fat)
1 egg
100g (3½oz) virtually fat-free quark,
   with garlic and herbs
Pinch of paprika
Black pepper

■ **ATTACK**   ■ **CONSOLIDATION**
■ **CRUISE**   ■ **STABILIZATION**

Preheat the oven to 200°C/400°F/Gas 6 and line a baking tray with greaseproof paper or aluminium foil.

In a bowl, mix the beef with the other ingredients and season generously with black pepper. Stir everything together thoroughly with a spatula.

Using the palms of your hands, quickly roll the meat into small balls – try to minimize contact with your hands, otherwise the mixture will warm up and turn sticky.

Place the meatballs on the baking tray and bake in the oven for 10–12 minutes, depending on how well done you like them. Serve hot or cold.

Spicy Indian pollock

Filets de lieu à l'indienne

2 servings
Preparation time
20 minutes
Cooking time
7 minutes
Ingredients
300g (10½oz) pollock or coley fillets
250ml (9fl oz) low-salt court-
    bouillon or fish stock
1 medium onion, finely chopped
1 egg yolk
Salt and black pepper
½ teaspoon curry powder
Pinch of saffron
1 tablespoon finely chopped parsley,
    to garnish

■ **ATTACK**   ▨ **CONSOLIDATION**
▨ **CRUISE**   ■ **STABILIZATION**

Poach the fish fillets in the hot court-bouillon for about 5 minutes.

In the meantime, brown the onion in a non-stick frying pan. Moisten with a cup of the court-bouillon and reduce for 2 minutes.

Add the egg yolk, diluted in a little of the liquid, and allow the sauce to thicken gradually.

Season to taste with salt and black pepper and then add the curry powder and saffron.

Arrange the fish fillets in a hot serving dish and pour over the sauce. Serve sprinkled with the chopped parsley.

2 servings
Preparation time
20 minutes
Cooking time
25 minutes
Ingredients
150g (5½oz) small mussels,
    scrubbed and rinsed well
300g (10½oz) whiting fillets
1 bay leaf
A few sprigs of thyme
1 teaspoon chopped garlic
1 teaspoon tomato purée
4 teaspoons fat-free fromage frais
Salt and black pepper

Normandy whiting fillets

Filets de merlan à la normande

■ **ATTACK**   ■ **CONSOLIDATION**
■ **CRUISE**   ■ **STABILIZATION**

Cook the mussels for 8–10 minutes, covered, in a frying pan until all the shells have opened. Discard any that refuse to open.

Remove the shells and keep back 100ml (3½fl oz) of the liquid.

Simmer the fish fillets in a flameproof casserole with the bay leaf, thyme, garlic and reserved liquid from the mussels for 10 minutes.

Transfer the fish to a warmed serving dish and put the tomato purée, fromage frais and mussels in the casserole. Season and cook the mussels for 2 minutes over a very gentle heat, then pour the sauce over the fish before serving.

4 servings
Preparation time
30 minutes
Cooking time
20 minutes
Ingredients
For the base
12 tablespoons oat bran
12 tablespoons fat-free fromage
  frais
12 tablespoons powdered skimmed
  milk
4 egg whites
Salt and black pepper
For the topping
8 scallops
300g (10½oz) virtually fat-free
  quark
100g (3½oz) tinned tuna in brine or
  spring water (drained weight)
200g (7oz) cooked and shelled
  small prawns
4 tablespoons fat-free fromage frais
A few sprigs of dill
A few chives, chopped
Juice of 1 lemon

Dukan seafood pizza

Pizza Dukan terre et mer

■ ATTACK   ▨ CONSOLIDATION
■ CRUISE   ■ STABILIZATION

Preheat the oven to 200°C/400°F/Gas 6.

Make the pizza base by combining the oat bran, fromage frais and skimmed milk. Whisk the egg whites until stiff and gently fold them in. Season with salt and black pepper.

Spread the dough out to the size of a plate on some greaseproof paper and bake on a baking sheet in the middle of the oven for a few minutes. Keep an eye on the base as it cooks to make sure that it turns golden brown but does not swell up.

For the topping, fry the scallops very quickly in a non-stick pan. and put to one side.

Preheat the grill to high.

Mix together the quark, tuna, scallops, prawns, fromage frais, dill and chives. Season with salt and black pepper and drizzle over the lemon juice.

Spread the topping over the pizza base and cook under the grill for a few minutes. Serve hot.

Omelette mille-feuilles with smoked salmon

Mille-feuilles d'omelette au saumon fumé

4 servings
Preparation time
25 minutes
Cooking time
15 minutes
Ingredients
8 eggs
8 tablespoons skimmed milk
Salt and black pepper
100g (3½oz) fat-free fromage frais
Juice of ½ lemon
¼ bunch chives, finely chopped, plus extra to garnish
200g (7oz) smoked salmon
A little salmon roe, to garnish

■ **ATTACK**   ■ **CONSOLIDATION**
■ **CRUISE**   ■ **STABILIZATION**

Preheat the oven to 180°C/350°F/Gas 4 and prepare two rectangular ovenproof dishes by lining them with some greaseproof paper.

In a bowl, whisk the eggs with the milk until smooth. Season very sparingly with salt (the smoked salmon contains a lot) and add some black pepper. Divide the mixture between the two dishes to make a very thin omelette in each and bake in the oven for about 15 minutes until cooked. Remove from the oven and leave to cool down.

Once the omelettes are completely cold, peel them away from the greaseproof paper and cut each one into 8 equal rectangles.

In a small bowl, combine the fromage frais with the lemon juice and chopped chives. Add a little salt and black pepper to taste.

Place a first rectangle of omelette on your serving plate and cover it with fromage frais sauce, then with a piece of smoked salmon. Next place another omelette rectangle on top and continue building layers until the fourth rectangle. Assemble the remaining three mille-feuilles in the same way

Finish off by topping the mille-feuilles with a little fromage frais sauce and garnishing with some salmon roe and a few chives. Serve well chilled.

Lemongrass chicken

Poulet à la citronnelle

8 servings
Preparation time
30 minutes
Cooking time
55 minutes
Ingredients
1.5kg (3lb 5oz) chicken breasts
2 small shallots, finely chopped
3 lemongrass stalks, finely chopped
Pinch of chilli powder
2 tablespoons fish sauce
2 tablespoons soy sauce
1 teaspoon Hermesetas liquid
   sweetener
Salt and black pepper

■ **ATTACK**   ▨ **CONSOLIDATION**
■ **CRUISE**   ■ **STABILIZATION**

Cut the chicken breasts into thin strips and sear in a large non-stick pan. Cook for about 10 minutes to brown the meat.

Add the rest of the ingredients and cook, covered, over a gentle heat for 45 minutes. Serve straightaway.

2 servings
Make a day in advance
Preparation time
25 minutes
Cooking time
50 minutes
Marinating time
8 hours
Ingredients
1 bouquet garni
Juice of 2 limes
1 onion, chopped
1 × 400–500g (14oz–1lb 2oz)
  poussin
2 egg whites
2kg (4lb 8oz) coarse sea salt

Lime and salt-crusted poussin

Coquelet au citron vert en croûte de sel

- ■ **ATTACK**
- ■ **CRUISE**
- ■ **CONSOLIDATION**
- ■ **STABILIZATION**

The day before you intend serving the dish put the bouquet garni, juice of half a lime, the onion and poussin in 1 litre (1¾ pints) cold water to marinate.

The following day, stuff the inside of the poussin with the seasoning bits from the marinade.

Preheat the oven to 200°C/400°F/Gas 6.

Mix together the egg whites and the sea salt and use some of this mixture to cover the bottom of a baking dish. Place the poussin in the middle of the dish and cover it with the remaining salt.

Bake the poussin in the oven for 50 minutes, then turn off the heat.

Allow the the poussin to rest in the switched-off oven for 10 minutes.

To serve, break the sea-salt crust with a hammer or the back of a spoon, halve the poussin and drizzle over the remaining lime juice.

Strain the juices carefully and serve as a sauce with the poussin.

4 servings
Preparation time
10 minutes
Cooking time
10 minutes
Ingredients
2 pieces fresh ginger, grated
2 tablespoons soy sauce
4 x 110g (4oz) sea bass fillets (with
   the skin)

You will need a steamer

Ginger steamed sea bass fillets

Filets de bar à la vapeur de gingembre

■ ATTACK   ■ CONSOLIDATION
■ CRUISE   ■ STABILIZATION

In the bottom of a steamer, warm a little water with half the grated ginger and half the soy sauce.

Steam the sea bass fillets in the upper part of the steamer for 10 minutes.

Serve the fish with the rest of the grated ginger and soy sauce.

4 servings
Preparation time
5 minutes
Cooking time
10 minutes
Ingredients
150g (5½oz) virtually fat-free quark
Salt and black pepper
4 x 240g (9oz) salmon steaks
   (without the skin)
10 tablespoons oat bran

Oat-bran-coated salmon steaks

Pavés de saumon panés

■ ATTACK   ■ CONSOLIDATION
■ CRUISE   ■ STABILIZATION

Stir the quark with a fork, add 1 tablespoon water and season with salt and black pepper.

Dip the salmon steaks into the quark mixture, then coat them in the oat bran.

Warm a non-stick frying pan and cook the steaks for 5 minutes on each side. Serve immediately.

4 servings
Preparation time
10 minutes
Cooking time
10 minutes
Ingredients
4 x 130g (4½oz) sole fillets
Salt and black pepper
4 tablespoons balsamic vinegar
2 tablespoons finely chopped fresh
   herbs (parsley, tarragon, chervil,
   chives)

You will need a steamer and
4 wooden cocktail sticks

Fillets of sole with balsamic vinegar

Filets de sole au vinaigre balsamique

■ **ATTACK**   ■ **CONSOLIDATION**
■ **CRUISE**   ■ **STABILIZATION**

Starting with the thickest side, roll up the sole fillets and use wooden cocktail sticks to hold them in place. Season with a little salt. Heat some water in a steamer and steam the sole fillets for 10 minutes.

In the meantime, prepare the balsamic dressing: combine the vinegar with 4 tablespoons water and the finely chopped herbs. Season with salt and black pepper.

Once the fish is cooked, arrange on four warmed plates, pour over the balsamic vinegar dressing and serve straightaway.

Salt-crusted sea bream

Dorade en croûte de sel

■ **ATTACK**   ▨ **CONSOLIDATION**
■ **CRUISE**   ■ **STABILIZATION**

4 servings
Preparation time
10 minutes
Cooking time
1½ hours
Ingredients
1 × 800g–1kg (1lb 12oz–2lb 4oz)
 sea bream
2.5kg (5lb 8oz) coarse sea salt

Clean and gut the sea bream but do not remove the scales.

Preheat the oven to 230°C/450°F/Gas 8.

You will need an ovenproof casserole slightly larger than the fish. Line the bottom and sides with aluminium foil. Fill the bottom of the dish with a layer of sea salt 3cm (1¼in) thick. Place the sea bream on top and cover with the remaining salt. The fish should be completely covered.

Sprinkle with a little water to form the crust.

Cook for 1 hour in the oven, then lower the temperature to 180°C/350°F/Gas 4 and continue cooking for 30 minutes.

Turn the contents of the casserole out on to a chopping board. Use the back of a spoon or a hammer to extract the fish from the block of salt. Brush away the salt and carefully remove the skin of the fish before serving.

2 servings
Preparation time
10 minutes
Cooking time
10 minutes
Ingredients
1 onion, chopped
250g (9oz) chicken livers
A drizzle of balsamic vinegar
2 eggs
100ml (3½fl oz) skimmed milk
Salt and black pepper
¼ bunch chives, chopped

Scrambled chicken livers

Brouillade aux foies de volaille

■ ATTACK   ■ CONSOLIDATION
■ CRUISE   ■ STABILIZATION

Warm a non-stick frying pan over a high heat. Add the onion and then the chicken livers and cook for 7–8 minutes. Once the livers are cooked, deglaze with the balsamic vinegar. Put to one side.

In a small bowl, whisk together the eggs and skimmed milk and season with salt and black pepper. Pour this mixture into the frying pan and scramble using a wooden spoon.

Stir the chicken livers into the scrambled eggs and divide between two warmed plates.

Scatter over the chopped chives and serve immediately

4 servings
Preparation time
15 minutes
Cooking time
6 minutes
Ingredients
4 very thin veal slices
4 eggs
Salt and black pepper
4 tablespoons oat bran
Lime wedges, to serve

Milan-style veal escalopes

Escalopes de veau milanaises

■ ATTACK   ■ CONSOLIDATION
■ CRUISE   ■ STABILIZATION

Tenderize the veal slices by beating them with a meat hammer or rolling pin until they are nice and thin.

Whisk the eggs together in a dish and season to taste. Place the oat bran in another dish. Dip the escalopes into the beaten eggs and then dip them in the oat bran. Dip them once again very quickly into the eggs and then for a second time in the oat bran so that they get a good thick coating.

Heat a non-stick frying pan and cook the escalopes for 3 minutes on each side. Serve with a few wedges of lime.

6 servings
Preparation time
15 minutes
Cooking time
10 minutes
Ingredients
8 sprigs mint
8 sprigs coriander
1kg (2lb 4oz) chicken breasts
2 egg whites
Salt and black pepper
6 tablespoons oat bran

Chicken and herb balls

Boulettes de poulet aux herbes

■ **ATTACK**   ■ **CONSOLIDATION**
■ **CRUISE**   ■ **STABILIZATION**

Preheat the oven to 180°C/350°F/Gas 4 and line a baking sheet with greaseproof paper or aluminium foil.

Wash the mint and coriander and remove the leaves, discarding the stems. Cut the chicken into cubes and roughly blend in a food processor. Add the egg whites, mint and coriander leaves, some salt and black pepper. Blend so that the minced chicken is not too fine. Add the oat bran and quickly blend one last time.

Using the palms of your hands, shape the minced chicken into large balls and place them on the baking sheet. Bake in the oven for 15 minutes.

Arrange on a warmed plate and serve.

Mint-and-cinnamon-scented sea bass

Filets de bar à la vapeur de menthe-cannelle

4 servings

Preparation time

10 minutes

Cooking time

10 minutes

Ingredients

10g (¼oz) coarse sea salt

3 sprigs fresh mint

½ teaspoon ground cinnamon

4 x 110g (4oz) sea bass fillets (with the skin)

½ lemon

2 cinnamon sticks

Salt and black pepper

You will need a steamer

■ **ATTACK**   ▨ **CONSOLIDATION**

■ **CRUISE**   ■ **STABILIZATION**

Put some water in the bottom of a steamer along with the sea salt, mint and ground cinnamon. Reserve a few mint leaves to garnish.

Place the fish fillets in the upper part of the steamer and cook for 10 minutes.

Serve the fish on warmed plates. Squeeze a drizzle of lemon juice over each fillet and decorate with the reserved mint leaves and half a cinnamon stick.

4 servings
Preparation time
5 minutes
Cooking time
10 minutes
Ingredients
4 eggs
3 tablespoons Japanese dashi stock
2 teaspoons crystallized stevia
2 teaspoons soy sauce

You will need a rectangular
non-stick frying pan (10cm/4in)
–a Tamagoyaki pan– used in
Japanese cooking

Japanese rolled Tamagoyaki omelette

Omelette japonaise Tamagoyaki

■ **ATTACK**   ▨ **CONSOLIDATION**
▨ **CRUISE**   ■ **STABILIZATION**

In a small bowl, beat together the eggs, dashi and crystallized sweetener.

Warm the Tamagoyaki pan over a high heat.

Pour a thin layer of the omelette mixture into the pan and cook it gently. Once it is cooked, roll the omelette to one side of the pan. Make a second omelette and then roll this one around the first omelette and repeat until the Tamagoyaki omelette is finished.

You will end up with quite a large omelette roll. Cut it into slices and serve with the soy sauce.

4 servings
Preparation time
10 minutes
Cooking time
30 minutes
Ingredients
400ml (14fl oz) skimmed milk
4 level tablespoons granulated
   sweetener
2 eggs
8 drops of lavender flavouring
Lavender flowers (optional)

Lavender ramekins

Ramequins à la lavande

■ **ATTACK**   ■ **CONSOLIDATION**
■ **CRUISE**   ■ **STABILIZATION**

Preheat the oven to 180°C/350°F/Gas 4 and place a baking dish
with some water in the bottom on to a baking tray.

Bring the milk to the boil in a saucepan.

Meanwhile, in a bowl, stir the sweetener into the eggs and then
add the lavender flavouring. Gently stir in the hot milk, little by little.

Divide the lavender milk between four ramekins and place them
in the baking dish. Bake in the oven, in the bain-marie, for 25
minutes, keeping an eye on them to check when they are done.

Remove the ramekins from the oven and leave them to cool down.

Decorate with lavender flowers, if you like, before serving.

4 servings
Preparation time
25 minutes
Cooking time
40 minutes
Ingredients
1 quantity Sweet Galette mixture
   (see page 53)
3 eggs
4 tablespoons Splenda granules
60g (2¼oz) fat-free fromage frais
60g (2¼oz) virtually fat-free quark
1 tablespoon ground cinnamon
1 vanilla pod

Cinnamon tart

Tarte à la cannelle

■ **ATTACK**　　■ **CONSOLIDATION**
■ **CRUISE**　　■ **STABILIZATION**

Preheat the oven to 220°C/425°F/Gas 7 and line a tart dish with greaseproof paper. If you prefer, you can use individual tartlet tins, as shown in the photograph.

First make the galette dough for the tart base by following the recipe on page 53.

Place the galette dough over the bottom of the dish and bake in the oven for 10 minutes

Meanwhile, make the filling: break the eggs into a bowl and whisk them until smooth. Add the sweetener and whisk again until the mixture is creamy.

Drain any liquid from the fromage frais and quark and gently fold into the eggs along with the ground cinnamon.

Split the vanilla pod, scrape out all the seeds and add them to the mixture.

Pour the filling over the tart base and bake in the oven for 30 minutes. Serve warm or cold.

4 servings
Preparation time
5 minutes
Cooking time
10 minutes
Ingredients
1 litre (1¾ pints) skimmed milk
4 pinches ground cinnamon
1 teaspoon vanilla or honey
    flavouring
4 egg yolks
8 tablespoons Canderel granules
1 teaspoon rum flavouring

Egg flip
Lait de poule

■ **ATTACK**　　■ **CONSOLIDATION**
■ **CRUISE**　　■ **STABILIZATION**

Heat the milk in a pan and add the cinnamon and vanilla or honey flavouring.

In a bowl, whisk the egg yolks with the sweetener. Add the eggs to the hot milk, whisking continuously. Add the rum flavouring.

Serve hot in four large glasses.

1 serving
Preparation time
15 minutes
Cooking time
5 minutes
Refrigeration time
1 hour
Ingredients
4 gelatine leaves
Pinch of salt
3 egg whites
3 tablespoons Canderel granules
1 teaspoon violet flavouring

Violet marshmallow
Guimauve à la violette

■ **ATTACK**　　■ **CONSOLIDATION**
■ **CRUISE**　　■ **STABILIZATION**

Soften the gelatine in a little cold water in a bowl.

Add a pinch of salt to the egg whites and beat until very stiff.

Dissolve the gelatine in approximately 250ml (9fl oz) water in a panover gentle heat, then add the sweetener and a few drops of flavouring.

Gradually add the beaten egg whites, whisking all the time.

Pour the mixture into a mould (preferably silicone) and leave to set in the fridge for 1 hour.

Turn out the marshmallow to serve.

 Note: Take care not to dissolve your gelatine in too much water otherwise there will be more liquid than egg white.

2 servings
Make a day in advance
Preparation time
15 minutes
Cooking time
5 minutes
Refrigeration time
12 hours
Ingredients
3 gelatine leaves
2 egg whites
440g (15½oz) fat-free fromage frais
1 tablespoon vanilla flavouring
2 tablespoons Canderel granules

Vanilla fromage frais bavarois

Bavarois de fromage blanc à la vanille

■ ATTACK   ■ CONSOLIDATION
■ CRUISE   ■ STABILIZATION

Soak the gelatine leaves for 5 minutes in a little cold water.

Beat the egg whites until stiff.

Gently heat 3 tablespoons water in a pan. Wipe the gelatine leaves dry and place them in the hot water, stirring them so that they dissolve.

Whip the fromage frais, then add the vanilla flavouring, the stiffly beaten egg whites and liquid gelatine and continue beating for 2–3 minutes.

Add the sweetener and refrigerate overnight. Serve well chilled.

2 servings

Preparation time

20 minutes

Cooking time

40 minutes

Ingredients

2 eggs, separated

6 tablespoons fat-free fromage frais

1 tablespoon Hermesetas liquid
sweetener

1 teaspoon lemon juice (or orange
flower water)

Lisaline dessert

Dessert Lisaline

■ **ATTACK**   ▨ **CONSOLIDATION**

■ **CRUISE**   ■ **STABILIZATION**

Preheat the oven to 180°C/350°F/Gas 4.

Stir the egg yolks into the fromage frais along with the sweetener
and lemon juice or orange flower water. Keep stirring until the
mixture is completely smooth.

Whisk the egg whites until stiff. Gently fold the fromage frais
mixture into the egg whites.

Pour into ramekin dishes and bake in the oven for 25–30 minutes,
then brown the desserts under the grill for 5–10 minutes. Be careful
not to let them burn. Serve warm.

Blancmange

Blanc-manger

■ **ATTACK**   ▫ **CONSOLIDATION**
▫ **CRUISE**   ■ **STABILIZATION**

4 servings
Preparation time
25 minutes
Cooking time
5 minutes
Refrigeration time
2 hours minimum
Ingredients
2 gelatine leaves
400g (14oz) fat-free fromage frais
3 tablespoons Canderel granules
8–10 drops bitter almond flavouring
1 egg white

Soak the gelatine leaves in a little cold water in abowl.

Gently heat 50g (1¾oz) of the fromage frais in a small saucepan. Drain the gelatine, squeeze out any water and carefully stir into the fromage frais until completely dissolved.

Pour the rest of the fromage frais into a bowl along with 2 tablespoons of the sweetener and the almond flavouring. Beat until smooth, then stir this into the fromage frais and gelatine mixture.

Whisk the egg white until almost stiff, then add the remaining sweetener and continue whisking for a few more seconds. Gently fold the beaten egg white into the fromage frais.

Divide the mixture between four ramekin dishes and refrigerate for at least 2 hours before serving.

2 servings
Preparation time
20 minutes
Freezing time
25 minutes or 3½ hours, depending
on whether or not you use an
ice-cream maker
Ingredients
3 tablespoons China tea
Juice of 1 lemon
2 teaspoons crystallized stevia
2 fresh mint leaves

You will need an ice-cream maker

China tea sorbet
Sorbet au thé

■ ATTACK   ▨ CONSOLIDATION
■ CRUISE   ■ STABILIZATION

Boil 300ml (10fl oz) water, add the tea, cover and leave to infuse for 3 minutes.

Strain 240ml (8½fl oz) of the tea infusion through a conical strainer and pour into an ice-cream machine drum along with the lemon juice and sweetener. Churn for 25 minutes. If you are not using an ice-cream maker, freeze for 3½ hours.

Strain the remaining tea infusion and pour into a flat metal tray that can be put in the freezer.

Freeze, stirring with a fork every 10 minutes, until small ice crystals start to form.

When ready to serve, fill some pretty glasses – for example, champagne flutes – with the sorbet, creating a dome shape. Scatter over the iced tea crystals and place a fresh mint leaf on top to finish off.

4 servings
Preparation time
5 minutes
Cooking time
2 minutes
Refrigeration time
2 hours
Ingredients
800ml (28fl oz) skimmed milk
2 × 2g sachets agar-agar
20 drops lychee flavouring
4 egg yolks
4 teaspoons crystallized stevia

Lychee creams
Crèmes au litchi

■ ATTACK   ▨ CONSOLIDATION
■ CRUISE   ■ STABILIZATION

Heat the milk over a high heat, adding the agar-agar and lychee flavouring, and boil for 1½ minutes. Remove from the heat.

Combine the 4 egg yolks with the crystallized sweetener, then gently stir in the hot milk and leave to cool.

Pour the mixture into four dishes and refrigerate for 2 hours before serving.

2 servings
Preparation time
15 minutes
Freezing time
1 hour
Refrigeration time
15 minutes
Ingredients
500ml (18fl oz) hot black coffee
2 Canderel vanilla sticks
1 teaspoon ground cinnamon
3 cardamon seeds

Coffee and cinnamon granita

Granité de café à la cannelle

■ ATTACK   ■ CONSOLIDATION
■ CRUISE   ■ STABILIZATION

Mix together the hot coffee, sweetener and spices. Stir and leave to cool.

Pour into a metal dish and freeze for about 1 hour.

Blend the mixture for 1 minute and then return to the metal dish. Refrigerate for about 15 minutes.

Divide the granita between two sundae dishes and serve.

4 servings
Preparation time
10 minutes
Cooking time
20 minutes
Ingredients
4 eggs
400ml (14fl oz) skimmed milk
1 vanilla pod
1 teaspoon vanilla flavouring
½ teaspoon grated nutmeg, plus a
  little extra for sprinkling
4 tablespoons Splenda granules

Vanilla-nutmeg custards

Flans vanilla-muscade

■ **ATTACK**   ■ **CONSOLIDATION**
■ **CRUISE**   ■ **STABILIZATION**

Preheat the oven to 160°C/325°F/Gas 3.

Beat the eggs together in a bowl.

Put the milk in a pan. Split the vanilla pod, scrape out the seeds into the milk and add the pod. Warm the milk without allowing it to boil.

Remove the vanilla pod and pour the milk over the beaten eggs.

Add the vanilla flavouring and ground nutmeg along with the sweetener and pour the mixture into individual ramekin dishes.

Grate a little fresh nutmeg over the custards and bake in the oven, in a bain-marie, for about 20 minutes. Serve warm or cold.

1 serving
Preparation time
10 minutes
Cooking time
20 minutes
Ingredients
2 eggs, separated
1 teaspoon Hermesetas liquid
   sweetener
1 teaspoon vanilla or dark chocolate
   flavouring
1 tablespoon wheat bran
2 tablespoons oat bran (or 1½
   tablespoons in Attack phase)

Cookies

■ ATTACK   ▨ CONSOLIDATION
■ CRUISE   ■ STABILIZATION

Preheat the oven to 180°C/350°F/Gas 4 and line a baking sheet with greaseproof paper.

In a bowl, combine the egg yolks with the sweetener, flavouring and the wheat and oat brans.

Whisk the egg whites until very stiff and then gently fold them into the bran mixture.

Place small, cookie-sized portions of dough on the baking sheet. Bake in the oven for 15–20 minutes. Serve warm from the oven or allow to cool.

2 servings

Preparation time

15 minutes

Cooking time

20 minutes

Ingredients

500ml (18fl oz) skimmed milk

3 eggs

4 tablespoons Canderel granules

2 tablespoons vanilla flavouring

Pinch of grated nutmeg

Vanilla creams

Crèmes à la vanille

■ **ATTACK**   ■ **CONSOLIDATION**

■ **CRUISE**   ■ **STABILIZATION**

Preheat the oven to 180°C/350°F/Gas 4.

Whisk together the milk, eggs, sweetener and vanilla flavouring.

Pour the mixture into two individual shallow ovenproof dishes and sprinkle over some grated nutmeg.

Bake in the oven, in a bain-marie, for 20 minutes, until set.

The creams can be served either warm or cold.

1 serving
Preparation time
5 minutes
Refrigeration time
2 hours minimum
Ingredients
10g (¼oz) powdered skimmed milk
Pinch of instant coffee powder or
    granules
½ gelatine leaf
1 tablespoon Canderel granules

Japanese cream

Crème japonaise

■ **ATTACK**   ■ **CONSOLIDATION**
■ **CRUISE**   ■ **STABILIZATION**

Reconstitute the milk using 100ml (3½fl oz) water. Flavour with the instant coffee and heat without allowing to boil.

Soften the gelatine in 3 tablespoons cold water and let it swell. Add to the milk along with the sweetener.

Pour the cream mixture into a sundae dish and refrigerate for at least 2 hours before serving.

Lime sorbet

Sorbet au citron vert

2 servings
Preparation time
10 minutes
Freezing time
30 minutes or 3½ hours, depending
on whether or not you use an
ice-cream maker

Ingredients
4 unwaxed limes
500g (1lb 2oz) fat-free fromage
frais
3 teaspoons crystallized stevia (or
more, to taste)

You will need an ice-cream maker

■ **ATTACK**   ■ **CONSOLIDATION**
■ **CRUISE**   ■ **STABILIZATION**

Remove the zest from one of the limes with a zester. Chop very finely with a sharp knife.

Blend together the fromage frais, the juice from the 4 limes, the zest and sweetener.

Pour the mixture into an ice-cream machine drum and churn for 30 minutes before serving. Alternatively, place in the freezer for 3½ hours if you are not using an ice-cream maker.

4 servings
Preparation time
20 minutes
Cooking time
10 minutes
Refrigeration time
30 minutes
Ingredients
500ml (18fl oz) skimmed milk
½ vanilla pod
4 eggs, separated
4 tablespoons Splenda granules

Floating meringues

Oeufs à la neige

■ ATTACK   ■ CONSOLIDATION
■ CRUISE   ■ STABILIZATION

Put the milk in a pan, split the vanilla pod and scrape in the seeds. Bring to the boil.

Beat the egg yolks with the sweetener until they turn pale.

Gently stir the boiling milk, little by little, into the yolks. Pour the milk back into the saucepan and warm over a gentle heat, stirring all the time with a wooden spoon to prevent the mixture sticking to the bottom of the pan. As soon as the custard starts to set, remove the pan from the heat. Do not allow it to come to the boil, otherwise it will curdle.

Pour the custard into a bowl and, when it has cooled down a little, cover with clingfilm and refrigerate.

Whisk the egg whites until stiff. Using a tablespoon, place balls of egg white into a pan of boiling water. As soon as they start to swell up, lift them out with a slotted spoon and drain on some kitchen paper.

Divide the custard between four sundae dishes and arrange the egg whites on top. Serve well chilled.

2 servings
Preparation time
10 minutes
Freezing time
30 minutes or 3½ hours, depending
on whether or not you use an
ice-cream maker
Ingredients
2 unwaxed lemons
500g (1lb 2oz) fat-free yoghurt
3 teaspoons crystallized stevia (or
more, to taste)
2 tablespoons fat-free fromage frais
2 fresh mint leaves

You will need an ice-cream maker

Yoghurt sorbet

Sorbet au yaourt

■ **ATTACK**　　■ **CONSOLIDATION**
■ **CRUISE**　　■ **STABILIZATION**

Remove the zest from one of the lemons with a zester. Chop very
finely with a sharp knife.

Beat the yoghurt with a whisk. Add the lemon zest and then the
juice from both lemons, the sweetener and fromage frais. Stir all
the ingredients together thoroughly.

Pour the yoghurt mixture into an ice-cream machine drum and
churn for 30 minutes. Alternatively, place in the freezer for 3½
hours if you are not using an ice-cream maker. Serve each portion
decorated with a mint leaf.

Iced lemon mousse

Mousse glacée au citron

2–3 servings
Preparation time
10 minutes
Freezing time
40 minutes
Ingredients
4 egg whites
5 unwaxed lemons
500g (1lb 2oz) fat-free fromage
    frais
8 tablespoons Canderel granules

■ **ATTACK**   ▨ **CONSOLIDATION**
■ **CRUISE**   ■ **STABILIZATION**

Whisk the egg whites until very stiff. Remove the zest from one of the lemons.

Beat the fromage frais with a whisk. Gently stir in the lemon zest, the juice from all 5 lemons and the egg whites. Add the sweetener.

Freeze the mousse in one large dish or in individual sundae dishes until it has set firm and then serve.

209

No-pastry lemon tart

Tarte au citron sans pâte

■ **ATTACK**   ■ **CONSOLIDATION**
■ **CRUISE**   ■ **STABILIZATION**

4 servings
Preparation time
15 minutes
Cooking time
35 minutes
Ingredients
3 eggs, separated
8 tablespoons Splenda granules
Grated zest and juice of 1 unwaxed
   lemon
Pinch of salt

Preheat the oven to 180°C/350°F/Gas 4.

In a bowl, beat the egg yolks with the sweetener until they turn pale.

Add 30ml (1fl oz) cold water and the lemon zest and juice.

Half-fill with water a pan into which the bowl will fit snugly and place the bowl over it. Cook over a gentle heat, stirring with a spatula until the mixture thickens. Remove from the heat.

Add a pinch of salt to the egg whites and whisk until stiff. Gently fold the egg whites into the hot egg yolks.

Pour the mixture into a non-stick baking dish 28cm (11in) in diameter. Bake in the oven for about 35 minutes, until the tart turns golden brown on top. Serve warm.

2 servings
Preparation time
15 minutes
Cooking time
3 minutes
Refrigeration time
3 hours
Ingredients
400ml (14fl oz) skimmed milk
6 drops bitter almond flavouring
3 gelatine leaves
2 teaspoons crystallized stevia
  (or more, to taste)

Almond milk jellies

Gelées d'amande

■ **ATTACK**   ▨ **CONSOLIDATION**
■ **CRUISE**   ■ **STABILIZATION**

Heat the milk and bitter almond flavouring in a saucepan and bring to the boil.

Soak the gelatine leaves in a little cold water for a few minutes.

Drain the gelatine, then gently stir it into the boiled milk, which has been taken off the heat.

Stir until all the gelatine has dissolved and add the sweetener.

Pour the mixture into small moulds and leave to set in the fridge for at least 3 hours before serving.

You will have to wait until Phase 4 – Stabilization before you can eat the almonds shown in the photo.

Jasmine tea granita

Granité de thé au jasmin

■ **ATTACK**   ■ **CONSOLIDATION**
■ **CRUISE**   ■ **STABILIZATION**

4 servings
Preparation time
20 minutes
Cooking time
10 minutes
Freezing time
2 hours
Ingredients
1 unwaxed lemon
30g (1oz) Hermesetas liquid
    sweetener
1 tablespoon jasmine tea

Remove the zest from the lemon.

In a pan, heat 400ml (14fl oz) water with the sweetener and lemon zest and bring to the boil. Then add the tea and leave to infuse for 8 minutes.

Strain the tea through a conical strainer and place in the freezer.

After 1 hour, when ice crystals have started to form, stir the tea mixture thoroughly and return to the freezer until it starts to turn into a granita (about another hour).

Use a fork to serve the granita in small bowls or glass dishes.

Proteins + vegetables (PV)

Proteins + vegetables are the staple foods in **Phase 2 – Cruise**, which means you can now eat vegetables again. Of course, you have to alternate these recipes with the pure protein (PP) ones. Rediscover the fresh, crisp taste of vegetables and enjoy!

6 servings
Preparation time
10 minutes
Refrigeration time
1 hour
Ingredients
125g (4¼oz) tinned crab meat in
    brine or spring water (drained
    weight)
150g (5½oz) virtually fat-free quark
Drizzle of lemon juice
2 egg whites
2 chicory heads
2 carrots, cut into batons
2 celery sticks, cut into batons

Vegetable dip with crab mousse

Dip de légumes en mousse de crabe

■ **CRUISE PV**
■ **CONSOLIDATION EXCEPT FOR PP THURSDAYS**
■ **STABILIZATION EXCEPT FOR PP THURSDAYS**

Place the crab meat in a blender. Add the quark and lemon juice and purée until you have a smooth mixture.

Beat the egg whites in a bowl until very stiff and then gently fold them into the crab mixture. Refrigerate the crab mousse for at least 1 hour.

Cut out the base of the chicory heads and separate the leaves.

Serve the vegetables with the crab mousse so that everyone can dip in and enjoy!

Prawns with dill

Verrines de crevettes à l'aneth

4 servings
Preparation time
10 minutes
Refrigeration time
30 minutes
Ingredients
½ unwaxed lime
200g (7oz) fat-free fromage frais,
    beaten
½ shallot, finely chopped
1 small bunch dill, finely chopped
Salt and black pepper
1 lettuce
20 large cooked prawns

■ **CRUISE PV**
■ **CONSOLIDATION EXCEPT FOR PP THURSDAYS**
■ **STABILIZATION EXCEPT FOR PP THURSDAYS**

Remove the zest from the lime and cut into very thin strips with a sharp knife. Squeeze the juice from the lime.

In a small bowl, mix together the fromage frais, lime juice, shallot and dill. Season with salt and pepper and refrigerate for 30 minutes.

Wash and dry the lettuce, and shell the prawns.

When ready to serve, cut the lettuce leaves into thin strips and divide between four glass dishes. Arrange 5 prawns per dish on top of the lettuce and then drizzle over some of the fromage frais sauce. Garnish with the lime zest.

Serve well chilled.

4 servings
Preparation time
10 minutes
Cooking time
2 hours
Ingredients
10 round firm tomatoes
Generous pinch of mild paprika

Paprika tomato crisps

Chips de tomates au paprika

■ **CRUISE PV**
■ **CONSOLIDATION EXCEPT FOR PP THURSDAYS**
■ **STABILIZATION EXCEPT FOR PP THURSDAYS**

Preheat the oven to 160°C/325°F/Gas 3 and line a baking tray with greaseproof paper.

Cut the tomatoes into 2–3mm-($\frac{1}{8}$in)-thick slices.

Place the tomato slices on the greaseproof paper and sprinkle the mild paprika powder all over them.

Bake in the oven for 2 hours, keeping a careful eye on the crisps.

Allow to cool before storing in an airtight container in a dry place. Serve the paprika tomato crisps with your aperitif.

Spinach muffins with quark centres

Muffins aux épinards coeur de fromage frais

2 servings
Preparation time
20 minutes
Cooking time
30 minutes
Ingredients
500g (1lb 2oz) frozen leaf spinach
4 tablespoons oat bran
2 tablespoons wheat bran
4 tablespoons powdered skimmed milk
½ teaspoon baking powder
1 egg, beaten
Salt and black pepper
50g (1¾oz) virtually fat-free quark

■ **CRUISE PV**
■ **CONSOLIDATION EXCEPT FOR PP THURSDAYS**
■ **STABILIZATION EXCEPT FOR PP THURSDAYS**

Preheat the oven to 180°C/350°F/Gas 4.

You will need either two silicone muffin moulds or two ramekin dishes lined with greaseproof paper.

Thaw the frozen spinach over a very gentle heat and cook for about 10 minutes. Purée the spinach very quickly in a blender, drain off any liquid and leave to cool down.

In a bowl, mix together the spinach, oat bran, wheat bran, powdered milk, baking powder and beaten egg, and season with salt and black pepper.

Using half the mixture, spread a layer in each mould or ramekin, then divide the fromage frais between the two. Finally, cover with the remaining spinach mixture.

Bake in the oven for about 20 minutes, until the muffins have risen and are cooked on top.

Remove the muffins from the oven and leave to rest for 5 minutes before turning them out of the moulds or ramekins to serve.

4 servings
Preparation time
10 minutes
Refrigeration time
30 minutes
Ingredients
1 garlic clove, finely chopped
½ bunch chives, chopped
200g (7oz) virtually fat-free quark
8 slices extra-lean cooked ham
   (without fat or rind)
8 lettuce leaves
4 sprigs parsley, to garnish

Ham roulades

Roulades de jambon

■ **CRUISE PV**
■ **CONSOLIDATION EXCEPT FOR PP THURSDAYS**
■ **STABILIZATION EXCEPT FOR PP THURSDAYS**

Mix the garlic and chives into the quark.

Spread the quark mixture over the ham slices and roll them up.

Place the ham roulades in the fridge for 30 minutes so that the quark mixture sets.

Decorate each serving dish with 2 lettuce leaves. Cut the roulades into smaller slices and use wooden cocktail sticks to hold them together. Place a few on the bed of lettuce.

To garnish, add a sprig of parsley before serving.

4 servings
Preparation time
10 minutes
Ingredients
1 small cucumber
6 slices extra-lean cooked ham
    (without fat or rind)
400g (14oz) virtually fat-free quark
4 tablespoons skimmed milk
Handful of chopped chives

Ham, cucumber and quark starters

Verrines jambon-concombre-fromage

■ **CRUISE PV**
■ **CONSOLIDATION EXCEPT FOR PP THURSDAYS**
■ **STABILIZATION EXCEPT FOR PP THURSDAYS**

Wash the cucumber and cut into thin strips. Dice the ham.

Stir the quark and milk together until you have a nice creamy mixture.

Place a layer of cucumber strips at the bottom of four glass dishes, then add a layer of the quark mixture and finish off with a layer of diced ham. Sprinkle over the chopped chives.

Serve well chilled.

4 servings
Preparation time
20 minutes
Cooking time
10 minutes
Refrigeration time
2 hours
Ingredients
150g (5½oz) leeks (white part only)
2 gelatine leaves
200g (7oz) virtually fat-free quark
100ml (3½fl oz) skimmed milk
4 tablespoons low-fat crème fraîche
   (3% fat)
Salt and black pepper
4 cherry tomatoes, halved
Handful of chopped chives

Contains 1 tolerated food portion
per person

Quark and leek bavarois

Bavarois de fromage frais en habit de verdure

■ **CRUISE PV**
■ **CONSOLIDATION EXCEPT FOR PP THURSDAYS**
■ **STABILIZATION EXCEPT FOR PP THURSDAYS**

Wash the leeks and cut them into thin juliennes. In a frying pan, soften them quickly in a little water.

Place the gelatine leaves in a little cold water in a bowl.

In a saucepan, whisk together the quark, skimmed milk and crème fraîche and warm through over a low heat.

Stir the drained gelatine leaves and leeks into the pan and season with salt and pepper.

Pour the mixture into four small ramekin dishes. Add 2 cherry tomato halves to each and scatter over the chopped chives.

Refrigerate for at least 2 hours. Serve well chilled.

Mussels with sugar snap peas

Verrines de moules aux haricots plats

4 servings
Preparation time
25 minutes
Cooking time
30 minutes
Ingredients
1 fish stock cube
500g (1lb 2oz) fresh sugar snap peas
1 litre (1¾ pints) small mussels
1 shallot, finely chopped
1 teaspoon finely chopped fresh ginger
100ml (3½fl oz) white wine
2 tablespoons low-fat crème fraîche (3% fat)
Salt and black pepper
Handful of chopped parsley

Contains 1 tolerated food portion per person

■ **CRUISE PV**
■ **CONSOLIDATION EXCEPT FOR PP THURSDAYS**
■ **STABILIZATION EXCEPT FOR PP THURSDAYS**

Bring a large pan of water to the boil. Add the fish stock cube and sugar snap peas and cook for 20 minutes.

Meanwhile, wash and scrub the mussels. Cover the bottom of another large pan with water, add the shallot, ginger and white wine and cook the mussels, covered, for about 10 minutes. Drain the mussels, discarding any that have refused to open, and reserve the cooking juices. Remove the mussels one by one from their shells.

Strain 200ml (7fl oz) of the mussels' cooking juices and pour into a small pan. Add the crème fraîche and warm over a low heat for about 10 minutes. Season with a little salt and pepper to taste.

Place a layer of the sugar snap peas on the bottom of four large glass dishes, then add a generous layer of mussels. Divide the sauce equally among the dishes and finish off by scattering the chopped parsley over the top before serving.

4 servings
Preparation time
10 minutes
Cooking time
1 minute
Ingredients
200g (7oz) very fresh beef carpaccio
150g (5½oz) virtually fat-free quark
1 bag rocket leaves

Sizzling-hot carpaccio and quark roulades

Roulades de carpaccio aux carrés frais cuites à la plancha

■ **CRUISE PV**
■ **CONSOLIDATION EXCEPT FOR PP THURSDAYS**
■ **STABILIZATION EXCEPT FOR PP THURSDAYS**

Spread a little quark over each slice of beef carpaccio and then scatter a few rocket leaves on top.

Roll up the carpaccio slices and use wooden cocktail sticks to hold the roulades in place. Keep making up roulades until you run out of ingredients.

Heat a plancha (or stone grill) in the centre of your table so that everyone can cook their own roulades – about 20 seconds on each side are all that is needed! Otherwise cook on a griddle pan and then serve.

Green gazpacho

Gaspacho green

6 servings
Preparation time
20 minutes
Refrigeration time
2 hours minimum
Ingredients
2 garlic cloves
1 red onion
1½ unwaxed limes
2 sprigs basil
1 cucumber
1 green pepper
1 celery stick
1 tablespoon cider vinegar
Celery salt
Black pepper (optional)

■ **CRUISE PV**
■ **CONSOLIDATION EXCEPT FOR PP THURSDAYS**
■ **STABILIZATION EXCEPT FOR PP THURSDAYS**

Peel the garlic and onion and cut the onion into quarters. Cut the ½ lime into large cubes. Rinse the basil and discard everything except the leaves. Wash the cucumber and slice it lengthways. Rinse the green pepper and cut into large pieces, discarding the stalk, seeds and white fleshy parts. Cut the celery stick into several pieces.

Blend the ingredients in a juice extractor in the following order: cucumber, pepper, celery, basil, garlic, onion and lime cubes. Put the cider vinegar in a jug and pour in the vegetable juice. Add some celery salt and stir well. Refrigerate for at least 2 hours.

Slice the remaining lime and divide the gazpacho between six glasses. Garnish with the lime slices and, if you wish, season with a little pepper. Serve well chilled.

4 servings
Preparation time
10 minutes
Ingredients
1 tomato
1 small bunch chives
4 slices oat bran sandwich loaf
 (see page 48)
4 slices smoked salmon
100g (3½oz) virtually fat-free quark
Black pepper

Salmon and quark triangles

Délice de saumon au fromage frais

■ **CRUISE PV**
■ **CONSOLIDATION EXCEPT FOR PP THURSDAYS**
■ **STABILIZATION EXCEPT FOR PP THURSDAYS**

Place the tomato in some boiling water for 20 seconds. Remove, peel off the skin, deseed and dice the flesh. Finely chop the chives.

In a non-stick frying pan (without any fat), fry the oat bran loaf slices on both sides until golden brown. Cut the slices into triangles.

Cut the smoked salmon slices into triangles too and place them on top of the bread. Spread some quark over the smoked salmon and add a little chopped tomato and chives. Season with pepper and fold over each salmon slice. Use wooden cocktail sticks to hold the triangles in place.

Arrange the salmon triangles on a pretty dish to serve.

Carrot and celery galettes

Galettes de carottes et céleri

4 servings
Preparation time
20 minutes
Cooking time
10–12 minutes
Ingredients
4 medium carrots, grated
¼ celeriac head, grated
6 eggs
6 tablespoons cornflour
1 onion, finely chopped
1 tablespoon mild paprika
Salt and black pepper

Contains 1½ tolerated food portions per person

■ **CRUISE PV**
■ **CONSOLIDATION EXCEPT FOR PP THURSDAYS**
■ **STABILIZATION EXCEPT FOR PP THURSDAYS**

Boil the carrots and celeriac in water for 5 minutes and then drain well.

In a bowl, whisk together the eggs and cornflour. Sir in the onions, paprika and drained vegetables.

Shape the mixture into small rounds and gently fry, in batches if necessary, in a non-stick frying pan for 1 minute on each side. Serve hot.

Courgette pancakes

Crêpes de courgettes

3 servings
Preparation time
15 minutes
Cooking time
15 minutes
Ingredients
6 eggs, separated
6 courgettes, finely chopped
1 garlic clove, chopped
A few sprigs of parsley, chopped
Salt and black pepper

■ **CRUISE PV**
■ **CONSOLIDATION EXCEPT FOR PP THURSDAYS**
■ **STABILIZATION EXCEPT FOR PP THURSDAYS**

Beat the egg whites until stiff.

Mix the courgettes with the egg yolks, garlic and parsley, and season with salt and pepper. Gently fold in the egg whites.

Cook a third of the mixture at a time in a non-stick frying pan over a medium heat, to make 3 large pancakes. Serve hot.

Provençale vegetable tart

Flan de légumes à la provençale

■ **CRUISE PV**
■ **CONSOLIDATION EXCEPT FOR PP THURSDAYS**
■ **STABILIZATION EXCEPT FOR PP THURSDAYS**

4 servings
Preparation time
35 minutes
Cooking time
50 minutes
Ingredients
500g (1lb 2oz) courgettes
4 tomatoes
2 red peppers, deseeded and diced
1 onion, thinly sliced
Salt and black pepper
4 eggs
4 tablespoons skimmed milk
2 tablespoon extra-light cream
    cheese

*Contains ½ tolerated food portion
per person*

Wash the courgettes and cut into small pieces without removing the skin. Plunge the tomatoes in boiling water for a few seconds, then peel, deseed and dice.

Preheat the oven to 200°C/400°F/Gas 6.

Fry all the vegetables in a non-stick frying pan over a high heat for 20 minutes. Season with salt and pepper.

Beat the eggs until creamy, then add the milk and cream cheese and season with salt and pepper. Stir in all the vegetables, mix together well and pour into a non-stick loaf tin. Place the tin in a bain-marie and bake in the oven for 30 minutes. Serve warm or at room temperature.

4 servings

Preparation time

10 minutes

Cooking time

25 minutes

Ingredients

4 chicory heads

1 litre (1¾ pints) low-salt chicken
stock

1 tablespoon ground cumin

2 egg yolks

4 tablespoons low-fat crème fraîche
(3% fat)

4 tablespoons finely chopped fresh
herbs (chervil, tarragon, chives,
basil and parsley)

Salt and black pepper

*Contains 1 tolerated food portion
per person*

Cream of chicory soup with herbs

Velouté d'endives aux herbes

■ **CRUISE PV**

■ **CONSOLIDATION EXCEPT FOR PP THURSDAYS**

■ **STABILIZATION EXCEPT FOR PP THURSDAYS**

Wash and thinly slice the chicory.

Heat the stock and add the chicory. Add the cumin and leave to simmer over a low heat for around 20 minutes. Allow to cool down and then purée in a blender.

In a bowl, whisk together the egg yolks and crème fraîche. Stir this into the stock and add the herbs. Heat again gently, without allowing the soup to come to the boil.

Season with salt and black pepper and serve piping hot.

2 servings
Preparation time
15 minutes
Cooking time
30 minutes
Ingredients
4 eggs plus 1 egg white
4 tablespoons oat bran
2 tablespoons wheat bran
4 tablespoons fat-free fromage frais
8 tablespoons powdered skimmed
 milk
1 x 8g sachet dried baker's yeast
Salt and black pepper
6 dried tomatoes, halved
1 fresh tomato, chopped
6 slices bresaola, cut into small
 pieces

Oat bran bread with bresaola and fresh and dried tomatoes

Pain de son d'avoine à la viande de Grisons et aux deux tomates

■ **CRUISE PV**
■ **CONSOLIDATION EXCEPT FOR PP THURSDAYS**
■ **STABILIZATION EXCEPT FOR PP THURSDAYS**

Preheat the oven to 180°C/350°F/Gas 4 and line a 500g (1lb 2oz) loaf tin with greaseproof paper.

Beat the eggs in a bowl and stir in the oat bran, wheat bran, and egg white. Then add the fromage frais, powdered milk and yeast and stir well. Season to taste with salt and black pepper.

Pour half this dough into the loaf tin and cover with the dried tomatoes, pieces of fresh tomato and bresaola. Pour the rest of the dough on top and smooth over with a palette knife.

Place the loaf tin in a bain-marie and bake the bread in the oven for 30 minutes, keeping a careful eye on it, until it is firm and golden brown on top.

Remove the loaf from the oven and leave to cool down before turning out of the tin and serving.

8 servings
Preparation time
45 minutes
Cooking time
1½ hours
Refrigeration time
2 hours minimum
Ingredients
2 carrots
1 leek
1 onion
1 × 1.5kg (3lb 5oz) chicken,
   cut into pieces
Salt and black pepper
2 tomatoes
1 small bunch tarragon, leaves only
1 egg white
1 teaspoon pink peppercorns

Chicken terrine

Terrine de volaille

■ **CRUISE PV**
■ **CONSOLIDATION EXCEPT FOR PP THURSDAYS**
■ **STABILIZATION EXCEPT FOR PP THURSDAYS**

Peel the carrots, leek and onion and place them in a stock pot with 1 litre (1¾ pints) water. Bring to the boil and add the chicken pieces, salt and pepper. Skim off any foam, then leave to simmer gently, uncovered, for 1 hour.

Remove and drain the chicken pieces, then take all the meat off the bones and chop it up finely, discarding any skin. Reserve the chicken stock.

Peel and deseed the tomatoes and cut into chunks. Place the chicken meat in a non-stick loaf tin and layer with the tomato chunks and tarragon leaves, saving some tarragon for the top. Bring the reserved stock to the boil and reduce it to around 250ml (9fl oz).

Beat the egg white until stiff, add it to the stock and boil for 1 minute. Allow to cool and then strain through some muslin. Pour the stock over the chicken and sprinkle the pink peppercorns on top.

Arrange a few pieces of tomato and about 10 tarragon leaves evenly over the top of the terrine, cover with clingfilm and refrigerate for at least 2 hours.

Turn the terrine out of the mould and serve cold.

4 servings
Preparation time
10 minutes
Cooking time
15 minutes
Ingredients
8 frozen artichoke hearts
Salt and black pepper
2 tablespoons white wine vinegar
4 eggs
8 slices bresaola

Artichoke hearts with soft-boiled eggs

Cœurs d'artichauts aux œufs mollets

■ **CRUISE PV**
■ **CONSOLIDATION EXCEPT FOR PP THURSDAYS**
■ **STABILIZATION EXCEPT FOR PP THURSDAYS**

In a pan, cover the frozen artichoke hearts with salted water and bring to the boil. Cook for 10 minutes. Drain and keep the artichoke hearts warm on a serving dish.

Bring a pan of water to the boil with the vinegar and carefully add the eggs. Once the water comes back to the boil, cook the eggs for 5 minutes, then remove and rinse under cold running water so that they cool down a little.

Place a slice of bresaola over each artichoke heart.

Very carefully shell the eggs. Working directly over the artichoke hearts, halve the eggs and put a half on top of each one.

Season with salt and black pepper and serve immediately.

2 servings
Preparation time
15 minutes
Cooking time
20 minutes
Ingredients
Salt and black pepper
1 small bunch asparagus
2 eggs
100ml (3½fl oz) skimmed milk
1 tablespoon low-fat crème fraîche
(3% fat)
Pinch of grated nutmeg
½ bunch parsley, chopped

Contains ½ tolerated food portion
per person

Asparagus clafoutis

Clafoutis d'asperges vertes

■ **CRUISE PV**
■ **CONSOLIDATION EXCEPT FOR PP THURSDAYS**
■ **STABILIZATION EXCEPT FOR PP THURSDAYS**

Preheat the oven to 180°C/350°F/Gas 4.

Bring a large pan of salted water to the boil. In the meantime, wash the asparagus and prepare by removing the very hard part and cutting each spear into 3 pieces. Place the asparagus in the boiling water for 1 minute. Remove from the pan, drain in a colander and then transfer to some kitchen paper to drain.

In a bowl, whisk together the eggs and add the milk and crème fraîche. Season with salt and black pepper and add a pinch of grated nutmeg along with the chopped parsley. Pour this mixture into two ramekin dishes and divide the asparagus equally between them.

Place the ramekins in the oven and bake for 20 minutes, keeping a careful eye on them to check when the clafoutis are cooked. They should be slightly brown on top.

Remove from the oven and serve piping hot.

8 servings
Preparation time
30 minutes
Cooking time
1½ hours
Refrigeration time
4 hours
Ingredients
1kg (2lb 4oz) French beans
500ml (18fl oz) low-salt stock
1 carrot
1 celery stick
1 onion
5 sprigs tarragon, chopped
½ teaspoon chopped oregano
8 slices extra-lean cooked turkey
    or chicken
4 eggs
300g (10½oz) fat-free fromage frais
1 tablespoon extra-light cream
    cheese (5% fat)
Salt and black pepper

Summer terrine

Terrine estivale

■ **CRUISE PV**
■ **CONSOLIDATION EXCEPT FOR PP THURSDAYS**
■ **STABILIZATION EXCEPT FOR PP THURSDAYS**

Preheat the oven to 180°C/350°F/Gas 4 and line a 2-litre (3½-pint) rectangular cake tin with greaseproof paper, allowing the paper to overlap the longest sides of the tin.

Cook the French beans in the stock, uncovered, for 15 minutes. Drain, then cut them into smaller pieces.

Chop the carrot, celery and onion together in a food processor or blender. In a high-sided non-stick frying pan, fry this chopped mixture over a gentle heat for 10 minutes.

Add the beans to the frying pan and cook over a gentle heat, stirring from time to time, until the beans no longer give off any water. Add the tarragon and oregano.

Line the cake tin with 6 of the slices of turkey or chicken, allowing the slices to overlap. Spoon in the vegetables.

In a bowl, beat together the eggs, fromage frais and cream cheese. Season with salt and black pepper, then gently pour this mixture over the vegetables. Fold over the meat, top with the remaining slices and finally cover with a sheet of greaseproof paper or aluminium foil.

Place the tin in a bain-marie and cook in the oven for 1 hour.

Leave to cool, then refrigerate for 4 hours. Serve the terrine nice and cold, cut into slices.

Thai lemongrass soup

Soupe thaïe à la citronnelle

2 servings
Preparation time
15 minutes
Cooking time
6 minutes
Ingredients
500ml (18fl oz) chicken stock
2 button mushrooms, quartered
1 lemongrass stalk, chopped
2 kaffir lime leaves, chopped
1 tablespoon finely chopped
    fresh ginger
Pinch of chilli powder
1 tablespoon fish sauce
Juice of ½ lime
6 large cooked, shelled prawns
    (with tails left on)
10 coriander leaves, finely chopped

■ **CRUISE PV**
■ **CONSOLIDATION EXCEPT FOR PP THURSDAYS**
■ **STABILIZATION EXCEPT FOR PP THURSDAYS**

In a pan, bring the chicken stock to the boil with the mushrooms, lemongrass, kaffir lime leaves and ginger, and cook for 2–3 minutes. Turn down the heat and add the chilli powder, fish sauce and lime juice.

Bring the stock back to the boil, add the prawns and cook for 3 minutes.

Serve the soup very hot in individual warmed bowls and scatter the chopped coriander over the top.

6 servings
Preparation time
40 minutes
Cooking time
55 minutes
Ingredients
600g (1lb 5oz) fennel bulbs, diced
450g (1lb) salmon fillet (without
   the skin)
150g (5½oz) fat-free fromage frais
Salt and black pepper
Pinch of curry powder
2 egg whites
1 tablespoon finely chopped dill

Salmon and fennel terrine

Terrine du froid

■ **CRUISE PV**
■ **CONSOLIDATION EXCEPT FOR PP THURSDAYS**
■ **STABILIZATION EXCEPT FOR PP THURSDAYS**

Preheat the oven to 180°C/350°F/Gas 4 and line a 1-litre (1¾-pint) terrine dish with greaseproof paper.

Steam the fennel for 10 minutes.

Cut two-thirds of the salmon into big chunks and the other third into thin strips.

Once the fennel is cooked, drain, then whiz in a blender until it becomes a smooth purée and put aside 3 tablespoons. Next add the fromage frais, salt, black pepper, curry powder and 1 of the egg whites to the fennel purée. Mix the ingredients together well.

Blend the salmon chunks with the reserved 3 tablespoons of fennel purée. Add the remaining egg white and season.

Pour half the salmon purée into the terrine dish and sprinkle over a little of the dill. Cover with a third of the fennel purée, then with half the salmon strips. Add more fennel purée and salmon strips, then add the rest of the fennel purée. Scatter over the remaining dill and finish off with a final layer of salmon purée. Cover the dish, place it in a bain-marie and bake in the oven for 45 minutes.

Allow to cool and serve cold.

4 servings
Preparation time
30 minutes
Refrigeration time
45 minutes
Ingredients
2 small cucumbers, peeled and
deseeded
1 white onion
1 garlic clove
Juice of 2 lemons
2 tablespoons anisette (aniseed-
flavoured liqueur)
Salt and black pepper
4 sprigs coriander, very finely
chopped
8 large cooked and shelled prawns
A few drops of Tabasco
¼ red pepper, deseeded and thinly
sliced
½ red onion, thinly sliced

Iced cucumber soup with prawns

Soupe de concombre glacée aux crevettes roses

■ **CRUISE PV**
■ **CONSOLIDATION EXCEPT FOR PP THURSDAYS**
■ **STABILIZATION EXCEPT FOR PP THURSDAYS**

Whiz the cucumber finely in a blender with the onion, garlic, juice of 1 lemon, anisette, salt and black pepper. Dilute this purée with 400–500ml (14–18fl oz) water. Add half the coriander and put the soup in the fridge for 45 minutes.

Half an hour before you are ready to serve, split the prawns lengthways and spread them out on a plate. Sprinkle over the remaining lemon juice and a few drops of Tabasco, cover and put the prawns in the fridge for 30 minutes.

Adjust the seasoning for the soup and divide it among four large bowls. Arrange the red pepper and onion slices, prawns and remaining coriander on top of the soup and serve immediately.

Japanese cucumber and seaweed salad

Salade japonaise aux algues et au concombre

4 servings
Preparation time
10 minutes
Cooking time
5 minutes
Refrigeration time
30 minutes
Ingredients
40g (1½oz) wakame seaweed
1 cucumber
8 cooked and shelled prawns
For the sauce
2 tablespoons balsamic or Japanese
   rice vinegar
2 tablespoons soy sauce
1 teaspoon Hermesetas liquid
   sweetener
Pinch of black pepper

■ **CRUISE PV**
■ **CONSOLIDATION EXCEPT FOR PP THURSDAYS**
■ **STABILIZATION EXCEPT FOR PP THURSDAYS**

Make the sauce by stirring all the ingredients together in a pan. Add 2 tablespoons water and bring to the boil over a low heat. Remove from the heat and leave to cool down.

Place the seaweed in a bowl, cover with warm water and leave to soak for 10 minutes. Drain and chop the seaweed, taking care to remove the central stalk. Halve the cucumber, scoop out the seeds with a spoon and slice as thinly as possible. Halve the prawns lengthways and stir them into the sauce along with the seaweed and sliced cucumber. Refrigerate for 30 minutes.

Serve nice and cold.

6 servings
Preparation time
15 minutes
Cooking time
5 minutes
Refrigeration time
2 hours minimum
Ingredients
1 cucumber, peeled and cubed
1 bunch mint, leaves only
200g (7oz) virtually fat-free quark
    or extra-light cream cheese, with
    garlic and herbs
18 raw gambas (Mediterranean
    prawns)
Pinch of chilli powder

Cucumber gazpacho with quark, gambas and chilli

Gaspacho de concombre, fromage frais à la menthe et gambas au piment d'Espelette

■ **CRUISE PV**
■ **CONSOLIDATION EXCEPT FOR PP THURSDAYS**
■ **STABILIZATION EXCEPT FOR PP THURSDAYS**

Place the cucumber cubes and mint leaves in a blender along with the quark and 100ml (3½fl oz) water. Blend until you get a smooth mixture, then refrigerate for at least 2 hours.

Ten minutes before you are ready to serve, shell the gambas, keeping on the tails to enhance the garnish. Sprinkle a dusting of chilli powder over the prawns and then, in a non-stick frying pan, sear them over a fairly high heat for 2–3 minutes on each side. Leave them to cool down.

Divide the chilled cucumber gazpacho between six bowls, adding three prawns to each, and serve.

4 servings
Preparation time
20 minutes
Ingredients
350g (12oz) kale or green cabbage, thinly sliced
150g (5½oz) red cabbage, thinly sliced
2 carrots, grated
3 rounded tablespoons Dukan mayonnaise (see page 68)
Salt and red pepper
Pinch of cayenne pepper

Dukan coleslaw

Coleslaw léger

■ **CRUISE PV**
■ **CONSOLIDATION EXCEPT FOR PP THURSDAYS**
■ **STABILIZATION EXCEPT FOR PP THURSDAYS**

In a bowl, mix all the vegetables together and add the Dukan mayonnaise, stirring to coat them well.

Season the coleslaw with salt, red pepper and a pinch of cayenne pepper and serve cold in glass dishes.

2 servings
Preparation time
15 minutes
Ingredients
4 tomatoes
2 small cucumbers
2 onions
2 sweet peppers
A few mint leaves
3 sprigs flat-leaf parsley
Juice of ½ lemon
1 tablespoon olive oil
Salt and black pepper

Shepherd's salad

Salade du berger

■ **CRUISE PV**
■ **CONSOLIDATION EXCEPT FOR PP THURSDAYS**
■ **STABILIZATION EXCEPT FOR PP THURSDAYS**

Cut the tomatoes and cucumbers into small cubes and place in a salad bowl.

Thinly slice the onions, deseed and chop the peppers, finely chop the mint and parsley and add all these ingredients to the bowl.

Season with the lemon juice, oil, salt and black pepper. Serve straightaway.

2 servings
Preparation time
10 minutes
Cooking time
30 minutes
Ingredients
500g (1lb 2oz) virtually fat-free
    cottage cheese
1 tablespoon skimmed milk
2 eggs
50g (1¾oz) sorrel, finely chopped
50g (1¾oz) basil, finely chopped
50g (1¾oz) dandelion leaves, finely
    chopped
Pinch of ground cinnamon
Salt and black pepper

Spring herb cake

Gâteau aux herbes de printemps

■ **CRUISE PV**
■ **CONSOLIDATION EXCEPT FOR PP THURSDAYS**
■ **STABILIZATION EXCEPT FOR PP THURSDAYS**

Preheat the oven to 180°C/350°F/Gas 4 and line a cake tin or terrine dish with greaseproof paper.

In a bowl, beat together the well-drained cottage cheese, skimmed milk and eggs until the mixture is more or less smooth. Add the herbs, cinnamon, salt and black pepper.

Pour the mixture into the cake tin or terrine dish and bake in the oven for 30 minutes.

This herb cake can be eaten either warm or hot.

2 servings
Preparation time
30 minutes
Cooking time
35 minutes
Refrigeration time
6 hours
Ingredients
500g (1lb 2oz) aubergines
2 red peppers
2 garlic cloves
2½ tablespoons powdered gelatine
2 tablespoons sherry vinegar
300g (10½oz) fat-free yoghurt
Salt and black pepper

Aubergine mousse

Mousse d'aubergine

■ **CRUISE PV**
■ **CONSOLIDATION EXCEPT FOR PP THURSDAYS**
■ **STABILIZATION EXCEPT FOR PP THURSDAYS**

Preheat the oven to 200°C/400°F/Gas 6.

Wipe the aubergines and peppers and then bake them in the oven for about 30 minutes, depending on their size. Use the tip of a knife to check they are done.

Peel the garlic, remove the green sprout and crush using a garlic press.

In a small saucepan, dissolve the gelatine in the sherry vinegar. Then warm it for 5 minutes over a low heat, stirring all the time.

Peel the peppers and remove the stalk and seeds. Cut the aubergines in half and scoop out the flesh with a spoon.

Place the garlic, aubergine flesh and peppers in a blender and whiz until puréed. Add the gelatine and yoghurt, season with salt and black pepper, and mix everything together thoroughly.

Pour the mixture into a small terrine dish, cover with clingfilm and leave to set in the fridge for 6 hours. Serve well chilled.

4 servings
Preparation time
15 minutes
Cooking time
40 minutes
Ingredients
600g (1lb 5oz) small button
   mushrooms
4 tablespoons cornflour
200g (7oz) virtually fat-free quark
4 eggs
150ml (5fl oz) skimmed milk
Black pepper

Contains 1 tolerated food portion
per person

Little mushroom and quark clafoutis

Petits clafoutis de champignons aux carrés frais

■ CRUISE PV
■ CONSOLIDATION EXCEPT FOR PP THURSDAYS
■ STABILIZATION EXCEPT FOR PP THURSDAYS

Preheat the oven to 180°C/350°F/Gas 4.

Leaving the mushrooms whole, place them in a pan, add 50ml (2fl oz) water and bring to simmering point over a medium heat. Cook for about 10 minutes, until all the water has evaporated.

In a bowl, work the cornflour into the quark and then fold in the eggs one by one. Add the milk to thin down the mixture, then season with black pepper.

Divide the mushrooms among four small individual ovenproof casseroles then pour the quark mixture over. Place the casseroles on a baking try and bake in the oven for 30 minutes.

When the clafoutis are cooked, leave them to cool down a little before turning them out on to plates. Serve warm.

4 servings
Preparation time
25 minutes
Cooking time
15 minutes
Ingredients
125g (4½oz) button mushrooms,
   thinly sliced
150g (5½oz) virtually fat-free quark
16 cooked prawns
50ml (2fl oz) skimmed milk
2 tablespoons finely chopped
   flat-leaf parsley
4 large scallops
Cooking salt
4 tablespoons oat bran

Mushroom and quark scallops baked in their shells

Coquilles de la mer gratinées aux carrés frais

■ **CRUISE PV**
■ **CONSOLIDATION EXCEPT FOR PP THURSDAYS**
■ **STABILIZATION EXCEPT FOR PP THURSDAYS**

Preheat the oven to 180°C/350°F/Gas 4.

Fry the mushrooms in a non-stick frying pan without any fat. When they are cooked, stir in 30g (1oz) of the quark.

In the meantime, shell the prawns. In a bowl, mix the remaining quark with the skimmed milk and parsley.

Open the scallop shells, remove and discard the frill and black stomach sack, and take out the scallop, and coral if there is any. Clean the shells carefully.

Crumple some aluminium foil, and place on a baking tray. Spread over a layer of cooking salt and wedge the shells into the salt. Divide the mushroom mixture between the shells and place a scallop and 4 prawns on each. Cover with the quark sauce and sprinkle the oat bran on top.

Bake in the oven for 8 minutes. Allow the shells to cool down slightly before serving.

4 servings
Preparation time
20 minutes
Cooking time
50 minutes
Ingredients
400g (14oz) lean minced beef (5% fat)
400g (14oz) lean minced veal
2 eggs
1 onion, finely chopped
2 garlic cloves, crushed
Salt and black pepper
A few sprigs of thyme, rosemary and parsley, finely chopped
150g (5½oz) button mushrooms, finely chopped

Meat loaf with mushrooms

Pain de viande aux champignons

■ **CRUISE PV**
■ **CONSOLIDATION EXCEPT FOR PP THURSDAYS**
■ **STABILIZATION EXCEPT FOR PP THURSDAYS**

Preheat the oven to 240°C/475°F/Gas 9 and line a loaf tin with greaseproof paper.

Mix the minced beef and veal together in a large bowl. Stir in the eggs, onion and garlic. Season with salt and black pepper and then stir in the herbs.

Gently sweat the mushrooms in a non-stick frying pan, then stir them into the minced meat mixture.

Pour the mixture into the loaf tin and bake in the oven for 45–50 minutes.

Serve the loaf sliced; it can be eaten either hot or cold.

1 serving
Preparation time
20 minutes
Cooking time
35 minutes
Ingredients
1 Savoury Galette (see page 50)
1 large onion, finely chopped
500g (1lb 2oz) chopped tomatoes, drained
1 teaspoon herbs (thyme, oregano and basil)
2 pinches black pepper
Salt
175g (6oz) tinned tuna in brine or spring water
2 tablespoons capers
6 teaspoons low-fat cream cheese (optional)

Contains 1 tolerated food portion (optional) per person

Tuna pizza

Pizza au thon

■ **CRUISE PV**
■ **CONSOLIDATION EXCEPT FOR PP THURSDAYS**
■ **STABILIZATION EXCEPT FOR PP THURSDAYS**

Preheat the oven to 180°C/350°F/Gas 4.

For the pizza base, follow the oat bran galette recipe on page 50.

Gently fry the onion in a non-stick frying pan. Add the tomatoes, herbs, pepper and salt. Simmer over a gentle heat for 10 minutes.

Drain and chop the tuna, then put to one side.

Spread the tomato mixture over the cooked galette and scatter over the tuna, capers and cream cheese (if using).

Bake in the oven for 25 minutes. Serve hot from the oven or cooled to room temperature.

4 servings
Preparation time
20 minutes
Cooking time
4 hours
Ingredients
1 garlic head
500g (1lb 2oz) leaf spinach
500g (1lb 2oz) brisket of beef
1 bay leaf
1 bunch mint
1 bunch coriander
A little grated nutmeg
1 cinnamon stick
1 teaspoon ground cinnamon
2 eggs, beaten
Salt and white pepper

Spinach dafina

Dafina allégée aux épinards

■ CRUISE PV
■ CONSOLIDATION EXCEPT FOR PP THURSDAYS
■ STABILIZATION EXCEPT FOR PP THURSDAYS

Peel the garlic cloves.

In a large pan over a low heat, start by softening the spinach with 2–3 of the garlic cloves.

Place the beef in a casserole and add the remaining garlic cloves, the bay leaf, mint, coriander and nutmeg.

Add the cinnamon stick and ground cinnamon, spinach and eggs. Cover with cold water, season with salt and pepper and bring to the boil. Lower the heat as far as possible and leave to simmer for about 4 hours, keeping a careful eye on the liquid level and topping up with a little boiling water as necessary.

Carve the beef into four portions and serve hot with the spinach and cooking juices.

2 servings
Preparation time
15 minutes
Cooking time
25 minutes
Ingredients
4 chicory heads
Salt and black pepper
2 tablespoons low-fat crème fraîche
  (3% fat)
2 x 120g (4½ oz) cod fillets

*Contains 1 tolerated food portion
per person*

Oven-baked cod and chicory parcels

Papillottes de cabillaud aux endives

■ **CRUISE PV**
■ **CONSOLIDATION EXCEPT FOR PP THURSDAYS**
■ **STABILIZATION EXCEPT FOR PP THURSDAYS**

Preheat the oven to 200°C/400°F/Gas 6.

Wash the chicory heads and remove the hard, bitter core.

Blanch the chicory in boiling water for 2 minutes. Drain and then chop into thin strips.

Gently fry the chopped chicory in a non-stick frying pan for 10 minutes. Season with salt and black pepper and stir in the crème fraîche.

Cut out two squares of aluminium foil, divide half the chicory between them and lay the cod fillets on top. Arrange the remaining chicory on top of the fish. Seal the foil parcels, place on a baking tray and bake in the oven for 15 minutes. Serve immediately.

4 servings
Preparation time
25 minutes
Cooking time
40 minutes
Ingredients
2 tomatoes
1 onion, diced
400g (14oz) minced beef (5% fat)
Salt and black pepper
2 carrots, diced
½ courgette, diced
2 teaspoons ground cinnamon
3 garlic cloves, crushed
1 bunch coriander, finely chopped

You will need a pressure cooker

Chorba

■ **CRUISE PV**
■ **CONSOLIDATION EXCEPT FOR PP THURSDAYS**
■ **STABILIZATION EXCEPT FOR PP THURSDAYS**

Halve the tomatoes and crush them. Place the pulp in a bowl and put to one side.

In a non-stick frying pan, gently fry the onion in 3 tablespoons water until it has almost melted. Add the beef and fry for about 5 minutes. Season with salt and black pepper.

Add the carrots, courgette, tomato pulp, cinnamon, garlic, coriander and half a glass of warm water. Cook for a further 10 minutes over a medium heat and season again with salt and pepper.

In the meantime, bring a pan of water to the boil. Pour the meat and vegetable mixture into a pressure cooker and cover it with boiling water. Cook for 20 minutes over a medium heat. Serve piping hot.

Club sandwich

2 servings
Preparation time
15 minutes
Cooking time
4 minutes
Ingredients
2 lettuce leaves
1 tablespoon fat-free fromage frais
1 teaspoon mustard
1 tomato, sliced
6 slices cooked chicken
1 hard-boiled egg, sliced
For the bread
2 tablespoons oat bran
1 egg
1 tablespoon fat-free fromage frais
1 teaspoon instant dried yeast

■ **CRUISE PV**
■ **CONSOLIDATION EXCEPT FOR PP THURSDAYS**
■ **STABILIZATION EXCEPT FOR PP THURSDAYS**

Prepare the bread by mixing together all the ingredients. Pour the dough into a high-sided microwavable dish and bake in the microwave for 4 minutes.

Turn the bread out of the mould and cut it in three lengthways. Lightly toast the slices.

Chop the lettuce leaves and add the fromage frais and mustard.

Spread half of this mixture over one of the bread slices and arrange half of the tomato slices on top, then add half of the chicken and hard-boiled egg. Repeat with another slice of bread and the rest of the filling ingredients and top with the remaining bread slice.

When the sandwich is complete, use a wooden cocktail stick to keep it in place and cut it in two diagonally before serving.

6 servings
Preparation time
10 minutes
Cooking time
1½ hours
Ingredients
2 celery sticks
4 carrots
250g (9oz) Chinese cabbage
1 × 1.8–2kg (4– 4½lb) chicken
1 × 5cm (2in) piece fresh ginger,
  finely chopped
3 onions, quartered
2 teaspoons salt
1 teaspoon black pepper
A few chives, chopped
Soy sauce, to serve

Chicken with ginger broth

Poule et son bouillon de gingembre

■ **CRUISE PV**
■ **CONSOLIDATION EXCEPT FOR PP THURSDAYS**
■ **STABILIZATION EXCEPT FOR PP THURSDAYS**

Cut the celery and carrots into small sticks. Slice the cabbage into thin strips.

Pour 4 litres (7 pints) cold water into a large pan and add the chicken, ginger and all the vegetables. Season with the salt and black pepper and bring to the boil. Leave to simmer, covered, for at least 1½ hours until the chicken is tender.

Cut the chicken into portions and arrange on a large plate, surrounded by the vegetables and with the chives scattered on top. Accompany it with the broth in individual bowls, along with some soy sauce to add according to taste.

.

3 servings
Preparation time
15 minutes
Cooking timen
10 minutes
Ingredients
3 tomatoes, quartered
8 tinned anchovies, rinsed and dried
1 tablespoon capers
8 eggs
2 tablespoons skimmed milk
10 chives, finely chopped
5 sprigs coriander, finely chopped
5 sprigs parsley, finely chopped
Black pepper
6 sun-dried tomatoes, chopped

Anchovy omelette strips

Rubans d'omelette aux anchois

- CRUISE PV
- CONSOLIDATION EXCEPT FOR PP THURSDAYS
- STABILIZATION EXCEPT FOR PP THURSDAYS

Fry the tomatoes in a non-stick frying pan with the anchovies and capers for 5 minutes over a medium heat.

Beat the eggs until creamy, add the milk and herbs and season with black pepper. In a wide non-stick frying pan, make two large, thin omelettes with the eggs (about 5mm/¼in thick). Leave to cool and cut into strips about 2cm (¾in) wide.

Place the omelette strips in a dish along with the fried tomatoes and anchovies. Add the sun-dried tomatoes and mix everything together well. Serve at room temperature.

4 servings
Preparation time
20 minutes
Cooking time
1 hour
Ingredients
1 large onion, finely chopped
480g (1lb 1oz) tinned chopped
    tomatoes
1 sweet pepper, deseeded and diced
3 garlic cloves, finely chopped
1 bay leaf
A few sprigs of thyme
1 green chilli, crushed
Salt and black pepper
500g (1lb 2oz) calamari rings

Calamari Provençale

Calmars à la provençale

■ **CRUISE PV**
■ **CONSOLIDATION EXCEPT FOR PP THURSDAYS**
■ **STABILIZATION EXCEPT FOR PP THURSDAYS**

Fry the onion in a non-stick frying pan over a medium heat.

When the onion is nicely browned, add the tomatoes, diced pepper, garlic, bay leaf, thyme and chilli pepper. Season with salt and black pepper. Cook, covered, for 10 minutes over a gentle heat.

Wash and clean the calamari, then add to the sauce. Cook over a low heat, covered, for 45 minutes. Serve immediately.

Mexican-style scampi

Scampi à la mexicaine

3–4 servings
Preparation time
10 minutes
Cooking time
3 minutes
Ingredients
4 tomatoes
1 green chilli, chopped
2 tablespoons finely chopped
  coriander
Juice of 1 lime
1 garlic clove, crushed
Salt
32 cooked scampi (Dublin Bay
  prawns)

You will need a steamer

■ **CRUISE PV**
■ **CONSOLIDATION EXCEPT FOR PP THURSDAYS**
■ **STABILIZATION EXCEPT FOR PP THURSDAYS**

Peel, deseed and dice the tomatoes. Add the chilli, coriander, lime juice and garlic and cook over a low heat for 10 minutes. Season to taste with salt.

Steam the scampi for 2–3 minutes.

Stir the scampi into the tomato sauce and serve piping hot.

2 servings
Preparation time
15 minutes
Cooking time
15 minutes
Ingredients
2 large shallots, finely chopped
4 teaspoons fat-free fromage frais
200g (7oz) sorrel
6–8 scallops
Salt and black pepper

Scallops with sorrel

Coquilles Saint-Jacques à l'oseille

■ **CRUISE PV**
■ **CONSOLIDATION EXCEPT FOR PP THURSDAYS**
■ **STABILIZATION EXCEPT FOR PP THURSDAYS**

Warm the shallots and fromage frais in a non-stick frying pan.

Meanwhile wash the sorrel and cook in another non-stick pan for 10 minutes over a medium heat.

Season the scallops with salt and black pepper and sear them quickly in a third non-stick pan over a high heat. When they have browned, turn down the heat and continue to fry gently until they are just cooked through.

Arrange a bed of sorrel on warmed plates and place the scallops on top. Pour over the fromage frais sauce and serve.

Chinese fondue

Fondue chinoise

6 servings
Preparation time
25 minutes
Cooking time
10 minutes
Ingredients
600g (1lb 5oz) vegetables of
   your choice (cabbage, carrots,
   mushrooms, celery, tomatoes)
400g (14oz) fish (monkfish, cod or
   sea bream)
100g (3½oz) calamari, sliced
12 raw scampi (Dublin Bay prawns)
   or prawns
12 mussels, scrubbed and cleaned
1 unwaxed lemon, sliced
Salt and black pepper
1 litre (1¾ pints) fish stock, plus
   300ml (10fl oz) extra if you are
   not cooking the vegetables in a
   steamer
A few sprigs of chervil
Soy sauce, to serve

You will need a fondue set

■ **CRUISE PV**
■ **CONSOLIDATION EXCEPT FOR PP THURSDAYS**
■ **STABILIZATION EXCEPT FOR PP THURSDAYS**

Slice the vegetables and cook separately until *al dente*, either by steaming them or cooking them in an extra 300ml (10fl oz) stock. Leave to cool and arrange on a serving dish or in individual bowls.

Cut the fish into bite-sized pieces and place either on the dish or in the bowls along with the calamari, scampi or prawns and mussels. Garnish with lemon slices.

Season the stock with salt and black pepper so that it tastes nice and strong and add the chervil sprigs. Bring it to the table and place on a lighted fondue heater. Heat the stock until it is simmering.

Dip the vegetables and fish into the stock until cooked (discard any unopened mussels) and eat with the accompanying soy sauce.

4 servings
Preparation time
25 minutes
Cooking time
15 minutes
Ingredients
4 small courgettes
4 carrots
1 × 2cm (¾in) piece fresh ginger
Salt and black pepper
4 x 230g (8oz) salmon fillets
8 x 140g (5oz) sole fillets
1 small tin tomato purée
2 onions, finely chopped
2 garlic cloves, finely chopped

Small fish parcels with vegetables and ginger

Petits ballotins de la mer, légumes et gingembre

■ CRUISE PV
■ CONSOLIDATION EXCEPT FOR PP THURSDAYS
■ STABILIZATION EXCEPT FOR PP THURSDAYS

Use a large grater to grate the vegetables and ginger coarsely. Season with salt and black pepper and leave to drain for 10 minutes.

Stretch approximately 30cm (12in) clingfilm over a work top. Make the first parcel by layering the fish so that one fillet of salmon is sandwiched between two fillets of sole. Place a large spoonful of grated vegetables on top and roll up the fish. Then roll up the clingfilm very tightly around the fish and twist to seal the parcel at both ends. Repeat to make up three more parcels in this way and then poach them in gently simmering water for 10 minutes.

Meanwhile, prepare a light tomato sauce. In a saucepan, heat the tomato purée with 200ml (7fl oz) water and the onions and garlic. Leave to simmer and reduce for about 10 minutes.

When ready to serve, slit open the clingfilm parcels, carefully take out the fish and pour the sauce over the top.

4 servings
Preparation time
25 minutes
Cooking time
20 minutes
Ingredients
2 garlic cloves, crushed
1 onion, diced
600–800g (1lb 5oz–1lb 12oz)
   minced beef (5% fat)
1 red pepper, deseeded and diced
1 mild red chilli, finely chopped
3 tomatoes, peeled and chopped
200g (7oz) tinned tomato purée
1 low-salt beef stock cube, dissolved
   in 50ml (2fl oz) hot water
1 tablespoon ground cumin
A few drops of Tabasco
8 large lettuce leaves
4 tablespoons tomato sauce, to
   serve (see page 69)

Burritos salad wraps

Burritos en cœur de laitue

■ **CRUISE PV**
■ **CONSOLIDATION EXCEPT FOR PP THURSDAYS**
■ **STABILIZATION EXCEPT FOR PP THURSDAYS**

Warm a large non-stick frying pan and pour a little water in the bottom. Gently fry the garlic and onion until they are soft. Add the minced beef and stir until it is cooked through.

Next add the red pepper, chilli, half the chopped tomatoes, the tomato purée and dissovled stock cube. Turn down the heat and stir in the cumin and Tabasco. Leave to simmer for 10 minutes, stirring from time to time until the sauce thickens.

Spoon the minced beef into the hollow of each large lettuce leaf, garnish with the remaining chopped tomatoes and serve with the tomato sauce.

6 servings
Preparation time
30 minutes
Cooking time
1 hour
Ingredients
1 large carp, gutted
3 x 120g (4½oz) hake fillets
1 onion, finely chopped
1 egg yolk
Salt and black pepper
A little oat and wheat bran
6–8 carrots, sliced

Dukan-style gefilte fish balls

Boulettes gefilte fish façon Dukan

■ **CRUISE PV**
■ **CONSOLIDATION EXCEPT FOR PP THURSDAYS**
■ **STABILIZATION EXCEPT FOR PP THURSDAYS**

Make a stock from the head, tail and skin of the carp. Strain and discard the fish parts.

In a food processor, purée the meat from the carp with the hake fillets, onion and egg yolk and season with salt and black pepper.

Shape the fish mixture into small balls and, instead of using flour, dip them into the mixed oat and wheat bran to coat.

Reheat the fish stock, add the carrots and cook over a very low heat for about 10 minutes. Then add the fish balls to the stock and continue to simmer for another 45 nimutes.

Konjac Shirataki noodles bolognaise

Bolognaise de pâtes de Konjac

4 servings
Preparation time
25 minutes
Cooking time
35 minutes
Ingredients
1 low-salt beef stock cube
2 onions, finely diced
3 garlic cloves, finely chopped
400g (14oz) lean minced beef (5%
    fat)
240g (8½oz) tinned peeled tomatoes
1 carrot, finely diced
Herbes de Provence
1 bay leaf
Salt and black pepper
1 packet Konjac Shirataki noodles*

*Available online and in Asian or
health-food shops*

■ **CRUISE PV**
■ **CONSOLIDATION EXCEPT FOR PP THURSDAYS**
■ **STABILIZATION EXCEPT FOR PP THURSDAYS**

Dilute half the stock cube in 100ml (3½fl oz) water and pour into a frying pan. Heat over a high heat and add the onions and garlic. Cook until they soften, lowering the heat and adding more water if necessary.

Add the minced beef to the frying pan and brown. Tip in the tomatoes and carrot and season with some herbes de Provence, the bay leaf, salt and black pepper. Leave to simmer over a low heat, covered, for about 30 minutes (or longer if you prefer a well-cooked bolognaise sauce, but remember to keep adding water as it cooks to prevent it from becoming too dry).

Once the sauce is almost cooked, rinse the noodles in plenty of cold water two or three times. Bring a large pan of water to the boil, adding some salt and the remaining half stock cube. As soon as the water comes to the boil, add the noodles and cook for 1 minute. Drain the noodles and pour over the reduced bolognaise sauce. Serve piping hot.

2 servings
Preparation time
10 minutes
Cooking time
15 minutes
Ingredients
300g (10½oz) French beans
Salt and black pepper
1 low-salt beef stock cube
1 garlic clove, finely chopped
2 fillet steaks
2 teaspoons balsamic vinegar

Fillet steak with French beans

Filets de bœuf aux haricots verts

■ **CRUISE PV**
■ **CONSOLIDATION EXCEPT FOR PP THURSDAYS**
■ **STABILIZATION EXCEPT FOR PP THURSDAYS**

Blanch the French beans in salted boiling water for a few minutes, then drain thoroughly.

Dissolve half the stock cube in 2 tablespoons water in a non-stick frying pan and gently brown the garlic. Add the French beans and cook for 3–4 minutes. Season with salt and black pepper.

In another non-stick frying pan, dissolve the remaining half stock cube in a little water and sauté the fillet steaks for about 4 minutes, turning them once. Deglaze the pan with the balsamic vinegar.

Serve the steaks and French beans immediately on warmed plates and pour over the cooking juices.

2 servings
Preparation time
20 minutes
Cooking time
1 hour
Ingredients
2 hard-boiled eggs, shelled
2 × 100g (3½ oz) veal escalopes
Salt and black pepper
100g (3½ oz) onions, finely chopped
100g (3½ oz) button mushrooms,
  finely chopped
A few sprigs of thyme, chopped
1 small bay leaf
500ml (18fl oz) tomato juice

Jonquille's veal olives

Paupiettes de veau jonquille

■ **CRUISE PV**
■ **CONSOLIDATION EXCEPT FOR PP THURSDAYS**
■ **STABILIZATION EXCEPT FOR PP THURSDAYS**

Preheat the oven to 160°C/325°F/Gas 3.

Place a hard-boiled egg on each wide, flat escalope. Sprinkle over some salt and black pepper and roll the escalope carefully round the egg. Secure with some kitchen string.

Place the veal olives in a small ovenproof dish. Add the onions, mushrooms, thyme and bay leaf. Season with salt and black pepper and pour over the tomato juice to keep the meat moist.

Cover and bake in the oven for about 1 hour.

To serve, remove the string and cut the olives in two widthways, so that the egg yolk is visible on the outside. Spoon over the sauce and arrange the onions and mushrooms around the olives.

Scallop and Mediterranean vegetable salad

Marinade de Saint-Jacques aux légumes grillés

2 servings

Preparation time

10 minutes

Cooking time

25 minutes

Refrigeration time

1 hour

Ingredients

Juice and grated zest of 1 unwaxed
  lemon

2 tablespoons finely chopped fresh
  coriander

Salt and black pepper

16 scallops

1 aubergine, cut into cubes

2 courgettes, sliced

4 tablespoons tomato sauce (see
  page 69)

You will need a steamer

■ **CRUISE PV**

■ **CONSOLIDATION EXCEPT FOR PP THURSDAYS**

■ **STABILIZATION EXCEPT FOR PP THURSDAYS**

Make a marinade by mixing together the lemon juice and zest with the coriander, and season with salt and black pepper.

Steam the scallops for 3 minutes.

Steam the aubergine and courgettes for 10 minutes, then fry them for 10 minutes in a non-stick frying pan covered with a sheet of baking parchment. Pour the marinade over the vegetables.

Spread the tomato sauce over two plates, then add the vegetables and the scallops and leave to marinate in the fridge for 1 hour before serving.

2 servings
Preparation time
10 minutes
Refrigeration time
2 hours minimum
Cooking time
10 minutes
Ingredients
250g (9oz) chicken livers
2 tablespoons balsamic vinegar
2 tablespoons soy sauce
1 teaspoon freshly grated ginger
1 garlic clove, finely chopped
1 red pepper
12 cherry tomatoes
8 button mushroom caps
Salt and black pepper

Oriental chicken liver kebabs

Brochettes de foies de volaille à l'orientale

■ **CRUISE PV**
■ **CONSOLIDATION EXCEPT FOR PP THURSDAYS**
■ **STABILIZATION EXCEPT FOR PP THURSDAYS**

Wash and clean the chicken livers and cut into about 20 pieces.

In a bowl, combine the vinegar, soy sauce, ginger and garlic, then add the chicken liver pieces and stir thoroughly. Leave to marinate in the fridge for at least 2 hours.

Preheat either your barbecue or grill and start preparing the kebabs. Cut the red pepper into small pieces, discarding the seeds, and thread on to kebab sticks, alternating them with the chicken liver pieces, the cherry tomatoes and mushrooms.

Grill the kebabs for 4–5 minutes on each side and then season with salt and black pepper.

Serve as soon as they are cooked.

4 servings
Preparation time
35 minutes
Cooking time
1 hour
Ingredients
1 × 1.25kg (2lb 12oz) chicken
2 shallots, finely chopped
1 sprig thyme
1 low-salt chicken stock cube
600g (1lb 5oz) chanterelle
 mushrooms, stalks removed
Salt and black pepper
2 garlic cloves, finely chopped
1 small bunch parsley, finely
 chopped

Chicken with chanterelle mushrooms

Poulet aux girolles

■ **CRUISE PV**
■ **CONSOLIDATION EXCEPT FOR PP THURSDAYS**
■ **STABILIZATION EXCEPT FOR PP THURSDAYS**

Cut the chicken into large pieces, and remove the skin and as much fat as possible.

In a non-stick flameproof casserole, gently fry the shallots without any fat, then add the chicken pieces and brown them all over. Pour in 250ml (9floz) water and add the thyme and stock cube. Cover and leave to simmer for 45 minutes. If necessary, add a little more water as the chicken cooks, to prevent it drying out.

Using a small brush, carefully clean between the mushroom gills. Chop the mushrooms and gently fry in a non-stick frying pan without any fat. Add salt and black pepper and sprinkle over the chopped garlic and parsley.

Serve the chicken accompanied by the mushrooms and with the cooking juices in a separate jug or sauce boat.

2 servings
Preparation time
35 minutes
Resting time
1 hour
Cooking time
25 minutes
Ingredients
400g (14oz) aubergines
Salt and black pepper
200g (7oz) minced beef (5% fat)
1 onion, finely diced
240g (8½oz) tinned chopped
   tomatoes
1 tablespoon cornflour
125ml (4fl oz) skimmed milk
A little grated nutmeg

*Contains ½ tolerated food portion
per person*

Moussaka

■ **CRUISE PV**
■ **CONSOLIDATION EXCEPT FOR PP THURSDAYS**
■ **STABILIZATION EXCEPT FOR PP THURSDAYS**

Peel the aubergines and cut into thick slices lengthways. Either steam them or cook in a pan with the lid on until softened, about 20 minutes.

Sprinkle over some salt and leave them to drain for 1 hour.

Preheat the oven to 200°C/400°F/Gas 6.

In a non-stick frying pan, brown the minced beef, then add the onion. Next add the tomatoes, and season with salt and black pepper. Leave the bolognaise sauce to simmer away gently.

Dissolve the cornflour in a little of the cold milk and heat the rest of the milk. Pour the cornflour into the hot milk and stir continuously until the sauce starts to thicken slightly. As soon as the first bubbles appear, turn off the heat. Season with salt, black pepper and a little nutmeg.

Pour two-thirds of the bolognaise sauce into the bottom of an ovenproof dish, cover with half the béchamel sauce, then top with the aubergine slices and the remaining béchamel sauce. Finish off with the rest of the bolognaise sauce and bake in the oven for 10–15 minutes. Serve hot.

6 servings
Preparation time
25 minutes
Refrigeration time
1 hour
Cooking time
25 minutes
Ingredients
1kg (2lb 4oz) chicken breasts
4 teaspoons balsamic vinegar
2 garlic cloves, crushed
1 teaspoon coriander seeds
2 teaspoons pink peppercorns
Salt and black pepper
2kg (4½lb) courgettes
Juice of 2 lemons
1 small bunch parsley, finely
    chopped

Spicy marinated chicken strips with lemony courgettes

Filets de poulet marinés aux épices et courgettes au citron

■ **CRUISE PV**
■ **CONSOLIDATION EXCEPT FOR PP THURSDAYS**
■ **STABILIZATION EXCEPT FOR PP THURSDAYS**

Cut the chicken breasts into thin strips and place in a shallow dish.

In a bowl, mix together 2 teaspoons of the balsamic vinegar with one of the garlic cloves, the coriander seeds and pink peppercorns. Add a pinch of salt. Pour the marinade over the chicken strips and leave to marinate in the fridge for 1 hour, turning the chicken over two or three times.

Rinse and peel the courgettes, leaving alternate strips of skin. Slice the courgettes and steam for 10 minutes.

In a bowl, combine the remaining balsamic vinegar, the remaining garlic clove, the lemon juice and parsley, and season with salt and black pepper. Then add the warm courgette slices and mix well. Leave to cool down and then refrigerate.

Preheat a barbecue or grill.

Thread the chicken on to wooden kebab sticks and cook on the barbecue for 5 minutes on each side, or for 8 minutes each side under the grill.

Serve the kebabs piping hot with the chilled lemony courgettes.

4 servings
Preparation time
20 minutes
Cooking time
50 minutes
Ingredients
1 × 1kg (2lb 4oz) chicken, halved
Salt and black pepper
250g (9oz) button mushrooms
4 tomatoes, quartered
2 egg yolks
250g (9oz) fat-free fromage frais

Chicken fricassée

Fricassée de poulet

■ **CRUISE PV**
■ **CONSOLIDATION EXCEPT FOR PP THURSDAYS**
■ **STABILIZATION EXCEPT FOR PP THURSDAYS**

Season the chicken with salt and black pepper and brown it in a non-stick flameproof casserole over a medium heat for 10 minutes.

Clean the mushrooms and add to the chicken, cover with water and then cook, covered, for 40 minutes. After 30 minutes, add the tomato quarters.

Put the egg yolks in a small heatproof bowl, add the fromage frais and mix together well. Take two ladlefuls of the cooking sauce from the chicken and add to the bowl, mixing everything together thoroughly.

Heat this sauce by placing the bowl over a pan of simmering water, stirring constantly, then pour it over the chicken just before serving.

2 servings
Preparation time
10 minutes
Cooking time
45 minutes
Ingredients
1 litre (1¾ pints) small mussels
½ red pepper
2 tomatoes
1 sweet onion
Herbes de Provence
1 lemon
Salt and black pepper

Mussel kebabs

Brochettes de moules

■ CRUISE PV
■ CONSOLIDATION EXCEPT FOR PP THURSDAYS
■ STABILIZATION EXCEPT FOR PP THURSDAYS

Clean the mussels thoroughly by scrubbing them and rinsing several times in water.

In a large pan, cook the mussels over a high heat to open up (discard any that remain closed), then remove them from their shells.

Cut the red pepper into large cubes, discarding the seeds, and quarter the tomatoes, removing the pulp. Cut the onion into quarters and separate the layers.

Preheat the grill or barbecue.

Thread the mussels and vegetables alternately on to kebab sticks.

Sprinkle over the herbes de Provence and cook the kebabs either under the grill or on the barbecue, turning them occasionally. During cooking, squeeze the lemon over the kebabs and season with salt and black pepper. Serve as soon as the vegetables are cooked to your liking.

4 servings
Make a day in advance
Preparation time
25 minutes
Cooking time
15 minutes
Refrigeration time
2 hours minimum or overnight
Ingredients
Zest and juice of 1 unwaxed lemon
4 sprigs thyme, leaves only
3 garlic cloves, finely chopped
3 shallots, finely chopped
1 small tin tomato purée
240g (8½oz) tinned chopped
   tomatoes
Pinch of cayenne pepper
2 tablespoons saffron powder
Salt and black pepper
6 chicken breasts

Spanish-style chicken kebabs

Brochettes de poulet à l'espagnole

■ CRUISE PV
■ CONSOLIDATION EXCEPT FOR PP THURSDAYS
■ STABILIZATION EXCEPT FOR PP THURSDAYS

Use a sharp knife to chop the lemon zest very finely.

In a large bowl, mix together the thyme leaves, garlic, shallots and tomato purée with the chopped tomatoes and lemon zest. Add 4 tablespoons of the lemon juice. Season the marinade with the cayenne pepper, saffron powder and a pinch of black pepper. Add a little salt.

Cut the chicken breasts into 3cm cubes and add to the marinade. Stir, cover and refrigerate for at least 2 hours, or preferably overnight.

Preheat the oven to 180°C/350°F/Gas 4 or preheat the barbecue.

Skewer the chicken pieces on to kebab sticks and cook in the oven for 15 minutes, or grill on the barbebcue for 20 minutes, basting from time to time with the marinade. Serve piping hot.

2 servings
Preparation time
20 minutes
Cooking time
40 minutes
Ingredients
2 x 450g (1lb) poussins
5 sprigs thyme, leaves only
1 unwaxed lemon, sliced
500ml (18fl oz) hot chicken stock
2 medium onions, thinly sliced
700g (1lb 9oz) cherry tomatoes
2 garlic cloves, finely chopped
Salt and black pepper

Roast lemon poussin with cherry tomatoes

Coquelets au citron et aux tomates-cerises

■ **CRUISE PV**
■ **CONSOLIDATION EXCEPT FOR PP THURSDAYS**
■ **STABILIZATION EXCEPT FOR PP THURSDAYS**

Preheat the oven to 180°C/350°F/Gas 4.

Place the poussins in an ovenproof dish and scatter over the thyme leaves. Cover the birds with the lemon slices.

Bake in the oven for 10 minutes, then moisten with the hot chicken stock. Bake for a further 10 minutes.

Take the dish out of the oven and arrange the onions, tomatoes and garlic around the poussins. Season with salt and black pepper and mix together so that the tomatoes are coated with cooking juices.

Return to the oven for 20 minutes. Remove the skin from the poussins before serving.

4 servings
Preparation time
45 minutes
Cooking time
25 minutes
Ingredients
4 quails
200g (7oz) virtually fat-free cottage cheese
400g (14oz) puréed celeriac (frozen and thawed, or see recipe page 344), plus extra to serve
2 bunches chives
4 pinches cumin seeds
Salt and black pepper

Quails stuffed with cottage cheese and celeriac

Cailles farcies à la faisselle et à la purée de céleri

■ **CRUISE PV**
■ **CONSOLIDATION EXCEPT FOR PP THURSDAYS**
■ **STABILIZATION EXCEPT FOR PP THURSDAYS**

Preheat the oven to 150°C/300°F/Gas 2.

Debone the quails by the backbone, making sure that both sides remain firmly attached. Or get your butcher to debone the birds for you.

Mix the cottage cheese into the puréed celeriac. Add the chives, cumin seeds and some salt and black pepper.

Stuff the quails with this mixture, then close the birds up and place them in individual ovenproof dishes with the fold underneath. Roast in the oven for 25 minutes.

Serve piping hot, accompanied, for example, by some extra puréed celeriac.

6 servings
Preparation time
20 minutes
Cooking time
1 hour
Ingredients
1.25kg (2lb 12oz) cauliflower
600g (1lb 5oz) minced beef (5% fat)
1 onion, finely chopped
2 garlic cloves
1 small bunch parsley
Salt and black pepper

You will need a steamer

Cauliflower shepherd's pie

Hachis au chou-fleur

■ **CRUISE PV**
■ **CONSOLIDATION EXCEPT FOR PP THURSDAYS**
■ **STABILIZATION EXCEPT FOR PP THURSDAYS**

Preheat the oven to 180°C/350°F/Gas 4.

Break the cauliflower into florets and steam for 15 minutes. Whiz in a blender to produce a purée.

Next, combine the minced beef, onion, garlic and parsley and season with salt and black pepper.

Spread the minced meat evenly in a baking dish, then pour over the cauliflower purée and bake in the oven for 45 minutes.

Basque chicken

Poulet basquaise

4 servings
Preparation time
15 minutes
Cooking time
1 hour 10 minutes
Ingredients
1 × 1kg (2lb 4oz) chicken
Salt and black pepper
1kg (2lb 4oz) tomatoes, peeled and deseeded
1 carrot, cut into chunks
2 red peppers, deseeded and diced
2 garlic cloves, chopped
1 bouquet garni

■ **CRUISE PV**
■ **CONSOLIDATION EXCEPT FOR PP THURSDAYS**
■ **STABILIZATION EXCEPT FOR PP THURSDAYS**

Cut the chicken into pieces, season with salt and black pepper and brown in a flameproof non-stick casserole over a medium heat.

Add the tomatoes, carrot, red peppers, garlic and bouquet garni.

Season, cover and cook for 1 hour over a very gentle heat.

Serve the chicken with the skin removed.

4 servings
Preparation time
20 minutes
Cooking time
20 minutes
Ingredients
2 tomatoes
4–6 chicken breasts
4 courgettes
1 garlic clove, chopped
1 lemon, thinly sliced

Oven-baked chicken and courgette parcels

Papillottes de poulet aux courgettes

- **CRUISE PV**
- **CONSOLIDATION EXCEPT FOR PP THURSDAYS**
- **STABILIZATION EXCEPT FOR PP THURSDAYS**

Preheat the oven to 220°C/425°F/Gas 7 and cut out four rectangles of greaseproof paper.

Plunge the tomatoes into boiling water for 30 seconds, then peel them.

Cut the chicken breasts into tiny strips. Wash the courgettes and cut into strips.

In a non-stick frying pan, fry the courgettes, tomatoes, garlic and lemon slices over a high heat. Stir thoroughly and remove from the heat.

Divide the chicken and vegetables equally among the greaseproof paper rectangles, fold up the parcels and seal tightly.

Place on a baking tray and bake in the oven for 15–20 minutes. Serve hot.

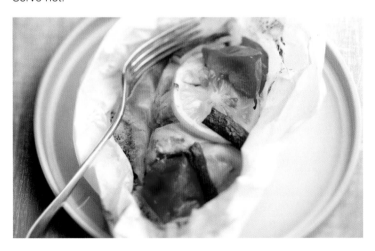

4 servings
Preparation time
15 minutes
Cooking time
10 minutes
Refrigeration time
1 hour
Ingredients
350g (12oz) chicken breasts
6 tomatoes, peeled and deseeded
150g (5½oz) virtually fat-free quark,
  with garlic and herbs
150g (5½oz) fat-free natural yoghurt
1 teaspoon balsamic vinegar
Black pepper
1 white onion, thinly sliced
2 sprigs flat-leaf parsley, chopped

You will need a steamer

Chicken and quark salad niçoise

Salade de poulet à la niçoise et au fromage frais

■ **CRUISE PV**
■ **CONSOLIDATION EXCEPT FOR PP THURSDAYS**
■ **STABILIZATION EXCEPT FOR PP THURSDAYS**

Cut the chicken into thin strips, steam for 10 minutes until cooked through, then leave to cool.

In the meantime, slice the tomatoes into thin segments.

In a bowl, stir the quark and yoghurt together until smooth and then add the balsamic vinegar and some black pepper.

In a salad bowl, mix the chicken strips with the tomato segments and onion slices. Pour the quark dressing over the top and place in the fridge for 1 hour.

Serve scattered with the chopped parsley – an ideal dish for hot summer days.

Tarragon chicken with chanterelle mushrooms

Poulet à l'estragon et aux girolles

4–6 servings
Preparation time
35 minutes
Cooking time
40 minutes
Ingredients
1 low-fat chicken stock cube
6 chicken legs or thighs
Salt and black pepper
1 sprig tarragon
1kg (2lb 4oz) chanterelle
   mushrooms
1 garlic clove, finely chopped
1 bunch parsley, finely chopped
250g (9oz) fat-free fromage frais

■ **CRUISE PV**
■ **CONSOLIDATION EXCEPT FOR PP THURSDAYS**
■ **STABILIZATION EXCEPT FOR PP THURSDAYS**

Dissolve the stock cube in 100ml (3½fl oz) boiling water.

Season the chicken pieces with salt and black pepper, and brown them in a flameproof non-stick casserole. Add the stock and the sprig of tarragon. Bring to the boil, cover, lower the heat and cook for 25 minutes.

Meanwhile, in a non-stick frying pan, gently fry the chanterelle mushrooms with the garlic and parsley. Season and keep warm.

When the chicken is ready to be served, discard the tarragon the casserole and deglaze with the fromage frais over a gentle heat. Adjust the seasoning.

Serve the chicken hot with the sautéed chanterelle mushrooms.

4 servings
Preparation time
20 minutes
Cooking time
2 hours
Ingredients
1 low-salt beef stock cube
500g (1lb 2oz) lean fillet of beef, cut
   into cubes
1 teaspoon cornflour
1 teaspoon chopped parsley
1 garlic clove, finely chopped
1 bay leaf
Salt and black pepper
3 medium onions, finely chopped
150g (5½oz) button mushrooms,
   sliced

Beef bourguignon

Boeuf bourguignon

■ **CRUISE PV**
■ **CONSOLIDATION EXCEPT FOR PP THURSDAYS**
■ **STABILIZATION EXCEPT FOR PP THURSDAYS**

Preheat the oven to 200°C/400°F/Gas 6.

Dissolve the stock cube in 250ml (9fl oz) boiling water.

Brown the beef in a high-sided non-stick frying pan, then transfer the meat to an ovenproof casserole.

Pour the beef stock into the frying pan and add the cornflour, parsley, garlic, bay leaf and salt and black pepper. Bring to the boil and allow to thicken slightly.

Pour the sauce over the beef (add some water if the meat is not covered). Cover the casserole and cook in the oven for 2 hours.

Fry the onions and mushrooms in a non-stick frying pan over a medium heat and add them to the meat during the last 30 minutes of cooking.

Serve the casserole piping hot.

4 servings
Make a day in advance
Preparation time
15 minutes
Cooking time
8 minutes
Refrigeration time
12 hours
Ingredients
600g (1lb 5oz) fresh tuna
4 large tomatoes
2 onions
4 rashers fat-reduced bacon
1 red pepper
For the marinade
200ml (7fl oz) lemon juice
2 tablespoons tomato purée
1 tablespoon chopped tarragon
1 tablespoon chopped basil
4 garlic cloves, finely chopped
A few black peppercorns
40g (1½oz) fennel seeds
Salt

Tuna and fennel kebabs
Brochettes de thon au fenouil

■ **CRUISE PV**
■ **CONSOLIDATION EXCEPT FOR PP THURSDAYS**
■ **STABILIZATION EXCEPT FOR PP THURSDAYS**

Cut the tuna into 4cm (1½in) cubes. Cut each tomato into 8 pieces and remove the pulp. Cut the onions into quarters and separate the layers. Wash and deseed the pepper, then cut into square pieces.

Thread the tuna cubes on to kebab sticks, alternating with the bacon and vegetables, and then place the kebabs in a wide, shallow bowl.

In another bowl, combine the ingredients for the marinade and pour over the kebabs. Leave to marinate in the fridge for 12 hours, or overnight.

Preheat a barbecue or grill.

Cook the kebabs either on the barbecue or under the grill for 8 minutes, moistening the fish with the marinade during cooking so that it does not become dry. Serve hot.

4 servings
Preparation time
35 minutes
Cooking time
1¼ hours
Ingredients
1 bouquet garni
1 teaspoon ground coriander
Salt and black peppercorns
Pinch of grated nutmeg
6 carrots
2 fennel bulbs
2 leeks
1 celery stick
2 turnips
4 shallots
500g (1lb 2oz) mussels
500g (1lb 2oz) cockles
500g (1lb 2oz) clams

Seafood stew

Pot-au-feu de fruits de mer

■ **CRUISE PV**
■ **CONSOLIDATION EXCEPT FOR PP THURSDAYS**
■ **STABILIZATION EXCEPT FOR PP THURSDAYS**

Bring 2.5 litres (4½ pints) water to the boil in a large pan. Add the bouquet garni, coriander, 1 teaspoon black peppercorns and a pinch of nutmeg.

Prepare the vegetables. Peel and roughly chop the carrots, cut the fennel into quarters, slice the leeks, chop the celery into several pieces and the turnips into cubes but leave the shallots whole. Put the carrots and turnips into the stock and cook, covered, for 30 minutes. Then add the remaining vegetables and cook for a further 30 minutes.

Scrub all the shellfish and rinse under cold running water. Remove the beards from the mussels. Take the vegetables out of the stock and divide them between four individual bowls. Add the shellfish to the stock and cook until they open, about 1 minute (discard any that refuse to open). Remove the shellfish and arrange over the vegetables.

Strain the stock and shellfish juices through a conical strainer, adjust the seasoning and pour the broth into the bowls. Serve immediately.

Burritos galette wrap

Burritos dans leur galette

■ **CRUISE PV**
■ **CONSOLIDATION EXCEPT FOR PP THURSDAYS**
■ **STABILIZATION EXCEPT FOR PP THURSDAYS**

In a lightly oiled non-stick frying pan wiped with kitchen paper, fry the onions over a high heat. After a few moments, add 4 tablespoons water. Add the minced beef and paprika. Dilute the tomato purée with a little water and add to the frying pan. Cook for 10 minutes.

In the meantime, chop the tomatoes into small pieces. Wash the lettuce leaves and cut into strips.

Prepare four galettes by mixing together the oat bran, wheat bran, egg whites, fromage frais and baking powder. Cook for 20 minutes in a non-stick frying pan over a very low heat, turning halfway through.

Place each galette on a warmed plate and cover one half with some shredded lettuce. Add the cooked mince, then the grated cheese and finish off with the chopped tomatoes. Complete the burritos by folding over the galettes. Serve straightaway.

4 servings
Preparation time
25 minutes
Cooking time
30 minutes
Ingredients
2 large onions, finely chopped
500g (1lb 2oz) minced beef (5% fat)
1 teaspoon paprika
4 tablespoons tomato purée
4 tomatoes
4 large lettuce leaves
60g (2¼oz) low-fat Emmental cheese (6% fat), grated

For the galettes
8 tablespoons oat bran
4 tablespoons wheat bran
4 egg whites
8 tablespoons fat-free fromage frais
1 teaspoon baking powder

1 serving
Preparation time
20 minutes
Cooking time
40 minutes
Ingredients
70g (2½oz) carrots
1 leek (white part only)
70g (2½oz) celery
1 bouquet garni
½ onion
1 clove
Salt and black pepper
250g (9oz) fillet of beef

Beef on a string

Bœuf à la ficelle

■ **CRUISE PV**
■ **CONSOLIDATION EXCEPT FOR PP THURSDAYS**
■ **STABILIZATION EXCEPT FOR PP THURSDAYS**

Roughly chop the vegetables.

Pour 1 litre (1¾ pints) water into a flameproof casserole. Add the bouquet garni, the half onion studded with the clove and the chopped vegetables. Season with salt and black pepper and bring to the boil.

Tie a piece of string around the beef and drop it into the simmering stock. Cover and cook over a medium heat for about 30 minutes.

Take the meat out, cut into pieces and arrange on a warmed plate. Served accompanied by the vegetables.

Thinly sliced beef with raspberry vinegar and courgettes

Eminé de bœuf au vinaigre et courgettes

4 servings
Preparation time
20 minutes
Cooking time
40 minutes
Ingredients
600g (1lb 5oz) lean beef
3 garlic cloves, chopped
1 onion, chopped
4 courgettes, cut into strips
100ml (3½fl oz) raspberry vinegar
2 sprigs parsley, chopped
¼ bunch tarragon, chopped
Salt and black pepper

■ **CRUISE PV**
■ **CONSOLIDATION EXCEPT FOR PP THURSDAYS**
■ **STABILIZATION EXCEPT FOR PP THURSDAYS**

Cut the beef into small, thin, even-sized pieces.

Fry the garlic, onion and courgettes in a non-stick frying pan. Stir well so that the vegetables brown on all sides. Pour in a cup of water, cover and cook over a gentle heat for 20 minutes. Remove the vegetables and put to one side.

In the same frying pan, sear the meat over a high heat for 5 minutes and add the vinegar. Mix together before returning the vegetables to the frying pan.

Simmer the beef and vegetables for 15 minutes and, at the very last moment, add the parsley and tarragon. Season with salt and black pepper and serve piping hot.

6 servings
Make a day in advance
Preparation time
20 minutes
Marinating time
8 hours
Cooking time
2 hours
Ingredients
1.25kg (2lb 12oz) stewing venison
2 shallots, finely chopped
2 onions, finely chopped
2 carrots, sliced
250ml (9fl oz) red wine
4 cloves
10 pink peppercorns
10 coriander seeds
4 bay leaves
1 sprig thyme
1 sprig rosemary
2 pinches ground ginger
½ teaspoon ground allspice
Salt and black pepper
For the celeriac purée
1 small celeriac, cut into large cubes
250ml (9fl oz) skimmed milk

*Contains 1 tolerated food portion
per person*

Venison stew with celeriac purée

Civet de biche et sa purée de céleri

■ **CRUISE PV**
■ **CONSOLIDATION EXCEPT FOR PP THURSDAYS**
■ **STABILIZATION EXCEPT FOR PP THURSDAYS**

Place the venison in a large bowl and add all the other ingredients with 500ml (18fl oz) water. Leave to marinate for 8 hours, or preferably overnight.

Remove the meat from the marinade and brown it in a cast-iron casserole. Then pour in the marinade juices and leave to simmer, uncovered, for 1 hour. Then cover and simmer for a further hour.

While the venison is cooking, prepare the celeriac purée. Steam the celeriac for 10–15 minutes, until tender. Then mash it with a potato masher, adding the skimmed milk to loosen the purée. Season with salt and black pepper.

Serve the venison stew on warmed plates, with the cooking juices in a separate jug or sauce boat and accompanied by the celeriac purée.

6 servings
Preparation time
20 minutes
Cooking time
10 minutes
Ingredients
36 native or Pacific oysters
Coarse sea salt
250ml (9fl oz) small mussels
50g (1¾oz) sea lettuce* or samphire
2 garlic cloves, chopped
½ bunch parsley, chopped
½ teaspoon melted butter flavouring

*Order from the fishmonger or
organic food stores*

Warm oysters with sea lettuce

Huîtres tièdes à la laitue de mer

■ **CRUISE PV**
■ **CONSOLIDATION EXCEPT FOR PP THURSDAYS**
■ **STABILIZATION EXCEPT FOR PP THURSDAYS**

Wash the oyster shells if they are grubby, then open them very carefully, preferably using an oyster knife. Cut the meat free and place back inside the bottom half of the shells. Spread the sea salt over a baking sheet and arrange the shells on top, ensuring they are firmly wedged.

Scrub and clean the mussels and cook in a pan over a medium heat until they have opened. Drain them and keep them to one side to be used in another dish (remember to discard any that have not opened). Strain the mussel cooking juices and reserve.

Preheat the grill.

Rinse the sea lettuce and shred it finely. Place the garlic in a saucepan along with 200ml (7fl oz) of the cooking juice from the mussels and the parsley. Bring to the boil and add the melted butter flavouring and half a glass of water. Add a little sea lettuce too.

Pour this sauce over the oysters and brown them for a few minutes under the grill.

Spread a thick layer of sea salt over six plates, arrange the oysters on top and garnish with the shredded sea lettuce. Serve straightaway.

Cretan moussaka

Mille-feuille d'aubergines à la crétoise

4 servings
Preparation time
20 minutes
Cooking time
30 minutes
Ingredients
600g (1lb 5oz) minced beef (5% fat)
2 garlic cloves, crushed
15 mint leaves, finely chopped
400g (14oz) tomato passata
2 aubergines
200g (7oz) fat-free yoghurt
Salt and black pepper

■ **CRUISE PV**
■ **CONSOLIDATION EXCEPT FOR PP THURSDAYS**
■ **STABILIZATION EXCEPT FOR PP THURSDAYS**

Preheat the oven to 200°C/400°F/Gas 6.

Brown the beef in a non-stick frying pan, then add the garlic, mint and tomato passata. Cover and simmer for 20 minutes, stirring from time to time.

Meanwhile, wash the aubergines and cut into 1cm -(½in)- thick slices. In another non-stick frying pan over a medium heat, gently fry them, without any fat, for 3 minutes on both sides. Then place the aubergine slices on some kitchen paper.

Pour the yoghurt over the meat, stir and season with salt and black pepper.

In each of four small gratin dish, arrange 2 slices of aubergine, side by side. Cover them with some of the meat sauce, then continue building up alternate layers, finishing off with a layer of aubergine. Bake in the oven for 5 minutes and serve.

4 servings
Preparation time
20 minutes
Cooking time
15 minutes
Ingredients
1 bunch asparagus
Salt and black pepper
8 eggs (very fresh)
50ml (2fl oz) skimmed milk
100g (3½oz) virtually fat-free quark

Asparagus and quark scrambled eggs

Œufs brouillés aux asperges et aux carrés de fromage frais

■ **CRUISE PV**
■ **CONSOLIDATION EXCEPT FOR PP THURSDAYS**
■ **STABILIZATION EXCEPT FOR PP THURSDAYS**

Prepare the asparagus and cook it in boiling salted water for about 3 minutes.

Carefully remove the asparagus spears from the pan using a slotted spoon, then refresh them in a large bowl of iced water (to preserve their flavour and colour). Keep back four spears and cut the remainder into chunks.

Whisk the eggs and skimmed milk until thick and creamy. Pour into a pan and warm over a very low heat, stirring continuously with a wooden spoon or spatula until you have a smooth, slightly thick cream. Then immediately turn off the heat and stir in the quark. This will stop the mixture from cooking and you will end up with very creamy scrambled eggs. Season with salt and black pepper. Add the asparagus chunks and fold them in carefully.

Divide this mixture between four warmed ramekin dishes and garnish with the reserved asparagus. Serve straightaway.

Stuffed courgettes

Courgettes farcies

4 servings
Preparation time
10 minutes
Cooking time
30 minutes
Ingredients
4 courgettes
Salt and black pepper
500g (1lb 2oz) minced beef (5% fat)
1 jar or tin salsa verde (Mexican
    green sauce)
200g (7oz) fat-free fromage frais

■ **CRUISE PV**
■ **CONSOLIDATION EXCEPT FOR PP THURSDAYS**
■ **STABILIZATION EXCEPT FOR PP THURSDAYS**

Preheat the oven to 240°C/475°F/Gas 9.

Halve the courgettes lengthways and deseed. Season with salt and black pepper.

Brown the minced beef in a non-stick frying pan, then mix together with the salsa verde and fromage frais. Fill the courgettes with this stuffing mixture and bake in the oven for 30 minutes. Serve hot.

Tagine with sardine balls

Tajine de sardines en boulettes

4 servings
Preparation time
25 minutes
Refrigeration time
3–4 hours
Cooking time
1 hour
Ingredients
600g (1lb 5oz) sardine fillets
1 teaspoon paprika
1 teaspoon ground cumin
4 tablespoons chopped parsley, plus
 extra to serve
4 tablespoons chopped coriander,
 plus extra to serve
4 garlic cloves, finely chopped
Juice of 2 lemons
4 tomatoes
3 preserved lemons, halved

■ **CRUISE PV**
■ **CONSOLIDATION EXCEPT FOR PP THURSDAYS**
■ **STABILIZATION EXCEPT FOR PP THURSDAYS**

Place the sardine fillets in a food processor and add the spices, parsley, coriander and garlic along with half of the lemon juice. Whiz until blended and then leave to rest in the fridge for 3–4 hours.

Remove the mixture from the fridge and form into small balls.

Bring a large pan of water to the boil and add the tomatoes for 15 seconds so that the skins can be easily peeled. Slice the tomatoes very thinly and spread them over the bottom of a tagine. Place the dish over a very gentle heat, pour in half a glass of water and the remaining lemon juice.

Carefully add the sardine balls to the sauce and place the preserved lemon halves in between them. Cover the tagine with its lid and cook for 1 hour.

When ready to serve, scatter some chopped herbs on top.

4 servings
Preparation time
25 minutes
Cooking time
1 hour 10 minutes
Ingredients
2 large courgettes
Salt and black pepper
1 low-salt chicken stock cube
2 eggs, separated, plus 2 egg whites
4 slices cooked turkey, cut into thin
  strips
A little grated nutmeg
30g (1oz) low-fat Emmental cheese,
  grated

Contains ¼ tolerated food portion
per person

Courgette and turkey soufflé

Soufflé de courgette à la dinde

■ **CRUISE PV**
■ **CONSOLIDATION EXCEPT FOR PP THURSDAYS**
■ **STABILIZATION EXCEPT FOR PP THURSDAYS**

Preheat the oven to 220°C/425°F/Gas 7.

Wipe the courgettes and grate with the skin on. Add some salt and cook them in a non-stick frying pan over a low heat for 10 minutes so that they release as much water as possible. Crumble in the stock cube. Drain the courgettes in a colander.

In a bowl, whisk the 4 egg whites with a pinch of salt until very stiff.

In another bowl, mix together the 2 egg yolks, turkey, nutmeg, cheese and cooked courgettes. Season with black pepper and gently fold in the egg whites.

Pour the mixture into a high-sided non-stick mould and place in the oven for 50 minutes, keeping a careful eye on the soufflé to check when it is cooked. Serve straightaway.

Kefta kebabs

Brochettes de keftas aux carrés frais

■ **CRUISE PV**
■ **CONSOLIDATION EXCEPT FOR PP THURSDAYS**
■ **STABILIZATION EXCEPT FOR PP THURSDAYS**

4 servings
Preparation time
25 minutes
Refrigeration time
10 minutes
Cooking time
8 minutes
Ingredients
500g (1lb 2oz) minced beef (5% fat)
1 onion, finely chopped
2 garlic cloves, finely chopped
1 egg
150g (5½oz) virtually fat-free quark,
  with herbs and garlic
Pinch of paprika
Pinch of ground cumin
Pinch of grated nutmeg
1 red pepper
1 green pepper
1 white onion

Place the minced beef in a bowl and work in the onion and garlic. Add the egg, quark and spices. Stir all the ingredients together until you get a smooth mixture and then refrigerate for 10 minutes.

Preheat a barbecue or grill.

Cut the red and green peppers into quarters and deseed. Peel the white onion, cut into quarters and separate the layers.

Shape the minced beef mixture into balls the size of golf balls with the palms of your hands. Thread the keftas on to kebab sticks, alternating with the pieces of pepper and white onion.

Cook the kebabs on the barbecue for about 8 minutes, or grill them turning them over halfway through. Serve sizzling hot.

4 servings
Preparation time
20 minutes
Cooking time
25 minutes
Ingredients
4 large cabbage leaves
400g (14oz) cooked sauerkraut
400g (14oz) fish fillets (salmon,
    pollock, smoked haddock),
    cut into strips
4 tablespoons low-fat cream
    (3% fat)
1 unwaxed lemon, sliced
Salt and black pepper
A few chives

You will need a steamer

*Contains 1 tolerated food portion
per person*

Fish sauerkraut wraps

Choucroute de la mer en papillotes

■ **CRUISE PV**
■ **CONSOLIDATION EXCEPT FOR PP THURSDAYS**
■ **STABILIZATION EXCEPT FOR PP THURSDAYS**

Blanch the whole cabbage leaves in boiling water for 5 minutes,
then drain.

On each cabbage leaf, place some sauerkraut, strips of fish,
1 tablespoon low-fat cream and a slice of lemon. Season sparingly
with salt and black pepper. Fold over the cabbage leaves and use
the chives to tie up each wrap.

Transfer the wraps to a steamer basket. Lay them side by side and
steam for 15–20 minutes. Serve immediately

4 servings
Preparation time
20 minutes
Cooking time
1½ hours
Ingredients
1 × 1kg (2lb 4oz) free-range chicken
3 onions, finely chopped
250g (9oz) tomatoes, diced
3 garlic cloves, crushed
½ teaspoon saffron powder
Salt and black pepper
400g (14oz) porcini or chanterelle
    mushrooms

Free-range saffron chicken

Poulet de Bresse au safran

■ **CRUISE PV**
■ **CONSOLIDATION EXCEPT FOR PP THURSDAYS**
■ **STABILIZATION EXCEPT FOR PP THURSDAYS**

Cut the chicken into large pieces and brown in a wide non-stick frying pan with a little water.

Add the onions, tomatoes and garlic.

Season the chicken pieces with the saffron, some salt and black pepper and leave to simmer over a very low heat for 1¼ hours, adding a little hot water from time to time to prevent it from becoming too dry.

Meanwhile, clean the mushrooms and chop them. Heat another non-stick frying pan and fry the mushrooms until they have released all their water, then add salt and black pepper.

Serve the chicken and mushrooms together, piping hot.

4 servings
Preparation time
35 minutes
Marinating time
20 minutes
Cooking time
30 minutes
Ingredients
4 × 200g (7oz) sea bream fillets
200g (7oz) sea salt
400g (14oz) baby spinach
20 basil leaves
20 mint leaves
4 sprigs flat-leaf parsley, leaves only
4 sprigs coriander, leaves only
1 spring onion, chopped
For the 'glazing' sauce
1 low-salt veal stock cube
1 teaspoon honey flavouring
100ml (3½fl oz) soy sauce
For the yoghurt dressing
2 tablespoons lemon juice
1 tablespoon soy sauce
5 chives, finely chopped
150g (5½oz) fat-free yoghurt
Black pepper

You will need a steamer

Sea bream and herb salad

Dorade en fraîcheur d'herbes

■ **CRUISE PV**
■ **CONSOLIDATION EXCEPT FOR PP THURSDAYS**
■ **STABILIZATION EXCEPT FOR PP THURSDAYS**

First make the 'glazing' sauce. In a pan, over a moderate heat, simmer the crumbled stock cube, honey flavouring, soy sauce and 50ml (2fl oz) water for 10 minutes until reduced.

Place the sea bream fillets in a large bowl. Add the sea salt and leave to marinate for 20 minutes. Rinse the fish repeatedly and dab dry.

Prepare the yoghurt dressing. In a bowl, combine the lemon juice, soy sauce, chives and yoghurt. Add black pepper and whisk with a fork to emulsify.

Remove the stalks from the baby spinach, rinse and dry. Rinse the herbs, add the spring onion and put to one side. Pour half the yoghurt dressing over the baby spinach and the other half over the herbs and onion.

Steam the sea bream fillets for 6–8 minutes, depending on how thick they are.

Arrange a bed of baby spinach on each of four plates and place a sea bream fillet on top. Pour over the 'glazing' sauce and scatter over the herb salad. Serve immediately.

Diet bouillabaisse

Bouillabaisse minceur

4–6 servings
Preparation time
45 minutes
Cooking time
1 hour
Ingredients
1.5kg (3lb 5oz) fresh fish (monkfish, bass, scorpion fish, mullet, conger eel, etc.)
1 leek, cut into large chunks
1 large onion, finely chopped
4 garlic cloves, crushed
3 tomatoes, diced
1 low-salt fish stock cube
2 fennel stalks
½ bunch parsley
2 sprigs thyme
3 bay leaves
1 sprig savory (or sweet marjoram)
Salt and black pepper
5–6 pinches saffron powder
1kg (2lb 4oz) shellfish (crayfish, crab, mussels, prawns, Dublin bay prawns, etc.)

■ **CRUISE PV**
■ **CONSOLIDATION EXCEPT FOR PP THURSDAYS**
■ **STABILIZATION EXCEPT FOR PP THURSDAYS**

Do not scale the fresh rock fish (mullet, scorpion fish, etc.). Rinse the fish and gut the larger ones.

Place a large pot over a low heat and gently fry the vegetables with the stock cube, half a glass of water and the herbs. Cook for 15 minutes. Add just the rock fish, season with salt and black pepper, and leave all the ingredients to brown for 15 minutes. Then pour in 3 litres (5¼ pints) boiling water and leave to simmer for a further 10 minutes.

Remove the pan from the heat and take out the fennel stalks. Put the rest of the contents through a food mill, with a large-holed disc, then through a seive. Add the saffron, adjust the seasoning and put to one side.

To serve, bring the soup to the boil and poach the rest of the fresh fish, starting with any firm-fleshed pieces. Cook for 6–10 minutes over a gentle heat then, at the very last moment, add the shellfish. Serve the bouillabaisse in a large warmed dish.

4 servings
Preparation time
25 minutes
Cooking time
5 minutes
Ingredients
2 garlic cloves
1 bunch parsley
500g (1lb 2oz) button mushrooms
500g (1lb 2oz) seafood sticks
   (surimi)
500g (1lb 2oz) large cooked prawns
Salt and black pepper

Stir-fried garlic prawns and mushrooms

Poêlée de surimi et crevettes aux champignons

■ **CRUISE PV**
■ **CONSOLIDATION EXCEPT FOR PP THURSDAYS**
■ **STABILIZATION EXCEPT FOR PP THURSDAYS**

Finely chop the garlic and parsley together and put to one side. Clean the mushrooms and wipe them dry. Slice thinly and put to one side too.

Cut the seafood sticks into cubes. Shell and cut up the prawns.

In a large non-stick frying pan, fry the prawns over a medium heat for 1 minute. Add the mushrooms, cook for 3 minutes and then add the cubed seafood sticks and cook for 1 minute more or until they are heated through.

Season with salt and black pepper, stir in the chopped parsley and garlic mixture and serve immediately.

2 servings
Preparation time
25 minutes
Cooking time
25 minutes
Ingredients
250ml (9fl oz) small mussels
500g (1lb 2oz) fish (monkfish, John
   Dory), cut into chunks
75g (2¾oz) button mushrooms,
   finely chopped
250ml (9fl oz) fish stock
Juice of ½ lemon
2 tablespoons fat-free fromage frais
1 egg yolk
Salt and black pepper

Fish stew

Blanquette de poisson

■ **CRUISE PV**
■ **CONSOLIDATION EXCEPT FOR PP THURSDAYS**
■ **STABILIZATION EXCEPT FOR PP THURSDAYS**

Scrub and thoroughly rinse the mussels.

Fry the fish pieces and mushrooms in a non-stick frying pan. As
soon as they turn golden brown, add the mussels and pour in the
fish stock. Cook for a further 10–15 minutes, then drain and reserve
the cooking liquid. Shell the mussels and keep them warm with the
fish and mushrooms. Discard any mussels that have failed to open.

Return the cooking liquid to a small pan, reduce by half and strain.
Stir in the lemon juice and, over a very gentle heat, bind the sauce
with the fromage frais and egg yolk, without allowing it to boil.
Season with salt and black pepper.

Pour this sauce over the fish and mushrooms and serve.

2 servings
Preparation time
10 minutes
Cooking time
40 minutes
Ingredients
2 garlic cloves, crushed
1 teaspoon ground cumin
1 teaspoon ground coriander
1 teaspoon ras el hanout (or
   garam masala)
1 low-salt chicken stock cube
2 tablespoons tomato purée
4 courgettes, thickly sliced
Juice of 1 lemon
A few sprigs of fresh coriander, to
   garnish

Courgette tagine

Tajine de courgettes

■ **CRUISE PV**
■ **CONSOLIDATION EXCEPT FOR PP THURSDAYS**
■ **STABILIZATION EXCEPT FOR PP THURSDAYS**

Gently fry the garlic and spices in a high-sided non-stick frying pan.

Add 500ml (18fl oz) water, the crumbled stock cube, tomato purée and courgettes. Cover and cook for 35 minutes over a medium heat.

Transfer the courgettes to a tagine or other serving dish, drizzle over the lemon juice and garnish with sprigs of coriander.

Provençal tian

Tian provençal

6 servings
Preparation time
25 minutes
Cooking time
55 minutes
Ingredients
5 tomatoes, sliced
2 aubergines, sliced
1 courgette, sliced
2 red peppers, deseeded and thinly
   sliced
2 green peppers, deseeded and
   thinly sliced
8 garlic cloves
1 sprig thyme, finely chopped
1 sprig savory (or sweet marjoram),
   finely chopped
5 basil leaves, finely chopped
Salt and black pepper

■ **CRUISE PV**
■ **CONSOLIDATION EXCEPT FOR PP THURSDAYS**
■ **STABILIZATION EXCEPT FOR PP THURSDAYS**

Preheat the oven to 190°C/375°F/Gas 5.

Arrange the tomato, aubergine and courgette slices around the edges of an ovenproof dish, alternating each vegetable, then place the peppers in the centre along with the unpeeled garlic cloves. Scatter the herbs over the vegetables and season with salt and black pepper.

Bake in the oven for 55 minutes. After about 30 minutes, moisten with a cup of water so that the vegetables do not dry out. Squeeze the garlic cloves out of their skin on to the vegetables to serve.

6 servings
Preparation time
30 minutes
Cooking time
35 minutes
Refrigeration time
20 minutes
Ingredients
1 garlic head
1kg (2lb 4oz) mixed red and green
  peppers
240g (8½oz) tinned chopped
  tomatoes
Salt and black pepper

Tchoutchouka

■ **CRUISE PV**
▦ **CONSOLIDATION EXCEPT FOR PP THURSDAYS**
■ **STABILIZATION EXCEPT FOR PP THURSDAYS**

Preheat the oven to 180°C/350°F/Gas 4.

Peel and crush the garlic cloves.

Roast the peppers in the oven for 10 minutes on each side. Take them out of the oven, place in a plastic bag and seal tightly. Leave for a few minutes and you will be able to remove the skin more easily. Skin the peppers and cut them into thin strips.

In either a large non-stick pan or a frying pan, gently fry the tomatoes with the garlic for 10 minutes and then add salt and black pepper.

Next add the sliced peppers and simmer for 10–15 minutes over a gentle heat. Stir regularly with a wooden spoon so that the vegetables do not stick to the bottom of the pan. Once the mixture has reduced, it is ready.

Transfer to a serving dish, leave to cool, refrigerate and serve chilled.

6 servings
Preparation time
15 minutes
Cooking time
40 minutes
Ingredients
1kg (2lb 4oz) carrots, sliced
Salt
50ml (2fl oz) vinegar
5 garlic cloves, crushed
1 tablespoon ground cumin
1 tablespoon paprika
Harissa, to taste (optional)

Cumin carrots

Carottes au cumin

■ **CRUISE PV**
■ **CONSOLIDATION EXCEPT FOR PP THURSDAYS**
■ **STABILIZATION EXCEPT FOR PP THURSDAYS**

Boil the carrots in 1 litre (1¾ pints) salted water for 30 minutes.

Warm the vinegar in a frying pan. Drain the carrots and add them immediately to the pan. Stir in the garlic and cumin. Gently fry for 10 minutes over a low heat. Season with salt and add the paprika.

You can also add a little harissa if you like your carrots to taste spicier.

Transfer to a dish and leave to cool. Serve the carrots cold.

2 servings
Preparation time
15 minutes
Cooking time
35 minutes
Ingredients
3 eggs, separated
2 heaped tablespoons cornflour
½ teaspoon Hermesetas liquid
  sweetener
Grated zest of 1 unwaxed lemon
3 heaped tablespoons fat-free
  fromage frais

*Contains 1 tolerated food portion
per person*

Nana's cake

Gâteau Nana

- CRUISE PV
- CONSOLIDATION EXCEPT FOR PP THURSDAYS
- STABILIZATION EXCEPT FOR PP THURSDAYS

Preheat the oven to 180°C/350°F/Gas 4.

Beat the egg whites until stiff.

Stir the cornflour, sweetener and lemon zest into the egg yolks. Mix together thoroughly.

Fold the stiffly beaten egg whites into the rest of the mixture.

Pour the mixture into a non-stick cake tin and bake in the oven for 30–35 minutes.

Serve straight from the oven or allow to cool before serving.

2 servings
Preparation time
10 minutes
Refrigeration time
2 hours
Ingredients
4 teaspoons sugar-free, fat-reduced
cocoa powder
2 egg yolks plus 4 egg whites
150g (5½oz) fat-free fromage frais
4 tablespoons Canderel granules
1 teaspoon instant coffee powder
Pinch of salt

*Contains 2 tolerated food portions
per person*

Chocolate mousse

Mousse chocolatée

■ **CRUISE PV**
■ **CONSOLIDATION EXCEPT FOR PP THURSDAYS**
■ **STABILIZATION EXCEPT FOR PP THURSDAYS**

In a bowl, mix together the cocoa powder, egg yolks, fromage frais, sweetener and instant coffee.

Beat the egg whites with salt until stiff. Gently fold the egg whites into the chocolaty mixture.

Pour the mixture into sundae dishes and refrigerate for 2 hours before serving.

Cocoa meringues

Meringues au cacao

Makes about 12 meringues

Preparation time
10 minutes

Cooking time
20 minutes

Ingredients
3 egg whites
6 tablespoons Canderel granules
2 teaspoons sugar-free, fat-reduced cocoa powder
2 teaspoons very strong coffee powder

Contains 2 tolerated food portions per person

■ **CRUISE PV**
■ **CONSOLIDATION EXCEPT FOR PP THURSDAYS**
■ **STABILIZATION EXCEPT FOR PP THURSDAYS**

Preheat the oven to 150°C/300°F/Gas 2.

Beat the egg whites until very stiff.

Sprinkle in the sweetener along with the cocoa powder, and then the coffee. Continue beating for a further 30 seconds.

Place small piles of the mixture on a baking sheet and bake in the oven for 15–20 minutes. Serve cold.

2 servings
Preparation time
35 minutes
Cooking time
20 minutes
Ingredients
3 Canderel vanilla sticks
1 teaspoon rum flavouring
1 egg white
30g (1oz) virtually fat-free quark
30g (1oz) fat-free fromage frais
½ teaspoon vanilla flavouring
For the dough
2 tablespoons Splenda granules
2 tablespoons oat bran
1 teaspoon wheat bran
1 tablespoon cornflour
1 teaspoon baking powder
80ml (2¾oz) skimmed milk
2 eggs, separated

*Contains ½ tolerated food portion
per person*

Rum babas

Babas au rhum

■ **CRUISE PV**
■ **CONSOLIDATION EXCEPT FOR PP THURSDAYS**
■ **STABILIZATION EXCEPT FOR PP THURSDAYS**

Preheat the oven to 180°C/350°F/Gas 4.

First make the dough. Combine the sweetener, oat and wheat brans, cornflour, baking powder and skimmed milk with the egg yolks. Whisk the egg whites until stiff and fold them into the dough. Pour the mixture into two small baba moulds or ramekin dishes and bake in the oven for 20 minutes.

In a pan, mix 1 of the vanilla sticks and the rum flavouring in a glass of water and heat.

Once the babas are cooked, turn them out of their moulds into serving dishes and pour the rum syrup over them. Allow the syrup to soak right into the cakes.

Now make a Chantilly cream. Beating the egg white in a bowl until just stiff. In another bowl, combine the quark, fromage frais, the remaining vanilla sticks and the vanilla flavouring. Gently fold the egg white into the quark mixture.

Use an icing bag to decorate the babas with the Chantilly cream. Serve without delay.

2 servings
Preparation time
10 minutes
Cooking time
20 minutes
Ingredients
4 eggs, separated
1 teaspoon Hermesetas liquid
   sweetener
½ teaspoon walnut flavouring
1 teaspoon vanilla flavouring
2 tablespoons wheat bran
4 tablespoons oat bran

Walnut-flavoured diet cookies

Cookies légers arôme noix

■ **CRUISE PV**
■ **CONSOLIDATION EXCEPT FOR PP THURSDAYS**
■ **STABILIZATION EXCEPT FOR PP THURSDAYS**

Preheat the oven to 180°C/350°F/Gas 4 and line a baking sheet with greaseproof paper.

In a bowl, combine the egg yolks, sweetener, flavourings and brans.

Whisk the egg whites until very stiff, then gently fold them into the bran mixture.

Place small, cookie-sized piles at regular intervals on the baking sheet.

Bake in the oven for 15–20 minutes and enjoy straightaway.

Prune delight

Délices aux pruneaux

■ **CRUISE PV**
■ **CONSOLIDATION EXCEPT FOR PP THURSDAYS**
■ **STABILIZATION EXCEPT FOR PP THURSDAYS**

3 servings
Preparation time
20 minutes
Refrigeration time
2 hours
Ingredients
1 gelatine leaf
450g (1lb) fat-free prune yoghurt
2 teaspoons crystallized stevia
3 tablespoons fat-free cottage
    cheese, drained for at least ½ day
3 egg whites

*Contains 1 tolerated food portion
per person*

Soak the gelatine in a little cold water in a bowl until it has softened completely and then dissolve it in a tablespoon of boiling water.

Stir the yoghurt very thoroughly and add the dissolved gelatine. Pour into three sundae dishes and refrigerate for at least 2 hours.

Meanwhile, prepare the Chantilly cream. Stir the sweetener into the cottage cheese in a bowl. Beat the egg whites until stiff in another bowl. Combine the egg whites carefully with the cottage cheese and refrigerate.

When ready to serve, top each prune delight with 3 tablespoons of the Chantilly cream.

4 servings
Preparation time
25 minutes
Cooking time
40 minutes
Refrigeration time
3 hours
Ingredients
4 tablespoons oat bran
2 tablespoons wheat bran
1 tablespoon powdered skimmed
 milk
½ teaspoon baking powder
3 tablespoons fat-free fromage frais
2 eggs plus 2 egg whites
½ teaspoon bitter almond flavouring
1½ teaspoons Hermesetas liquid
 sweetener
For the orange cream
1 gelatine leaf
1 vanilla pod
250ml (9fl oz) skimmed milk
2 egg yolks
3 tablespoons Canderel granules
3 tablespoons cornflour, plus extra
 for dusting
½ teaspoon orange flavouring

Contains ¾ tolerated food portion
per person

Bitter almond cake with orange cream

Gâteau à l'amande amère et sa crème à l'orange

■ **CRUISE PV**
■ **CONSOLIDATION EXCEPT FOR PP THURSDAYS**
■ **STABILIZATION EXCEPT FOR PP THURSDAYS**

Preheat the oven to 180°C/350°F/Gas 4 and line a round cake tin with greaseproof paper.

In a bowl, mix together the oat and wheat brans with the skimmed milk and baking powders. Add the fromage frais and stir very thoroughly. Next add the eggs and the egg whites and stir until the mixture is smooth. Stir in the almond flavouring and sweetener.

Pour the mixture into the cake tin and bake in the oven for 30 minutes – a thin metal skewer pushed into the centre should come out clean when the cake is cooked.

In the meantime, make the orange cream. Place the gelatine in a little cold water in a bowl for 5 minutes to soften. Split the vanilla pod, scrape out the seeds, place both pod and seeds in a pan with the milk and heat.

In a bowl, mix the egg yolks with the sweetener, cornflour and orange flavouring. Once the milk has come to the boil, remove the pan from the heat and take out the vanilla pod. Pour the milk slowly over the egg mixture and stir well. Pour the milk back into the pan and let the mixture thicken while stirring with a wooden spoon. Add the drained gelatine. Allow the mixture to cool down to room temperature for 30 minutes, then refrigerate for 3 hours.

Cut the cake into two layers. Spread the orange cream over one cake half, place the other half on top and, lastly, sprinkle over a spoonful of powdered sweetener. Serve cut into wedges.

5 servings
Preparation time
10 minutes
Cooking time
5 minutes
Ingredients
200g (7oz) silken tofu
5 tablespoons cornflour
10 doses Protifar*
4 eggs
½ teaspoon butter flavouring
2 teaspoons vanilla flavouring
½ teaspoon rum flavouring
2 tablespoons Canderel granules (or more, to taste)
500ml (18fl oz) skimmed milk

Contains 1 tolerated food portion per person

*Available from health-food stores

Vanilla and white rum superprotein pancakes

Crêpes superprotéinés vanille/rhum blanc

■ **CRUISE PV**
■ **CONSOLIDATION EXCEPT FOR PP THURSDAYS**
■ **STABILIZATION EXCEPT FOR PP THURSDAYS**

In a large bowl, mix together the silken tofu, cornflour, Protifar and eggs. Next add the flavourings and sweetener and stir again thoroughly. Then pour in the milk very gradually and keep stirring until you get a nice, smooth, lump-free mixture.

Warm a non-stick frying pan and pour in a ladleful of the pancake mixture. Cook until golden brown on one side and then turn the pancake over and cook the other side. Continue cooking pancakes in this way until you have used all the mixture. Enjoy!

4 servings
Preparation time
15 minutes
Cooking time
1 hour
Refrigeration time
3 hours
Ingredients
200g (7oz) silken tofu
1 tablespoon cornflour
½ teaspoon sachet baking powder
3 tablespoons fat-free fromage frais
5 drops butter flavouring
1 tablespoon pistachio flavouring
Grated zest of 1 unwaxed lemon
1 tablespoon Hermesetas liquid
   sweetener
3 eggs

Contains ¼ tolerated food portion
per person

Pistachio-flavoured custard cake

Mi-gâteau, mi-flan pistache

■ **CRUISE PV**
■ **CONSOLIDATION EXCEPT FOR PP THURSDAYS**
■ **STABILIZATION EXCEPT FOR PP THURSDAYS**

Preheat the oven to 200°C/400°F/Gas 6.

In a large bowl, mix together all the ingredients. Pour the mixture into a silicone loaf tin.

Bake in the oven for 1 hour. Halfway through, cover the tin with some aluminium foil. When the cake is cooked, switch off the oven and leave the cake to cool in the oven with the door closed.

Turn the custard cake out of the loaf tin and refrigerate for 3 hours before serving.

Rhubarb ice cream

Glace à la rhubarbe

4 servings
Preparation time
15 minutes
Cooking time
15 minutes
Refrigeration time
30 minutes
Freezing time
35 minutes or 3½ hours, depending on whether or not you use an ice-cream maker

Ingredients
500g (1lb 2oz) rhubarb
8 tablespoons Canderel granules
1 tablespoon vanilla flavouring
1 egg white
150g (5½oz) fat-free natural yoghurt

You will need an ice-cream maker

■ **CRUISE PV**
■ **CONSOLIDATION EXCEPT FOR PP THURSDAYS**
■ **STABILIZATION EXCEPT FOR PP THURSDAYS**

Prepare the rhubarb by washing and peeling it and then cutting it into chunks. Cook over a gentle heat with the sweetener and vanilla flavouring for about 15 minutes, stirring occasionally. Remove from the heat and leave to cool.

Beat the egg white until stiff and gently fold into the yoghurt. Once the rhubarb has cooled down, stir the yoghurt mixture into the rhubarb and refrigerate to chill thoroughly, about 30 minutes.

Pour the rhubarb mixture into an ice-cream or sorbet machine and churn for 35 minutes. If you are not using an ice-cream maker, freeze for 3½ hours and use a fork to break any ice crystals that are starting to form on the surface of the ice cream every 30 minutes.

 Rhubarb is the only fruit-vegetable allowed in the Cruise phase – so make the most of it!

Low-fat ice cream

Glace allégée

4 servings
Preparation time
15 minutes
Freezing time
3 hours
Ingredients
90g (3¼oz) fat-free fromage frais
90g (3¼oz) virtually fat-free quark
2 eggs plus 1 egg yolk
3 tablespoons low-fat crème fraîche
   (3% fat)
8 Canderel vanilla sticks
A few drops of the flavouring of your
   choice

Contains ½ tolerated food portion
per person

- **CRUISE PV**
- **CONSOLIDATION EXCEPT FOR PP THURSDAYS**
- **STABILIZATION EXCEPT FOR PP THURSDAYS**

Separate the eggs. In a bowl, mix together the fromage frais, quark, 3 egg yolks, crème fraîche, sweetener and flavouring of your choice. Beat vigorously for 2 minutes.

Whisk the 2 egg whites until stiff and then gently fold into the mixture.

Pour into a metal ice tray and place in the freezer for 3 hours. Every 30 minutes, use a fork to break any ice crystals that are starting to form on the surface of the ice cream.

You can also use an ice-cream maker.

355

Savoy biscuit

Biscuit de Savoie

4 servings
Preparation time
15 minutes
Cooking time
40 minutes
Ingredients
3 eggs, separated
6 tablespoons Splenda granules
1 tablespoon vanilla flavouring
8 tablespoons cornflour
½ × 8g sachet instant dried yeast

Contains 2 tolerated food portions per person

■ **CRUISE PV**
■ **CONSOLIDATION EXCEPT FOR PP THURSDAYS**
■ **STABILIZATION EXCEPT FOR PP THURSDAYS**

Preheat the oven to 180°C/350°F/Gas 4 and line a 22–24cm (8½–9½in) sandwich tin with greaseproof paper.

In a bowl, beat together the egg yolks with the sweetener and vanilla flavouring until the mixture is creamy. Add the cornflour and yeast.

Beat the egg whites until very stiff and gently fold them in. Pour the mixture into the sandwich tin and bake in the oven for 35–40 minutes.

Turn out while still warm and leave to cool on a rack before serving.

4 servings
Preparation time
20 minutes
Cooking time
10 minutes
Freezing time
1 hour
Ingredients
4 tablespoons oat bran
2 tablespoons wheat bran
300ml (10fl oz) skimmed milk
2 eggs
2 tablespoons orange flower
  flavouring
For the pistachio cream
2 tablespoons cornflour
300ml (10 fl oz) skimmed milk
20 drops pistachio flavouring
4 egg yolks
1½ tablespoons Hermesetas liquid
  sweetener

*Contains ½ tolerated food portion
per person*

Pistachio 'semifreddo' pancakes

Crêpes 'semifreddo' à la pistache

■ **CRUISE PV**
■ **CONSOLIDATION EXCEPT FOR PP THURSDAYS**
■ **STABILIZATION EXCEPT FOR PP THURSDAYS**

In a large bowl, mix together all the pancake ingredients. Lightly oil a non-stick frying pan, then wipe with kitchen paper. Pour a quarter of the mixture into the pan, taking care to spread it out thinly to form a pancake. Cook one side, then flip the pancake over with a spatula to cook the other. Use the remaining mixture to make three more pancakes.

Make the pistachio cream. Dissolve the cornflour in a little of the milk. Heat the rest of the milk and add the pistachio flavouring. In a bowl, combine the egg yolks with the sweetener and stir in the cornflour. Pour the hot milk slowly over the yolks and stir continuously with a wooden spoon. Return the milk to the pan and heat for 3 minutes over a low heat, stirring all the time. Remove from the heat and leave to cool down.

Place each pancake on a sheet of clingfilm. Spread the pistachio cream over the pancakes, roll them up and twist the clingfilm at both ends to seal the rolls. Place in the freezer for 1 hour.

Take out of the freezer and discard the clingfilm. Cut the pancake rolls into 1cm (½in) slices and serve.

Cottage cheese cake

Gâteau paysan à la faisselle

4 servings
Make a day in advance
Preparation time
20 minutes
Cooking time
1 hour
Refrigeration time
2 hours
Ingredients
250g (9oz) fat-free cottage cheese
4 eggs, separated
6 tablespoons Splenda granules
2 tablespoons cornflour
200ml (7fl oz) skimmed milk
1 teaspoon ground cinnamon
Grated zest of 1 unwaxed orange

*Contains ½ tolerated food portion
per person*

■ **CRUISE PV**
■ **CONSOLIDATION EXCEPT FOR PP THURSDAYS**
■ **STABILIZATION EXCEPT FOR PP THURSDAYS**

Leave the cottage cheese to drain overnight.

Preheat the oven to 180°C/350°F/Gas 4 and line a cake tin with greaseproof paper.

In a large bowl, stir the egg yolks into the cottage cheese.

Add the sweetener, cornflour, milk, cinnamon and orange zest to the cottage cheese mixture.

Beat the egg whites until stiff and fold them into the mixture.

Pour into the cake tin and bake in the oven for 1 hour, keeping a careful eye on it as it cooks.

Leave the cake to cool down and then refrigerate for 2 hours before turning it out of the tin to serve.

2 servings
Preparation time
15 minutes
Cooking time
15 minutes
Ingredients
3 eggs, separated
2 tablespoons Splenda granules
4 teaspoons sugar-free, fat-reduced
 cocoa powder
Pinch of grated nutmeg

Contains 2 tolerated food portions
per person

Chocolate ramekins

Gâteaux au chocolat

■ **CRUISE PV**
■ **CONSOLIDATION EXCEPT FOR PP THURSDAYS**
■ **STABILIZATION EXCEPT FOR PP THURSDAYS**

Preheat the oven to 180°C/350°F/Gas 4.

In a bowl, beat the egg yolks with the sweetener and cocoa.

Beat the egg whites until stiff and gently fold them into the chocolate mixture. Add the nutmeg and pour into ramekin dishes.

Bake in the oven for 10–15 minutes. Serve straightaway.

Violet blancmange

Blanc-manger à la violette

4 servings
Preparation time
25 minutes
Cooking time
10 minutes
Refrigeration time
4–6 hours
Ingredients
10 gelatine leaves
450ml (16fl oz) skimmed milk
1 teaspoon bitter almond flavouring
6 tablespoons Canderel granules
2 teaspoons violet flavouring
8 tablespoons low-fat single cream
   (3% fat)

Contains 2 tolerated food portions
per person

■ **CRUISE PV**
■ **CONSOLIDATION EXCEPT FOR PP THURSDAYS**
■ **STABILIZATION EXCEPT FOR PP THURSDAYS**

Soak the gelatine leaves in a little cold water in a bowl for 10 minutes or so.

Pour the skimmed milk and bitter almond flavouring into a saucepan and warm over a medium heat until the milk is just about to boil. At that point, add the sweetener and violet flavouring. Drain off the gelatine, squeeze out any water and carefully stir into the milk.

Take the pan off the heat and stir in the single cream. Check the mixture is sweet enough for your taste and adjust if necessary, then pour into four sundae dishes or glasses and refrigerate for 4–6 hours. Serve very cold.

Chocolate and ginger charlotte

Charlotte au chocolat et au gingembre

4 servings
Make a day in advance
Preparation time
45 minutes
Cooking time
20 minutes
Refrigeration time
8 hours
Ingredients
3 eggs, separated, plus 2 egg whites
2 tablespoons cornflour
5 tablespoons Splenda granules
1 teaspoon vanilla flavouring
½ teaspoon baking powder
Pinch of salt
350g (12oz) fat-free fromage frais
4 teaspoons sugar-free, fat-reduced cocoa powder
2 teaspoons dark chocolate flavouring
2 teaspoons chopped stem ginger
6 tablespoons Canderel granules
A little warm milk

Contains 1½ tolerated food portions per person

■ **CRUISE PV**
■ **CONSOLIDATION EXCEPT FOR PP THURSDAYS**
■ **STABILIZATION EXCEPT FOR PP THURSDAYS**

Preheat the oven to 180°C/350°F/Gas 4 and line a baking tray with greaseproof paper.

In a bowl, combine the egg yolks with the cornflour, Splenda granules, vanilla flavouring and baking powder until the mixture is nice and smooth.

Add a pinch of salt to the 3 egg whites and beat until very stiff. Gently fold them into the egg-yolk mixture.

Spread the dough out on the baking tray in two rectangular shapes, 1cm (½in) thick. Smooth the surface and place the tray in the middle of the oven. Bake for 15–20 minutes, keeping a careful eye on the sponges.

Remove from the oven, leave to cool, then cut one of the sponges into fingers. Keep the other sponge to use as a base for the charlotte.

In the meantime, mix together the fromage frais, cocoa powder, dark chocolate flavouring, ginger and Canderel granules. Whisk the remaining 2 egg whites until stiff and gently fold them into the fromage frais mousse.

Quickly dip the sponge fingers in the warm milk and arrange them on end around the sides of a silicone charlotte mould or a mould covered with clingfilm. Pour in the mousse mixture and cover with the remaining sponge. Refrigerate overnight. Carefully invert the mould to turn out the charlotte. Serve chilled.

Rhubarb gratin

Gratin de rhubarbe

6 servings
Preparation time
20 minutes
Cooking time
10 minutes
Ingredients
300g (10½oz) homemade rhubarb compote (see page 71)
3 eggs, separated
150g (5½oz) fat-free fromage frais
3 tablespoons Splenda granules
1 teaspoon rum flavouring
1½ teaspoons vanilla flavouring
Pinch of salt
1 teaspoon ground cinnamon

■ **CRUISE PV**
■ **CONSOLIDATION EXCEPT FOR PP THURSDAYS**
■ **STABILIZATION EXCEPT FOR PP THURSDAYS**

Preheat the oven to 150°C/300°F/Gas 2.

Purée the rhubarb compote in a food processor or blender.

Spoon 2 tablespoons of the compote into each of six ramekin dishes.

In a small bowl, stir the egg yolks into the fromage frais. Add the sweetener, and flavourings, and combine all the ingredients thoroughly.

In another bowl, add a pinch of salt to the egg whites and beat until stiff. Gently fold the egg whites into the fromage frais mixture.

Pour into the ramekins, on top of the compote, and finish off with a dusting of ground cinnamon. Bake in the oven for 10 minutes. Serve warm.

Rhubarb is the only fruit-vegetable allowed in the Cruise phase – so make the most of it!

4 servings
Preparation time
10 minutes
Cooking time
5–10 minutes
Ingredients
8 egg whites
Pinch of salt
4 tablespoons wheat bran
8 tablespoons oat bran
4 tablespoons fat-free fromage frais
4 tablespoons cornflour
½ × 8g sachet instant dried yeast
2 teaspoons matcha green tea
   powder
12 drops butter flavouring
4 tablespoons Hermesetas liquid
   sweetener

*Contains 1 tolerated food portion
per person*

Matcha green tea sponge fingers

Financiers au thé vert matcha

■ **CRUISE PV**
■ **CONSOLIDATION EXCEPT FOR PP THURSDAYS**
■ **STABILIZATION EXCEPT FOR PP THURSDAYS**

Preheat the oven to 180°C/350°F/Gas 4.

Whisk the egg whites with a pinch of salt until stiff.

In a large bowl, mix together all the remaining ingredients.

Gently fold in the egg whites and pour the mixture into a bun tin. Place in the oven, immediately reduce the temperature to 150°C/300°F/Gas 2 and bake for 5–10 minutes. Keep a careful eye on the sponge fingers to make sure they do not burn on top.
.

Chocolate canneles

Choco-cannelés

4 servings
Preparation time
20 minutes
Cooking time
1¼ hours
Ingredients
250ml (9fl oz) skimmed milk
2 teaspoons dark chocolate
    flavouring
4 tablespoons cornflour
4 tablespoons Splenda granules
4 teaspoons sugar-free, fat-reduced
    cocoa powder
1 egg, plus 1 egg yolk
½ teaspoon rum flavouring

Contains 2 tolerated food portions
per person

■ **CRUISE PV**
■ **CONSOLIDATION EXCEPT FOR PP THURSDAYS**
■ **STABILIZATION EXCEPT FOR PP THURSDAYS**

Preheat the oven to 240°C/475°F/Gas 9.

Bring the milk and dark chocolate flavouring to the boil in a pan.

In the meantime, in a large bowl, mix together the cornflour, sweetener and cocoa powder with the egg and egg yolk. Pour the boiling milk over the egg mixture, then add the rum flavouring. Gently stir the ingredients together until you have a smooth mixture and leave to cool.

Pour the mixture into four individual silicone moulds and bake in the oven for 5 minutes, then lower the temperature to 180°C/350°F/Gas 4 and bake for a further 30 minutes, until the canneles have a nice brown crust and are gooey inside. Serve hot.

2 servings
Preparation time
10 minutes
Cooking time
12 minutes
Ingredients
5 tablespoons fat-free fromage frais
2 tablespoons cornflour
2 egg yolks, plus 3 egg whites
2 tablespoons lemon juice
3 tablespoons Splenda granules

Contains 1 tolerated food portion per person

Cheesecake

■ CRUISE PV
■ CONSOLIDATION EXCEPT FOR PP THURSDAYS
■ STABILIZATION EXCEPT FOR PP THURSDAYS

Preheat the oven to 180°C/350°F/Gas 4.

Mix together the fromage frais, cornflour, egg yolks, lemon juice and sweetener, and beat until the mixture is frothy.

Whisk the egg whites until stiff, then gently fold them into the fromage frais mixture. Pour into a soufflé dish and bake in the oven for 12 minutes.

Allow to cool before serving.

Vegetarian food

Vegetable proteins (tofu, seitan, etc.) also have their part to play in the Dukan method, so here is a selection of recipes that are ideal for vegetarians.

Starters p. 372   **Main courses** p. 380   **Desserts** p. 396

4 servings
Preparation time
10 minutes
Refrigeration time
35 minutes
Ingredients
450g (1lb) firm tofu
1 onion, finely chopped
1 garlic clove, finely chopped
4 tablespoons nutritional yeast*
½ teaspoon crystallized stevia
1 tablespoon balsamic vinegar
1 tablespoon Dijon mustard
2 tablespoons soy sauce
Pinch of cayenne pepper
¼ glass Dukan mayonnaise
    (see page 68)

*Available in organic or
health-food stores*

Tofu spread

Tartinade de tofu

■ **ATTACK**   ■ **CONSOLIDATION**
■ **CRUISE**   ■ **STABILIZATION**

In a small bowl, crush the firm tofu using a fork.

Add all the remaining ingredients, the mayonnaise last, and refrigerate.

The tofu spread can be eaten either on oat bran galettes (see page 50) or as a dip with raw vegetable sticks.

4 servings
Preparation time
35 minutes
Cooking time
1 hour 10 minutes
Ingredients
2 onions, chopped
2 garlic cloves, chopped
250ml (9fl oz) low-salt chicken stock
150g (5½oz) textured soya protein*
1 tablespoon soy sauce
2 teaspoons dried oregano
1 teaspoon dried thyme
240g (8½oz) tinned whole peeled
    tomatoes
200g (7oz) courgettes, diced
100g (3½oz) celery sticks, diced
Salt and black pepper
Handful of chopped parsley

*Available in organic or
health-food stores*

Tomato and textured soya protein Mediterranean soup

Soupe méditerranéenne à la tomate et aux protéines de soja texturées

■ **CRUISE PV**
■ **CONSOLIDATION EXCEPT FOR PP THURSDAYS**
■ **STABILIZATION EXCEPT FOR PP THURSDAYS**

Warm a large pan and gently cook the onions and garlic in 3 tablespoons water. Add the chicken stock, textured soya protein, 250ml (9fl oz) water, the soy sauce and herbs. Bring to the boil, then turn the heat down, cover and leave to simmer for 30 minutes.

Next add the tomatoes, courgettes and celery and bring the soup back to the boil. Lower the heat and simmer for 20–30 minutes more.

Taste before serving and add salt and black pepper as necessary.

When ready to serve, pour the soup into large bowls and scatter over the chopped parsley.

2 servings
Preparation time
20 minutes
Cooking time
20 minutes
Ingredients
300g (10½oz) firm or semi-firm tofu
2 tablespoons wheat bran
4 tablespoons oat bran
2 tablespoons dried onion
2 tablespoons soy sauce
½ teaspoon dried basil
½ teaspoon dried oregano
Salt and black pepper
2 tomatoes, sliced
A few cornichons

Tofu galettes

Galettes au tofu

■ **CRUISE**
■ **CONSOLIDATION EXCEPT FOR PP THURSDAYS**
■ **STABILIZATION EXCEPT FOR PP THURSDAYS**

Preheat the oven to 160°C/325°F/Gas 3 and line a baking tray with greaseproof paper.

In a large bowl, combine all the ingredients except the tomatoes and cornichons. Mix together to form a dough. Knead the dough for a few minutes and then shape into galettes.

Place the galettes on the baking tray and bake in the oven for 20 minutes, keeping a careful eye on them.

Serve with the sliced tomatoes and cornichons, like a hamburger without the bread.

4 servings
Preparation time
25 minutes
Cooking time
50 minutes
Ingredients
600g (1lb 5oz) carrots, sliced
300g (10½oz) broccoli, cut into
  florets
4 tablespoons low-fat cream (3%
  fat)
Salt and black pepper
2 eggs
Pinch of grated nutmeg
240g (8½oz) tofu, cut into small
  cubes
1 teaspoon dried thyme
10 chives, finely chopped

*Contains 1 tolerated food portion
per person*

You will need a steamer

Carrot, broccoli and thyme loaf

Pain de carottes et brocolis au thym

■ **CRUISE PV**
■ **CONSOLIDATION EXCEPT FOR PP THURSDAYS**
■ **STABILIZATION EXCEPT FOR PP THURSDAYS**

Preheat the oven to 150°C/300°F/Gas 2.

Place the carrots and broccoli on separate sides of a steamer basket and steam them for 15 minutes. Put the broccoli to one side and leave to cool down.

Blend the carrots with the cream to make a purée and season with salt and black pepper. Lightly beat the eggs with a fork and add to the carrot purée along with a pinch of nutmeg. Stir together thoroughly.

Stir the tofu, thyme and chives into the carrot purée. At the last moment, add the broccoli florets, folding them in very carefully so that they do not break up.

Pour the mixture into a small non-stick loaf tin and bake in a bain-marie in the oven for 35 minutes.

Leave the loaf to cool down before turning it out of the tin. Serve cold.

4 servings
Preparation time
15 minutes
Ingredients
600g (1lb 5oz) smoked tofu, sliced
8 tablespoons soy sauce
400g (14oz) black winter radish
4 carrots
2 uncooked beetroot
2 bags sprouting seeds of your
   choice
1 quantity Maya sauce (see page 66)

Tofu, root vegetable and sprouting seed salad

Salade de tofu, légumes racines et graines germées

■ **CRUISE PV**
■ **CONSOLIDATION EXCEPT FOR PP THURSDAYS**
■ **STABILIZATION EXCEPT FOR PP THURSDAYS**

Gently fry the tofu slices in a non-stick frying pan with 6 tablespoons of the soy sauce.

Peel the root vegetables and slice them very thinly using a mandoline cutter.

In a large bowl, mix the Maya sauce with the remaining soy sauce and add the sliced vegetables, tofu and sprouting seeds. Stir together well and serve.

6 servings
Preparation time
35 minutes
Cooking time
1 hour 5 minutes
Ingredients
1 × 4kg (8lb 13oz) pumpkin
1 low-salt vegetable stock cube
2 large onions, finely chopped
4 garlic cloves, crushed
2cm (½inch) piece fresh ginger,
  chopped
1 tablespoon curry powder
250ml (9fl oz) glasses soya milk
2 tablespoons miso
½ teaspoon salt

*Contains ½ tolerated food portion
per person*

Soup in the pumpkin

Soupe dans la citrouille

■ **CRUISE PV**
■ **CONSOLIDATION EXCEPT FOR PP THURSDAYS**
■ **STABILIZATION EXCEPT FOR PP THURSDAYS**

Preheat the oven to 180°C/350°F/Gas 4.

Prepare the pumpkin by cutting off the top to use as a lid and scooping out the seeds and fibre. Place the pumpkin, with the opening at the top, on a baking tray and bake in the oven for about 45 minutes. After 30 minutes, check to see how cooked the pumpkin is by pricking the skin with the tip of a small, sharp knife. The skin should be tender without disintegrating.

In the meantime, dissolve the stock cube in 250ml (9fl oz) of hot water and set aside.

Warm a non-stick frying pan and gently fry the onions and garlic for about 15 minutes. Then add the ginger and curry powder, stir and cook for a few minutes so that the mixture softens slightly.

Once the pumpkin is ready, take it out of the oven and carefully scoop out the flesh, leaving a decent thickness around the skin. Purée the pumpkin flesh in a blender, adding enough soya milk to get a smooth texture. Put the pumpkin purée back inside the pumpkin shell and add the onion mixture, the remaining soya milk and the vegetable stock. Season with the salt.

Place the lid on the pumpkin and return it to the oven. Bake for 20 minutes or so, keeping a careful eye on it.

Dissolve the miso in a small bowl and stir it into the soup.

Serve the soup piping hot in its pumpkin tureen.

4 servings
Preparation time
25 minutes
Cooking time
25 minutes
Ingredients
4 small tomatoes
8 large button or portobello
    mushrooms
400g (14oz) seitan, diced
2 garlic cloves, crushed
½ bunch parsley, finely chopped
8 tablespoons fat-free fromage frais
120g (4¼oz) low-fat Emmental
    cheese (4% fat), grated
A few herbes de Provence
Salt and black pepper

Contains 1 tolerated food portion
per person

Seitan-stuffed tomatoes and mushrooms

Tomates et champignons farcis
au seitan

■ **CRUISE PV**
■ **CONSOLIDATION EXCEPT FOR PP THURSDAYS**
■ **STABILIZATION EXCEPT FOR PP THURSDAYS**

Preheat the oven to 180°C/350°F/Gas 4.

Cut the tops off the tomatoes to make lids and scoop out the insides, reserving the pulp. Clean the mushrooms, chop off the stalks and carefully scoop out and retain a little of the flesh, creating a hollow in which to put the stuffing. Using a fork, mix the mushroom flesh with the tomato pulp and keep on one side.

Lightly oil a non-stick frying pan and wipe with kitchen paper. Warm the pan over a very high heat and fry the seitan along with the garlic, tomato and mushroom mixture and parsley. Fry over a high heat for 2 minutes, stirring all the time.

Pour the seitan mixture into a large bowl and add the fromage frais, 40g (1½oz) of the Emmental cheese and the herbes de Provence. Season with salt and black pepper.

Fill each tomato and mushroom hollow with the stuffing and replace the tomato lids. Place in an ovenproof dish, scatter over the remaining grated cheese and bake in the oven for 20 minutes. Serve hot.

Vegetarian lasagne

Lasagnes végétariennes

2 servings
Preparation time
30 minutes
Cooking time
40 minutes
Ingredients
1 medium aubergine, thinly sliced
Salt and black pepper
1 courgette, thinly sliced
100g (3½oz) firm tofu, thinly sliced
1 onion, finely chopped
1 garlic clove, finely chopped
2 tomatoes, thinly sliced
60g (2¼oz) low-fat Emmental
  cheese (4% fat), grated
1 sprig thyme
1 small bunch oregano, finely
  chopped
1 small bunch basil, finely chopped
Pinch of chilli powder

Contains 1 tolerated food portion
per person

■ **CRUISE PV**
■ **CONSOLIDATION EXCEPT FOR PP THURSDAYS**
■ **STABILIZATION EXCEPT FOR PP THURSDAYS**

Preheat the oven to 230°C/450°F/Gas 8.

Sprinkle salt over the aubergine slices and leave to drain for at least 30 minutes. Rinse and wipe dry with kitchen paper.

In a non-stick frying pan, fry the aubergine slices in a little water for a few minutes, until they turn slightly golden brown. Put to one side. Do the same, separately, with the courgette and tofu slices, and put to one side.

Gently fry the onion and garlic for a minute or two and then add the tomatoes. Sprinkle over the herbs and chilli powder and season with salt and black pepper.

In an ovenproof dish, first arrange a layer of aubergine slices, cover with tofu and put the courgettes on top. Then add another layer of aubergine with a second layer of tofu. Add the tomatoes (with the onions and garlic) and finish off with a layer using up the rest of the aubergine slices.

Bake in the oven for 20 minutes. Sprinkle over the grated cheese and return to the oven for a further 5 minutes for the lasagne to turn golden brown on top. Serve immediately.

Potofu

4 servings
Preparation time
20 minutes
Cooking time
10 minutes
Ingredients
1 low-salt vegetable stock cube
1 packet miso soup
2 leeks
2 small courgettes
8 button mushrooms
4 spring onions
400g (14oz) herb tofu
70g dried seaweed (approx.)
Soy sauce, to serve

■ **CRUISE PV**
■ **CONSOLIDATION EXCEPT FOR PP THURSDAYS**
■ **STABILIZATION EXCEPT FOR PP THURSDAYS**

Make a broth with 1.5 litres (just over 2½ pints) water, the stock cube and packet of miso soup.

Wash the vegetables and cut them as thinly as possible, either into slices or strips. Slice the tofu. Add all the ingredients to the broth along with dried seaweed and cook for about 10 minutes.

Serve the broth piping hot accompanied by some soy sauce to taste.

2 servings
Preparation time
20 minutes
Cooking time
25 minutes
Ingredients
500g (1lb 2oz) chard
400g (14oz) spinach
½ onion, finely chopped
240g (8½oz) tofu, cut into small
  cubes
1 teaspoon soy sauce
Salt and black pepper
1 teaspoon finely chopped mint,
  plus 1–2 sprigs to garnish
A few coriander seeds

Tofu chard

Blettes au tofu

■ CRUISE PV
■ CONSOLIDATION EXCEPT FOR PP THURSDAYS
■ STABILIZATION EXCEPT FOR PP THURSDAYS

Wash the chard and spinach. Drain thoroughly, then chop.

In a large non-stick frying pan, gently fry the onion until it becomes translucent.

Add the spinach and chard, cover and leave to cook for 10 minutes.

In another non-stick frying pan, fry the tofu with the soy sauce for 5 minutes over a very low heat. Season with salt and black pepper and cook for a further 5 minutes.

Serve the hot vegetables on a warmed serving dish with the tofu. Scatter over the chopped mint and coriander seeds, and drizzle the cooking juices over the top. Garnish with a sprig or two of mint.

4 servings
Preparation time
15 minutes
Cooking time
5 minutes
Ingredients
4 eggs
2 tablespoons soy sauce
1 garlic clove, finely chopped
½ onion, finely chopped
Black pepper
400g (14oz) firm tofu, cut into small
    cubes
½ green pepper, deseeded and diced
1 tablespoon finely chopped parsley,
    plus a few sprigs to garnish

Tofu omelette

Omelette au tofu

■ **CRUISE PV**
■ **CONSOLIDATION EXCEPT FOR PP THURSDAYS**
■ **STABILIZATION EXCEPT FOR PP THURSDAYS**

Whisk the eggs together in a bowl and add the soy sauce, garlic, onion and some black pepper.

Stir in the tofu along with the green pepper.

Warm a non-stick frying pan and pour in the mixture. Cover and cook the omelette over a gentle heat.

When ready to serve, scatter over the chopped parsley and garnish with a few extra sprigs .

4 servings
Preparation time
25 minutes
Cooking time
45 minutes
Ingredients
300g (10½oz) button mushrooms
2 garlic cloves, finely chopped
2 sprigs parsley, finely chopped
400g (14oz) silken tofu
4 eggs
100g (3½oz) virtually fat-free quark,
    with herbs and garlic
Salt and black pepper
12 cherry tomatoes

Silken tofu and button mushroom quiche

Quiche au tofu soyeux et champignons de Paris

■ **CRUISE PV**
■ **CONSOLIDATION EXCEPT FOR PP THURSDAYS**
■ **STABILIZATION EXCEPT FOR PP THURSDAYS**

Preheat the oven to 200°C/400°F/Gas 6.

Clean and chop the mushrooms.

In a non-stick frying pan, gently fry the garlic and parsley for 2 minutes. Add the mushrooms and cook for about 10 minutes, stirring from time to time.

Beat the silken tofu together with the eggs, then add the quark and fried mushrooms. Season with salt and black pepper. Pour the mixture into a non-stick quiche dish. Arrange the cherry tomatoes on top, pushing them gently into the mixture.

Bake in the oven for 30 minutes, keeping a careful eye on the quiche as it cooks.

Serve hot from the oven or cooled to room temperature.

4 servings
Preparation time
15 minutes
Cooking time
35 minutes
Ingredients
2 onions
1 bunch flat-leaf parsley
200g (7oz) silken tofu, well drained
2 garlic cloves, crushed
Salt and black pepper
2 eggs
30g (1oz) virtually fat-free quark
30g (1oz) fat-free fromage frais
2 teaspoons baking powder
8 tablespoons oat bran
4 tablespoons wheat bran

No-pastry tofu and oat tartlets

Tartelettes sans pâte avoine-tofu

■ CRUISE
■ CONSOLIDATION ■ STABILIZATION

Preheat the oven to 180°C/350°F/Gas 4.

Peel the onions, then roughly blend them in a food processor with the flat-leaf parsley for 1 minute. Transfer this mixture to a bowl and add the silken tofu, garlic, salt and black pepper and mix everything together thoroughly.

Add the eggs, quark, fromage frais, baking powder and oat and wheat brans, and use a fork to stir all the ingredients together vigorously for 1 minute. Check the seasoning.

Fill four small silicone tartlet moulds with the mixture, place in the middle of the oven and bake for 35 minutes, keeping a careful eye on them as they cook.

Allow to cool a little, then turn the warm tartlets out of their moulds, place them on a baking sheet and leave them to dry out in the oven with the door open. Serve warm.

4 servings
Preparation time
10 minutes
Cooking time
12 minutes
Ingredients
1 onion, finely chopped
1 carrot, grated
Pinch of ground turmeric
1 low-salt vegetable stock cube
400g (14oz) firm or semi-firm tofu
Salt and black pepper
1 sprig parsley, chopped

Tofu broth

Bouillon de tofu

■ CRUISE PV

▨ CONSOLIDATION EXCEPT FOR PP THURSDAYS

■ STABILIZATION EXCEPT FOR PP THURSDAYS

In a non-stick frying pan, cook the onion for 5 minutes over a gentle heat until it has softened. Add the grated carrot and turmeric and cook for a further 2 minutes.

Meanwhile, bring 750ml (just over 1¼ pints) water to the boil in a pan and dissolve the stock cube.

Stir the vegetables into this broth, crumble in the tofu and cook for a further 5 minutes. Season with salt and black pepper.

Remove the pan from the heat, add the parsley and serve.

2 servings
Preparation time
30 minutes
Cooking time
50 minutes
Ingredients
1 × 350g (12oz) pack seitan mix*
1 large onion, finely chopped
12 garlic cloves, crushed
5 bay leaves
1 teaspoon dried thyme
1 teaspoon dried sage
1 teaspoon celery salt
2 tablespoons soy sauce
4 tablespoons nutritional yeast*
125ml (4fl oz) juice from tinned
   peeled tomatoes

*Available in organic or
health-food stores*

Homemade minced seitan

Haché de seitan maison

■ **CRUISE PV**
■ **CONSOLIDATION EXCEPT FOR PP THURSDAYS**
■ **STABILIZATION EXCEPT FOR PP THURSDAYS**

Preheat the oven to 180°C/350°F/Gas 4 and line a baking tray with greaseproof paper.

In a large bowl, stir the seitan mix into 375ml (13¼fl oz) water using a wooden spoon to form a dough. Knead the dough for about 5 minutes until it is smooth and flexible. Place it on the baking tray and leave to rest for 5 minutes. Then stretch the dough as much as possible into a wide strip about 2cm (¾in) thick and bake in the oven for 30 minutes. After 15 minutes use a pointed knife to pierce any bubbles that may have formed in the dough.

Remove the seitan from the oven and allow to cool down enough to handle. Cut it into four sections and then into pieces. Whiz in a food processor or blender until it looks like minced meat. This may need to be done in several batches.

In a non-stick frying pan, cook the onion, garlic and bay leaves over a gentle heat until all the ingredients have softened. Add the thyme, sage and celery salt and continue cooking. Next, stir in the soy sauce, nutritional yeast, tomato juice and seitan and mix all the ingredients together thoroughly. Cook for a further 10 minutes before serving.

Note: You can also freeze the minced seitan in single portions.

Tofu moussaka

Moussaka de tofu

4 servings
Preparation time
35 minutes
Resting time
1 hour
Cooking time
55 minutes
Ingredients
1 very large aubergine
Cooking salt
4 large onions, finely chopped
6 garlic cloves, finely chopped
1 teaspoon dried basil
1 teaspoon dried oregano
½ teaspoon ground cinnamon
125g (4½oz) tinned peeled tomatoes
300g (10½oz) silken tofu
Pinch of grated nutmeg
Pinch of ground turmeric
1 teaspoon sea salt

■ **CRUISE PV**
■ **CONSOLIDATION EXCEPT FOR PP THURSDAYS**
■ **STABILIZATION EXCEPT FOR PP THURSDAYS**

Leaving the skin on, cut the aubergine into slices 5mm (¼in) thick. Sprinkle over some cooking salt and leave to drain in a colander for about 1 hour. Then quickly rinse under cold running water and place on a clean tea towel to dry off.

Preheat the oven to 180°C/350°F/Gas 4.

In the meantime, heat a non-stick frying pan over a low heat and fry the onions, garlic, basil, oregano and cinnamon. Once the ingredients have softened, add the tomatoes. Stir and leave to simmer, still over a low heat, for 5 minutes.

Place the silken tofu, nutmeg, turmeric and sea salt in a food processor and blend until the mixture has a smooth, creamy texture.

Take a third of the aubergine slices and line the bottom of a large ovenproof dish. Next add a third of the garlic, onion and tomato mixture and then spread a third of the tofu mixture on top. Repeat this layering process twice more.

Bake the moussaka in the oven for 45 minutes, checking carefully that the aubergines are cooked through. Serve straightaway.

2 servings
Preparation time
30 minutes
Resting time
45 minutes
Cooking time
30 minutes
Ingredients
300g (10½oz) fresh spinach
1 teaspoon sea salt
2 eggs, beaten
200g (7oz) silken tofu
2 tablespoons dried onions
1 garlic clove, crushed
1 teaspoon dried basil
½ teaspoon dried oregano
4 teaspoons oat bran

Tofu and spinach pie

Tourte de tofu aux épinards

■ CRUISE PV
■ CONSOLIDATION EXCEPT FOR PP THURSDAYS
■ STABILIZATION EXCEPT FOR PP THURSDAYS

Preheat the oven to 180°C/350°F/Gas 4.

Wash and dry the spinach, then place in a colander and sprinkle with the salt. Rub the leaves between your hands and leave to rest for 45 minutes. Squeeze the spinach to extract all the water and chop.

Place the chopped spinach in a large bowl and add the eggs, silken tofu, dried onions, garlic, herbs and oat bran. Using your hands, mix all the ingredients together. Transfer the mixture to a non-stick flan dish.

Bake in the oven for 20 minutes, then cover the pie with some aluminium foil and bake for another 10 minutes. Serve hot.

4 servings
Preparation time
25 minutes
Cooking time
20 minutes
Ingredients
1 × 200g (7oz) tempeh roll*
4 tablespoons soy sauce
1 teaspoon curry powder
1 garlic clove, finely chopped
1 red pepper, deseeded and diced
1 green pepper, deseeded and diced
1 yellow pepper, deseeded and diced
50ml soya milk
10 drops coconut flavouring

Contains 1¼ tolerated food portions per person

Available in organic or health-food stores

Tempeh curry with three peppers, coconut and soya

Curry de tempeh, soja coco aux trois poivrons

■ **CRUISE PV**
■ **CONSOLIDATION EXCEPT FOR PP THURSDAYS**
■ **STABILIZATION EXCEPT FOR PP THURSDAYS**

Cut the tempeh roll into slices about 5mm (¼in) thick. Place in a dish and cover with the soy sauce mixed with the curry powder to marinate for 30 minutes.

In a non-stick frying pan, gently fry the garlic over a medium heat.

Drain the marinated tempeh slices and add them to the frying pan. Gently fry for about 5 minutes on each side, then add the peppers and continue to fry for about 5 minutes.

Pour the soya milk into the frying pan and add the coconut flavouring. Stir all the ingredients together and cook for a further 2–3 minutes. Serve piping hot.

4 servings
Preparation time
25 minutes
Marinating time
30 minutes
Cooking time
10 minutes
Ingredients
Juice of 1 lemon
1 teaspoon ground coriander
1 teaspoon ground ginger
1 tablespoon soy sauce
1 red pepper
1 green pepper
4 button mushrooms
500g (1lb 2oz) seitan
4 small onions

Marinated vegetarian kebabs

Brochettes végétariennes marinées

■ CRUISE PV
■ CONSOLIDATION EXCEPT FOR PP THURSDAYS
■ STABILIZATION EXCEPT FOR PP THURSDAYS

In a dish, mix together the lemon juice, coriander, ginger and soy sauce.

Clean the peppers and mushrooms. Cut the seitan and peppers (discarding the seeds) into kebab-sized cubes and halve the onions. Place them all in the dish with the marinade and leave to marinate for 30 minutes.

Preheat a barbecue or grill.

Remove the seitan and vegetables from the marinade and thread on to kebab sticks, alternating the pieces. Cook the kebabs on the barbecue or under the grill for about 10 minutes. Serve hot.

4 servings
Preparation time
20 minutes
Cooking time
25 minutes
Ingredients
4 beef tomatoes
200g (7oz) silken tofu
4 garlic cloves, crushed
1 small bunch basil
1 small bunch parsley
Salt and black pepper

Tofu-stuffed tomatoes

Tomates farcies au tofu

■ CRUISE PV
■ CONSOLIDATION EXCEPT FOR PP THURSDAYS
■ STABILIZATION EXCEPT FOR PP THURSDAYS

Preheat the oven to 200°C/400°F/Gas 6.

Slice the tops off the tomatoes to use as lids. Scoop out the insides, reserving the pulp. In a blender, whiz the tomato pulp with the tofu, garlic, basil and parsley. Season with salt and black pepper.
Fill the tomatoes with the stuffing and replace the lids. Put the tomatoes in an ovenproof dish and bake in the preheated oven for 25 minutes. Serve hot or cold.

4 servings
Preparation time
20 minutes
Marinating time
2 hours
Cooking time
10 minutes
Ingredients
8 tablespoons soy sauce
500g (1lb 2oz) firm tofu
4 tablespoons wheat bran
1 tablespoon chopped garlic
2 tablespoons fresh chopped ginger
200g (7oz) wakame seaweed

Tofu in a wheat bran crust on a bed of seaweed

Tofu pané au son de blé sur lit d'algues

■ **CRUISE PV**
■ **CONSOLIDATION EXCEPT FOR PP THURSDAYS**
■ **STABILIZATION EXCEPT FOR PP THURSDAYS**

Pour 4 tablespoons of the soy sauce into a dish. Chop the tofu into 1cm (½in) cubes and leave to marinate in the soy sauce for 2 hours in the fridge.

Drain the tofu cubes and roll them in the wheat bran. Heat a non-stick frying pan, add 3 drops of oil and immediately wipe off with kitchen paper. Add the garlic, ginger and tofu cubes and fry gently, stirring continuously. Once the cubes have turned golden brown on all sides, remove them from the pan and keep warm.

Rinse and drain the seaweed (or, if you are using dried seaweed, add water). Over a low heat, gently cook the seaweed in the frying pan with the remaining soy sauce for 2 minutes.

To serve, divide the seaweed between four warmed plates and arrange the wheat-bran-encrusted tofu cubes on top.

Tofu chocolate muffins

Muffins tofu-chocolat

Makes 6 muffins
Preparation time
15 minutes
Cooking time
30 minutes
Ingredients
3 eggs, separated
Pinch of salt
12 tablespoons oat bran
6 tablespoons wheat bran
400g (14oz) silken tofu
6 teaspoons sugar-free, fat-reduced
    cocoa powder
6 tablespoons Splenda granules
1 teaspoon baking powder
20 drops hazelnut flavouring

*Contains 1 tolerated food portion
per muffin*

■ **CRUISE PV**
■ **CONSOLIDATION EXCEPT FOR PP THURSDAYS**
■ **STABILIZATION EXCEPT FOR PP THURSDAYS**

Preheat the oven to 180°C/350°F/Gas 4.

Beat the egg whites with a pinch of salt until stiff.

In a large bowl, mix together the oat bran, wheat bran, silken tofu, cocoa powder, sweetener, baking powder, egg yolks and hazelnut flavouring. Gently fold in the stiffly beaten egg whites.

Divide the mixture between six silicone muffin moulds and bake in the oven for 30 minutes. Keep a careful eye on the muffins to make sure they do not burn on top.

These are nicest served warm from the oven.

4 servings
Preparation time
15 minutes
Cooking time
30 minutes
Ingredients
200g (7oz) silken tofu
4 teaspoons sugar-free, fat-reduced
    cocoa powder
2 tablespoons cornflour
3 tablespoons Splenda granules
2 eggs
½ teaspoon rum flavouring

*Contains 1½ tolerated food
portions per person*

Rum and cocoa cakes

Petits moelleux rhum-cacao

■ **CRUISE PV**
■ **CONSOLIDATION EXCEPT FOR PP THURSDAYS**
■ **STABILIZATION EXCEPT FOR PP THURSDAYS**

Preheat the oven to 180°C/350°F/Gas 4.

In a large bowl, combine the silken tofu, cocoa powder, cornflour
and sweetener. Mix the ingredients together with an electric whisk.
Add the eggs and flavouring and continue whisking.

Pour the mixture into individual rectangular silicone moulds and
bake in the oven for 30 minutes, keeping a careful eye on the
cakes to ensure they do not burn on top. And then enjoy!

4 servings
Preparation time
5 minutes
Cooking time
5 minutes
Refrigeration time
2 hours minimum
Ingredients
1 × 2g sachet agar-agar powder
4 teaspoons Matcha green tea
    powder
4 teaspoons crystallized stevia (or
    more, to taste)
1 teaspoon vanilla flavouring
200g (7oz) silken tofu

Matcha green tea silken tofu mousse

Verrines de mousse soyeuse au thé vert matcha

■ **ATTACK**　　■ **CONSOLIDATION**
■ **CRUISE**　　■ **STABILIZATION**

In a pan, bring 300ml (10fl oz) water to the boil and add the agar-agar. Boil for a minute or two, then turn off the heat. Add the green tea powder, sweetener and vanilla flavouring, stir and leave to cool.

In the meantime, beat the silken tofu with an electric whisk. Slowly add the green tea mixture and whisk again until the mixture turns slightly frothy. Taste and add extra sweetener if necessary.

Pour the mousse into four large sundae dishes and refrigerate for at least 2 hours. Serve chilled.

4 servings
Preparation time
5 minutes
Refrigeration time
6 hours minimum
Ingredients
375g (13 oz) silken tofu
500ml (18fl oz) skimmed milk
A few drops of vanilla flavouring
4 teaspoons sugar-free, fat-reduced
   cocoa powder
4 tablespoons crystallized stevia
300g (10½oz) fat-free vanilla
   yoghurt
8 mint leaves

*Contains 1 tolerated food portion
per person*

Mint and cocoa-flavoured silken tofu smoothie

Tofu soyeux fouetté à la menthe et au cacao

■ CRUISE
■ CONSOLIDATION EXCEPT FOR PP THURSDAYS
■ STABILIZATION EXCEPT FOR PP THURSDAYS

Blend all the ingredients together until you have a nice, frothy mixture.

Place in the fridge for at least 6 hours.

Serve well chilled.

Consolidation

These recipes are for **Phase 3 – Consolidation**. This is a very tricky time in your diet, when you have to follow certain rules scrupulously. You can now eat starchy foods, fruit and cheese, but with certain provisos. When it's your weekly pure protein day, don't forget to refer back to the PP recipes (pages 74–227).

Starters p. 404   **Main courses** p. 418   **Desserts** p. 454

4 servings
Preparation time
20 minutes
Cooking time
25 minutes
Ingredients
1 broccoli head
Salt
300g (10½ oz) chicken breasts
8 filo pastry sheets*
225g (8oz) virtually fat-free quark,
    with herbs and garlic
½ bunch chervil, finely chopped
2 egg yolks, beaten

*2 filo pastry sheets are equivalent
to 1 portion of starchy foods*

Chicken, broccoli and quark crispy parcels

Croustillants au poulet, brocoli et carrés frais

■ **CONSOLIDATION EXCEPT FOR PP THURSDAYS**
■ **STABILIZATION EXCEPT FOR PP THURSDAYS**

Preheat the oven to 180°C/350°F/Gas 4 and line a baking tray with greaseproof paper.

Cut the broccoli into florets and blanch them in boiling salted water for about 3 minutes. Drain and refresh under cold running water.

Cut the chicken breasts into thin strips.

Lay some strips of chicken and a few blanched broccoli florets in the middle of each filo pastry sheet and top with a portion of quark. Scatter over the chopped chervil and twist the filo parcels to seal. Brush with the beaten egg yolks using a small pastry brush.

Place the eight parcels on the baking tray and bake in the oven for about 20 minutes.

Leave to cool down slightly before serving.

4 servings
Preparation time
10 minutes
Cooking time
30 minutes
Ingredients
1 courgette
1 small onion, finely chopped
½ bunch basil, finely chopped
85g (3oz) low-fat feta cheese, crumbled
100g (3½oz) virtually fat-free quark, crumbled
3 tablespoons oat bran
2 eggs
Salt and black pepper

Courgette and feta cheese bites

Bouchées de courgette à la feta et au fromage frais

■ **CONSOLIDATION EXCEPT FOR PP THURSDAYS**
■ **STABILIZATION EXCEPT FOR PP THURSDAYS**

Preheat the oven to 220°C/425°F/Gas 7 and line a baking tray with greaseproof paper.

Roughly grate the unpeeled courgette.

In a large bowl, mix together the courgette, onion, basil, feta, quark, oat bran and eggs and season with salt and black pepper.

As soon as the mixture is nicely blended, place small piles on the baking tray and bake in the oven for 30 minutes. After 15 minutes, turn the courgette and feta bites over.

Serve warm from the oven or cooled to room temperature.

6 servings
Preparation time
15 minutes
Ingredients
200g (7oz) tinned tuna in brine or
spring water, drained
200g (7oz) virtually fat-free quark
A squeeze of lemon juice
White pepper
2 tablespoons finely chopped basil
4 slices wholemeal bread
1 cucumber
1 red pepper
1 fennel bulb

Provençal tuna and quark spread

Tartinades provençales de carrés frais au thon

■ **CONSOLIDATION EXCEPT FOR PP THURSDAYS**
■ **STABILIZATION EXCEPT FOR PP THURSDAYS**

Roughly flake the tuna and place in a blender along with the quark. Add the lemon juice and white pepper and whiz until you get a nice, smooth mixture. Then stir in the basil without blending the mixture any further and place in the fridge.

Toast the wholemeal bread slices and cut into triangles.

Cut the cucumber into slices about 5mm (¼in) thick and the red pepper and fennel into long, wide strips.

Spread the tuna and quark mixture over the toast and vegetables and arrange on a serving platter. Serve either as a tasty starter or as a canapé with drinks.

4 servings
Preparation time
15 minutes
Ingredients
2 grapefruit
2 chicory heads
20 cooked prawns
4 slices smoked salmon
150g (5½oz) virtually fat-free quark
75g (2¾oz) fat-free natural yoghurt
Juice of ½ lime
½ bunch dill, finely chopped

Gourmet salad served in grapefruit shells

Salade folle au carrés frais en coque de pamplemousse

■ **CONSOLIDATION EXCEPT FOR PP THURSDAYS**
■ **STABILIZATION EXCEPT FOR PP THURSDAYS**

Halve the grapefruit and scoop out the flesh without damaging the skin. Cut the flesh into cubes, taking care not to squash it and discard as much of the white pith as you can.

Cut out the base of the chicory heads, separate the leaves and cut each one in three. Shell the prawns, retaining the tails on a few to provide a garnish (if wished), and cut the smoked salmon into
thin strips.

In a bowl, stir together the quark, yoghurt and lime juice.

In another large bowl, mix together the grapefruit chunks, chicory leaves, prawns, smoked salmon strips and dill. Pour over the yoghurt and quark dressing and combine all the ingredients very carefully.

Divide the mixture between the half-grapefruit shells and serve immediately.

4 servings
Preparation time
15 minutes
Refrigeration time
30 minutes
Ingredients
4 slices smoked salmon
Juice of 1 lemon
Juice of 1 lime
A few pink peppercorns
1 clove
1 pink grapefruit
1 grapefruit
1 orange
1 small bunch dill, finely chopped

Salmon marinated in citrus fruit

Saumon mariné aux agrumes

■ **CONSOLIDATION EXCEPT FOR PP THURSDAYS**
■ **STABILIZATION EXCEPT FOR PP THURSDAYS**

Cut the smoked salmon slices into thin strips and place them in a dish. Pour over the lime and lemon juice and add the pink peppercorns and clove. Combine the ingredients and cover with clingfilm. Leave to marinate in the fridge for 30 minutes.

Peel the 2 grapefruit and the orange. Separate the segments over a bowl to collect all the juice.

Arrange the grapefruit and orange segments in four individual dishes and add the smoked salmon strips, along with the juice from the marinade and from the citrus fruit.

Garnish with the dill and serve well chilled.

4 servings
Preparation time
15 minutes
Refrigeration time
1 hour
Ingredients
2 cucumbers
150g (5½oz) fat-free natural yoghurt
1 garlic clove
1 small bunch mint
Salt and black pepper
200g (7oz) low-fat feta cheese, cut
 into small cubes

Chilled feta and cucumber soup

Soupe froide concombre-feta

■ **CONSOLIDATION EXCEPT FOR PP THURSDAYS**
■ **STABILIZATION EXCEPT FOR PP THURSDAYS**

Wash and peel the cucumbers. Cut one quarter of one cucumber into small cubes and set aside.

In a food processor, blend the remaining cucumber with the yoghurt, garlic and mint. Season with salt and black pepper.

Stir the feta and reserved cucumber cubes into the soup and refrigerate for 1 hour. Serve well chilled.

4 servings
Preparation time
20 minutes
Cooking time
20 minutes
Ingredients
200g (7oz) turkey escalope
4 dried tomatoes
200g (7oz) virtually fat-free quark
1 bunch fresh mint, finely chopped
Black pepper
8 filo pastry sheets*
2 egg yolks

*2 filo pastry sheets are equivalent
to 1 portion of starchy foods*

Turkey and minted quark samosas

Samoussas de dinde au carrés frais et à la menthe

■ **CONSOLIDATION EXCEPT FOR PP THURSDAYS**
■ **STABILIZATION EXCEPT FOR PP THURSDAYS**

Preheat the oven to 180°C/350°F/Gas 4 and line a baking tray with greaseproof paper.

Chop the turkey escalope into tiny chunks and gently fry them without using any fat in a non-stick frying pan.

Wipe any oil from the dried tomatoes and chop finely. Put the cooked turkey chunks in a bowl and add the quark, mint and dried tomatoes. Season with black pepper.

Cut the filo pastry sheets in two and place a spoonful of the mixture on to each piece, close to the edge. Fold the sheets into triangles to make 16 samosas.

Place them on the baking tray and brush with the egg yolks using a pastry brush.

Bake the samosas in the oven for about 12 minutes. They should be nice and crispy without turning brown on top.

Serve warm from the oven.

Alsatian tarte flambée

Tarte flambée alsacienne

4 servings
Preparation time
15 minutes
Cooking time
30 minutes
Ingredients
2 eggs, separated
4 tablespoons cornflour
200g (7oz) fat-free fromage frais
250g (9oz) shallots, finely chopped
Salt and black pepper
200g (7oz) cured ham, sliced
2 tomatoes, thinly sliced
85g (3oz) extra-light cream cheese

Contains 1½ tolerated food
portions per person

■ **CONSOLIDATION EXCEPT FOR PP THURSDAYS**
■ **STABILIZATION EXCEPT FOR PP THURSDAYS**

Preheat the oven to 200°C/400°F/Gas 6.

Beat the egg whites until very stiff.

Mix together the cornflour, egg yolks and fromage frais, then fold in the beaten egg whites.

Pour the mixture into a non-stick pie dish. Scatter over the shallots and season with salt and black pepper.

Top the flan with the ham, tomatoes and extra-light cream cheese, and bake in the oven for 25–30 minutes.

Serve either hot or cold.

Couscous with beef meatballs

Couscous, boulettes à la viande de boeuf

6–8 servings
Preparation time
40 minutes
Cooking time
1¾ hours
Ingredients
1kg (2lb 4oz) lean beef, fat removed and cut into chunks
1 teaspoon grated nutmeg
1 tablespoon ras el hanout
1 teaspoon ground cinnamon
1 tablespoon ground cumin
Salt and red pepper
1 garlic head
1 large onion
1 x 1.5kg (2lb 4oz) chicken, cut into pieces
500g (1lb 2oz) courgettes, chopped
200g (7oz) turnips, chopped
1 celery head, chopped
200g (7oz) carrots, chopped
200g (7oz) leeks, chopped
200g (7oz) marrow, chopped
440g (15½oz) quick-cook couscous
1 small bunch coriander
For the meatballs
500g (1lb 2oz) lean minced beef (5% fat)
A few sprigs of parsley, chopped
A few sprigs of coriander, chopped
A few mint leaves, chopped
½ teaspoon ground cumin
Pinch of grated nutmeg
1 onion, finely chopped
1 egg yolk
Salt and red pepper

▪ **CONSOLIDATION EXCEPT FOR PP THURSDAYS**
▪ **STABILIZATION EXCEPT FOR PP THURSDAYS**

Preheat the oven to 180°C/350°F/Gas 4 and line a baking tray with greaseproof paper.

Start by cooking the lean beef in a large pan with half of all the spices: nutmeg, ras el hanout, cinnamon and cumin. Season with salt and red pepper. Add the whole garlic head and the peeled onion. Cover with water. After 1 hour, add the chicken pieces and chopped vegetables.

Leave the meat and vegetables to simmer for 30 minutes. At the end of cooking add the rest of the spices and the coriander.

Meanwhile, make the meatballs. Mix together all the ingredients in a large bowl. Knead carefully and shape into small balls. Place the meatballs on the baking tray and cook in the oven for 15–20 minutes. Drain on some kitchen paper before adding them to the pot with the meat and vegetables. Cook everything together for 10 minutes so that the flavours combine.

Place the couscous in a large microwavable bowl and add an equal volume of salted warm water. Leave the couscous to swell for 3–4 minutes, then mix it with a fork. Cover with clingfilm and place in the microwave for 2 minutes on maximum. Carefully break up the couscous with a fork.

Serve the couscous (no more than 225g (8oz) per person) with the vegetables, meat and meatballs on top and some of the liquid from the stew spooned over.

4 servings
Preparation time
40 minutes
Cooking time
1¾ hours
Ingredients
800g (1lb 12oz) boned shoulder of
    lamb
2 garlic cloves, finely chopped
2 large onions, finely chopped
Salt and black pepper
1 tablespoon ground turmeric
1 teaspoon ground ginger
1 tablespoon ground cinnamon
2 tablespoons finely chopped
    coriander
1.5kg (3lb 5oz) globe artichokes
    (about 6)
2 preserved lemons, quartered
Juice of 1 lemon

You will need a steamer

Lamb tagine with artichokes

Tajine d'agneau aux artichauts

■ **CONSOLIDATION EXCEPT FOR PP THURSDAYS**
■ **STABILIZATION EXCEPT FOR PP THURSDAYS**

Wash the lamb and cut it into 5–6cm (2–2½in) chunks.

In a large pan, soften the garlic and onion in 4 tablespoons water. Add salt and black pepper, then the turmeric, ginger and cinnamon. Stir everything together, heat through for 1 minute and add the pieces of lamb. Leave to brown for 10 minutes.

Next, pour in enough water to cover the lamb, add half the coriander and simmer, covered, for 1 hour, stirring occasionally.

In the meantime, steam the artichokes and remove the hearts. Cut the hearts into quarters and mix with the preserved lemons.

When the meat has cooked for 1 hour, add the artichoke and preserved lemon quarters to the pan along with the lemon juice. Simmer for a further 30 minutes.

Serve the tagine in a warmed dish and scatter over the remaining coriander.

4 servings
Preparation time
15 minutes
Cooking time
20 minutes
Ingredients
½ bunch asparagus
Salt and black pepper
4 rashers fat-reduced bacon
6 eggs, plus 2 egg whites
A few sprigs of parsley, chopped
Pinch of ground cumin

Asparagus with bacon omelette

Asperges vertes aux œufs brouillés

▨ **CONSOLIDATION EXCEPT FOR PP THURSDAYS**
▨ **STABILIZATION EXCEPT FOR PP THURSDAYS**

Clean and remove the woody ends of the asparagus. Place the spears in a large pan of salted water and cook until tender.

Cut the bacon rashers into thin strips. Cook lightly in a non-stick frying pan for a few minutes, then remove from the pan and set aside.

Whisk the 6 eggs, season with salt and black pepper and add the parsley and cumin.

In a large bowl, beat the egg whites with a pinch of salt until they are very stiff. Gently fold them into the beaten egg mixture.

Reheat the frying pan and pour in half the egg mixture. While the omelette is still runny, scatter half the asparagus and the bacon over the uncooked side. Cover with the other half of the egg mixture and continue cooking the omelette.

Once the omelette is cooked through, serve straightaway with the remaining asparagus on top.

4 servings
Preparation time
25 minutes
Cooking time
25 minutes
Ingredients
4 slices leg of lamb (fat removed)
2 garlic cloves
4 tablespoons balsamic vinegar
Salt
2 bunches asparagus
100g (3½oz) lamb's lettuce
8 cherry tomatoes, halved

Balsamic lamb with asparagus salad

Agneau balsamique en salade d'asperges vertes

■ **CONSOLIDATION EXCEPT FOR PP THURSDAYS**
■ **STABILIZATION EXCEPT FOR PP THURSDAYS**

Preheat the oven to 200°C/400°F/Gas 6.

Place the lamb on a baking sheet. Peel and halve the garlic cloves and place them with the meat. Mix the balsamic vinegar with 2 tablespoons water and pour over the lamb. Season with salt and roast in the oven for 15 minutes.

Meanwhile, prepare the asparagus by cleaning it thoroughly and chopping the stalks in three, discarding the woody ends. Bring a large pan of salted water to the boil and cook the asparagus for about 8 minutes; it should still have some bite. Once it is ready, remove from the heat and transfer to a colander to drain.

Add the asparagus to the lamb, mix together and roast in the oven for 10 minutes.

Serve on four large warmed plates, scatter over a few lamb's lettuce leaves and garnish with 4 cherry tomato halves per person.

4 servings
Preparation time
15 minutes
Cooking time
30 minutes
Ingredients
½ Victoria pineapple
400g (14oz) pork tenderloin
1 × 2cm (¾in) piece fresh ginger,
    grated
2 garlic cloves, chopped
200g (7oz) virtually fat-free quark
4 pinches Colombo spice powder
265g (9½oz) brown rice

Creole pork tenderloin

Filet mignon au carrés frais
à la créole

■ **CONSOLIDATION EXCEPT FOR PP THURSDAYS**
■ **STABILIZATION EXCEPT FOR PP THURSDAYS**

Preheat the oven to 190°C/375°F/Gas 5, prepare 4 squares of aluminium foil measuring about 22cm (8½in) and line a baking tray with greaseproof paper.

Using a sharp-pointed knife, peel the pineapple and cut out any 'eyes'. (Victoria pineapples are tender in the middle, so the core does not need to be removed.) Chop the pineapple into cubes.

Cut the pork tenderloin into eight medallions and place two on each foil square. Divide the pineapple cubes among the squares, adding a little ginger, garlic and 50g (1¾oz) of the quark to each, along with a pinch of spice powder. Seal the foil parcels, place them on the baking tray and bake in the oven for 30 minutes.

Meanwhile, cook the brown rice in a large pan of water for about 20–30 minutes until just tender.

Serve the oven-baked parcels with a timbale of brown rice, 225g (8oz) maximum per person.

4 servings
Preparation time
25 minutes
Resting time
2 hours
Cooking time
1 hour
Ingredients
1 × 1.25kg (2lb 12oz) leg of lamb
1 bunch rosemary, leaves only
2 garlic heads
Salt and black pepper

Garlicky leg of lamb

Gigot à l'ail

■ **CONSOLIDATION EXCEPT FOR PP THURSDAYS**
■ **STABILIZATION EXCEPT FOR PP THURSDAYS**

Preheat the oven to 230°C/450°F/Gas 8.

Remove as much fat from the leg of lamb as possible and roll the meat in the rosemary to coat. Keep on one side any bits of rosemary that do not stick to the joint. Wrap the lamb in clingfilm and leave to rest in the fridge for 2 hours.

Separate the cloves from the garlic heads, but do not peel them – just rinse in water.

Remove the lamb from the clingfilm and put it in an ovenproof dish along with the reserved rosemary. Roast in the oven for 15 minutes, then turn the temperature down to 220°C/425°F/Gas 7 and add the garlic cloves. After 5 minutes, pour a glass of water into the dish, and after another 10 minutes baste the lamb and turn it over. Leave to cook for a further 30 minutes, basting several times.

Take the dish out of the oven, season lamb with salt and black pepper and baste once more. Cover with aluminium foil and leave to rest for about 15 minutes in a warm place before serving.

4 servings
Preparation time
35 minutes
Cooking time
20 minutes
Ingredients
4 x 150g (5oz) pork chops
1 red pepper, thinly sliced
1 green pepper, thinly sliced
1 yellow pepper, thinly sliced
2 courgettes, sliced
8 large button mushrooms, sliced
4 tablespoons balsamic vinegar
Salt and black pepper

Pork chops with balsamic grilled vegetables

Côtes de porc aux légumes grillés balsamiques

■ **CONSOLIDATION EXCEPT FOR PP THURSDAYS**
■ **STABILIZATION EXCEPT FOR PP THURSDAYS**

Preheat the grill and cook the pork chops for 7 minutes on each side. Next cook the vegetables, grilling them for about 3–5 minutes on each side, depending on the type. Then mix the vegetables together in a large bowl, pour in the balsamic vinegar and toss gently. Season with salt and black pepper.

Serve the chops accompanied by the grilled vegetables and balsamic sauce.

4 servings
Preparation time
15 minutes
Cooking time
50 minutes
Ingredients
480g (1lb 1oz) lean fillet of lamb,
  cut into pieces
2 onions, chopped
2 garlic cloves, crushed
400g (14oz) French beans, cut into
  pieces
8 artichoke hearts
2 low-salt beef stock cubes
Salt and black pepper
2 small sprigs thyme
2 tablespoons cornflour

Contains ½ tolerated food portion
per person

Sauté of lamb with artichokes and French beans

Sauté d'agneau aux artichauts et aux haricots verts

■ **CONSOLIDATION EXCEPT FOR PP THURSDAYS**
■ **STABILIZATION EXCEPT FOR PP THURSDAYS**

Brown the lamb pieces, onions, garlic, French beans and artichoke hearts in a large flameproof casserole. Dissolve the stock cubes in 1 litre (1¾ pints) hot water, pour into the casserole and season with salt and black pepper. Add the thyme and leave to simmer for 20 minutes.

Dissolve the cornflour in a little of the cooking liquid and stir into the casserole. Simmer for a further 15–20 minutes.

Serve the lamb sauté piping hot.

4 servings
Preparation time
25 minutes
Cooking time
45 minutes
Ingredients
16 button or large salad onions
2 carrots
280g (10oz) green lentils
Salt and black pepper
4 cloves
1 bouquet garni
4 × 100–120g (3½–4¼oz) salmon
  steaks (without the skin)
4 rashers fat-reduced bacon
A few chervil leaves, to garnish

Bacon-wrapped salmon with lentils

Petit salé de saumon et lentilles

■ **CONSOLIDATION EXCEPT FOR PP THURSDAYS**
■ **STABILIZATION EXCEPT FOR PP THURSDAYS**

Peel the onions and cut the carrots into thick slices.

Fill a large pan with cold water (about five times the volume of the lentils) and pour in the lentils. Bring to the boil over a high heat, then add the onions, carrots, cloves and bouquet garni. Cook for 30 minutes and add salt and black pepper.

Wash and wipe dry the salmon steaks. Wrap each in a rasher of bacon and, if necessary, tie with some kitchen string. Place the salmon rolls in the lentils, which by now are almost cooked. Cover and cook for another 10 minutes over a gentle heat.

Serve the lentils on a warmed dish, allowing 225g (8oz) at most per person (cooked weight). Arrange the salmon steaks on top, scattering over a few chervil leaves.

4 servings
Preparation time
25 minutes
Cooking time
20 minutes
Ingredients
2 x 120g (4½oz) skinless fillets of
  cod
1 onion, finely chopped
1 egg
2 tablespoons oat bran
1 tablespoon paprika
1 tablespoon chopped parsley
Salt and black pepper
280g (10oz) couscous (uncooked
  weight)

Couscous with fish balls

Couscous aux boulettes de poisson

■ CONSOLIDATION EXCEPT FOR PP THURSDAYS
■ STABILIZATION EXCEPT FOR PP THURSDAYS

In a food processor, blend the cod fillets with the onion. In a bowl, mix the cod and onion with the egg, oat bran, paprika and parsley. Add salt and black pepper and knead together well. Dampen your hands and form the mixture into small balls.

Heat a non-stick frying pan, add 3 drops of oil and immediately wipe off with kitchen paper. Fry the fish balls until lightly browned, then place them in a high-sided pan, cover with water and cook for 10 minutes over a low heat.

Meanwhile bring 1.2 litres (2 pints) salted water to the boil in a large pan. Pour the couscous into a large bowl. Add the boiling water, stir it into the couscous, cover the bowl and leave to swell for 5 minutes. Then use a fork to break up the couscous.

Serve the fish balls hot with the couscous.

Spicy tuna with chick peas

Emincé de thon aux épices et pois chiches

4 servings
Preparation time
30 minutes
Refrigeration time
2 hours
Cooking time
25 minutes
Ingredients
4 x 100g (4oz) tuna steaks
50ml (2fl oz) balsamic vinegar
50ml (2fl oz) soy sauce
2 onions, finely chopped
4 garlic cloves, finely chopped
240g (8½oz) tinned peeled
    tomatoes, crushed
1 teaspoon ground cumin
2 sprigs thyme
1 bay leaf
Salt and black pepper
800g (1lb 12oz) cooked chick peas
Harissa, to taste

■ **CONSOLIDATION EXCEPT FOR PP THURSDAYS**
■ **STABILIZATION EXCEPT FOR PP THURSDAYS**

Cut the tuna steaks into thin slices and place in a dish along with the balsamic vinegar and soy sauce. Leave to marinate in the fridge for at least 2 hours.

Soften the onions and garlic in a flameproof casserole with 4 tablespoons water. As soon as they turn translucent, add the tomatoes. Next add the cumin, thyme and bay leaf. Season with salt and black pepper and leave to reduce over a low heat.

In another pan, heat the chick peas with a little harissa for about 10 minutes.

In a non-stick frying pan, fry the tuna strips for 3 minutes on each side.

Serve on warmed plates, with the tuna on a bed of tomato sauce on one side and the chick peas on the other.

4 servings
Preparation time
15 minutes
Cooking time
40 minutes
Ingredients
600g (1lb 5oz) salmon fillet, cut into
   4 pieces
280g (10oz) wild rice
Salt and black pepper
250g (9oz) mushrooms, chopped
2 garlic cloves, finely chopped
¼ bunch parsley, finely chopped
4 tablespoons low-fat crème fraîche
   (3% fat)
Pinch of grated nutmeg
2 tablespoons chopped fresh ginger

Contains 1 tolerated food portion
per person

You will need a steamer

Salmon with wild rice and mushrooms

Saumon au riz sauvage et aux champignons

■ **CONSOLIDATION EXCEPT FOR PP THURSDAYS**
■ **STABILIZATION EXCEPT FOR PP THURSDAYS**

Steam the salmon for 10 minutes.

In the meantime, prepare the rice. Bring a large pan of salted water to the boil, pour in the rice and cook for about 40 minutes over a medium heat.

Warm a non-stick frying pan and cook the mushrooms in 4 tablespoons water along with the garlic and parsley. Once they are cooked, add the crème fraîche and leave to simmer over a gentle heat for 2–3 minutes.

Take the rice off the heat and drain. Stir in the mushrooms, add a pinch of nutmeg and the chopped ginger and serve with the steamed salmon.

4 servings
Preparation time
30 minutes
Cooking time
20 minutes
Ingredients
600g (1lb 5oz) smoked haddock
 fillets, cut into thin strips
Juice of 6 limes
4 preserved lemons, cut into small
 pieces
1 green chilli, finely chopped
4 spring onions, finely chopped
100g (3½oz) quinoa
100g (3½oz) bulgur wheat
100g (3½oz) quick-cook couscous
Salt and black pepper
100ml (3½fl oz) low-fat coconut
 milk

Lime and lemon smoked haddock carpaccio with quinoa, couscous and bulgur wheat

Carpaccio de haddock aux deux citrons et trois semoules

■ **CONSOLIDATION EXCEPT FOR PP THURSDAYS**
■ **STABILIZATION EXCEPT FOR PP THURSDAYS**

Place the haddock in a large dish and add half of the lime juice. Add half of the preserved lemons along with the chilli and spring onions. Now add the rest of the lime juice and refrigerate.

Rinse the quinoa thoroughly. Pour the quinoa and bulgur wheat into a pan and cover with water equal to twice their volume. Bring to the boil, then cook, covered, over a gentle heat until all the water is absorbed (about 10–15 minutes). Turn off the heat and leave for about 10 minutes for the grains to swell up. The quinoa and bulgur are ready once they have doubled their volume.

Bring 100ml (3½fl oz) water to the boil with a pinch of salt and add the couscous. Leave to rest and swell up for 5 minutes, then use a fork to break up the grains. Stir the couscous into the quinoa and bulgur wheat and add the remaining preserved lemons. Pour in half the coconut milk and cook in the microwave for 30 seconds.

Remove the haddock from the marinade and drain. Pour over the rest of the coconut milk. Divide the couscous mixture between four bowls, allowing no more than 225g (8oz) per person. Arrange the smoked haddock carpaccio on top and garnish with the chilli and preserved lemons from the marinade. Add salt and black pepper to taste and serve immediately.

2 servings
Preparation time
20 minutes
Cooking time
10 minutes
Ingredients
500ml (18fl oz) small mussels
2 tablespoons white wine
1 bunch parsley
1 garlic clove, peeled
40g (1½oz) Parmesan cheese
Salt and black pepper
150g (5½oz) linguine (uncooked
   weight)
1 tomato, chopped

*Contains 1 tolerated food portion
per person*

Mussel and parsley pesto linguine

Linguine aux moules et au persil

■ **CONSOLIDATION EXCEPT FOR PP THURSDAYS**
■ **STABILIZATION EXCEPT FOR PP THURSDAYS**

Wash and scrub the mussels, place them in a high-sided frying pan with the white wine and cook over a high heat for 2–3 minutes. Shake the pan while the mussels are cooking so that they open up, then leave them to cool. Discard any that have stayed shut.

Wash the parsley, remove all the leaves and place in a blender with the garlic and Parmesan. Purée the ingredients and add salt and black pepper.

Bring some salted water to the boil in a pan and add the linguine. Cook the pasta according to the instructions on the packet.

Shell the mussels and place them in a large serving dish with the linguine, tomato and parsley pesto. Mix everything together and serve immediately.

4 servings
Preparation time
20 minutes
Cooking time
1 hour
Ingredients
265g (9½oz) wild rice
Salt and black pepper
300ml (10fl oz) fish stock
2 large lobsters
1 glass white wine
4 egg yolks
2 vanilla pods

Contains 1 tolerated food portion
per person

Vanilla lobster with wild rice

Langouste gratinées à la vanille et leur riz sauvage

■ **CONSOLIDATION EXCEPT FOR PP THURSDAYS**
■ **STABILIZATION EXCEPT FOR PP THURSDAYS**

Cook the rice well in advance. Pour some salted water into a large pan and cook over a medium heat for about 40 minutes. The water should be three times the volume of the rice.

Boil the fish stock, add the lobsters and cook for 10 minutes. Remove the lobsters, cut them in half lengthways and keep them warm.

Strain the fish stock into a pan, add the white wine and reduce by half.

In a heatproof bowl, beat the egg yolks and scrape the seeds from the vanilla pods into the beaten yolks. Place the bowl over a pan filled with water and heat gently whilst very slowly pouring the reduced fish stock into the yolks, beating the mixture vigorously all the while. The resulting sabayon sauce should be thick and frothy. Taste and adjust the seasoning with salt and black pepper if necessary.

Arrange the lobster halves in a heatproof dish, pour over the sabayon sauce and grill them for a few minutes. Serve with the wild rice.

Dukan-style raclette

Raclette façon Dukan

4 servings
Preparation time
20 minutes
Cooking time
30 minutes
Ingredients
500g (1lb 2oz) waxy potatoes
Salt
200g (7oz) bresaola
150g (5½oz) raclette cheese
320g (11¼oz) extra-light
  cream cheese
A few cocktail onions
A few cornichons

You will need a raclette machine

*Contains 2 tolerated food portions
per person*

■ **CONSOLIDATION EXCEPT FOR PP THURSDAYS**
■ **STABILIZATION EXCEPT FOR PP THURSDAYS**

Cook the potatoes in a large pan of salted water for about 20 minutes. Check whether they are done by pricking with a knife – the tip should slide in easily.

Arrange the bresaola slices on a serving dish, put the raclette cheese in a raclette machine and switch on. Place the cooked potatoes on the top part of the machine so that they stay warm.

Place a portion of melted raclette cheese on each plate, and serve the cream cheese in individual bowls with the onions and cornichons in small dishes. Eat with the cooked potatoes.

4 servings
Preparation time
15 minutes
Cooking time
30 minutes
Ingredients
4 small aubergines, halved
4 garlic cloves, quartered
Salt and black pepper
1 x 400g (14oz) jar sugar-free
  tomato sauce
1 teaspoon chopped oregano, plus
  extra to garnish
150g (5½oz) Manchego cheese,
  cut into thin strips
75g (2¾oz) serrano ham,
  cut into thin strips

Spanish baked aubergines

Aubergines gratinées à l'espagnole

▢ **CONSOLIDATION EXCEPT FOR PP THURSDAYS**
▪ **STABILIZATION EXCEPT FOR PP THURSDAYS**

Preheat the oven to 230°C/450°F/Gas 8.

Stud each aubergine half with two garlic quarters. Season with salt and black pepper, then place in an ovenproof dish and bake in the oven for 20 minutes.

Pour the tomato sauce over the aubergines and sprinkle with the oregano. Cover each aubergine half with strips of Manchego cheese and serrano ham, return to the oven and bake for a further 10 minutes. Sprinkle with more oregano and serve.

2 servings
Preparation time
15 minutes
Cooking time
10 minutes
Ingredients
4 tomatoes
150g (5½oz) low-fat feta
  cheese, diced
4 eggs
Salt and black pepper

Turkish-style tomatoes and eggs

Tomates à la feta et aux œufs à la turque

▢ **CONSOLIDATION EXCEPT FOR PP THURSDAYS**
▪ **STABILIZATION EXCEPT FOR PP THURSDAYS**

Bring 1 litre (1¾ pints) water to the boil in a large pan. Add the tomatoes and leave for 1 minute, then drain and remove the skins. Chop the tomatoes into small pieces.

In a non-stick frying pan, fry the tomatoes for a few minutes. Then add the feta cubes, stirring them into the tomatoes. Break the eggs over the mixture and stir them in too. Add salt and black pepper and cook for a few more minutes over a gentle heat. Serve hot.

Spanish tortilla

Tortilla à l'espagnole

4 servings
Preparation time
20 minutes
Cooking time
30 minutes
Ingredients
600g (1lb 5oz) potatoes,
  thinly sliced
200g (7oz) onions, thinly sliced
Salt and black pepper
8 eggs

▨ **CONSOLIDATION EXCEPT FOR PP THURSDAYS**
▨ **STABILIZATION EXCEPT FOR PP THURSDAYS**

Heat 3 drops of oil in a non-stick frying pan and wipe off with kitchen paper. Add the sliced potatoes and after 5 minutes add the onions along with 4 tablespoons water and some salt. Cover and continue to cook over a high heat, stirring the vegetables from time to time so that they do not stick to the pan. When the potatoes and onions are soft, turn off the heat.

In a large bowl, beat the eggs together, season with salt and black pepper and then add the potatoes and onions.

Wipe the frying pan, pour in the omelette mixture and cook over a gentle heat for 10 minutes. Once the omelette is cooked but still runny in the centre, turn it over on to a plate and slip it back into the frying pan to cook the other side. This will take another 10 minutes or so. Serve immediately.

4 servings
Preparation time
30 minutes
Cooking time
1 hour 25 minutes
Ingredients
1 x 1kg (2lb 4oz) guinea fowl
½ lemon
1 Savoy cabbage
Salt and black pepper
1 onion
1 clove
1 bouquet garni
50g (2oz) blueberries
500ml (18fl oz) low-salt chicken
    stock, fat skimmed off

Guinea fowl and blueberries

Pintade au chou et aux myrtilles

■ **CONSOLIDATION EXCEPT FOR PP THURSDAYS**
■ **STABILIZATION EXCEPT FOR PP THURSDAYS**

Preheat the oven to 200°C/400°F/Gas 6 and preheat the grill to medium.

Rub the guinea fowl with the lemon half and brown it for 5 minutes under the grill.

In the meantime, cut the cabbage into 8 pieces and blanch in boiling salted water for 5 minutes. Drain.

Place the guinea fowl in a flameproof casserole and arrange the cabbage around it. Stud the onion with the clove and add to the casserole along with the bouquet garni, blueberries and seasoning. Pour over the stock. Cover and cook in the oven for 1–1¼ hours, basting the bird at regular intervals.

Once the guinea fowl is cooked, remove it from the casserole with the cabbage and keep warm. Place the casserole on a hob, discard the bouquet garni and boil the stock until it has reduced and thickened slightly. Serve this with the guinea fowl and cabbage.

Beef tagine with garden peas

Tajine de boeuf aux petits pois

4 servings
Preparation time
25 minutes
Cooking time
2 hours 20 minutes
Ingredients
500g (1lb 2oz) braising beef (chuck steak or shoulder)
4 garlic cloves, finely chopped
2 onions, finely chopped
Salt and black pepper
1 teaspoon ground ginger
½ teaspoon ground turmeric
½ teaspoon ground cinnamon
1 teaspoon ground cumin
880g (1lb 15oz) garden peas
1 tablespoon chopped fresh coriander

■ **CONSOLIDATION EXCEPT FOR PP THURSDAYS**
■ **STABILIZATION EXCEPT FOR PP THURSDAYS**

Cut the beef into small pieces and brown along with the garlic and onions in a flameproof casserole or tagine. Add salt, black pepper and 6 tablespoons hot water. Next add the spices and stir. Cook for 15 minutes.

Add 100ml (4fl oz) water and leave to simmer for at least 1 hour 40 minutes, adding more water if necessary. Then add the peas and cook for a further 20 minutes.

Adjust the seasoning, sprinkle over the coriander and serve.

Chili con carne

4 servings
Preparation time
20 minutes
Cooking time
45 minutes
Ingredients
400g (14oz) minced beef (5% fat)
2 onions, chopped
2 garlic cloves, chopped
1 red pepper, deseeded and cut into thin strips
Salt and black pepper
3 tablespoons Mexican spices (or chilli powder)
240g (8½oz) tomato passata
880g (1lb 15oz) tinned red kidney beans

■ **CONSOLIDATION EXCEPT FOR PP THURSDAYS**
■ **STABILIZATION EXCEPT FOR PP THURSDAYS**

Brown the minced beef in a deep non-stick frying pan, stirring it well so that it breaks up completely.

Once the meat is nicely browned, add the onions, garlic and red pepper. Season with salt and black pepper and add the spices and passata. Pour in about 200ml (7fl oz) water, cover and leave to simmer over a medium heat for 30 minutes.

Rinse and drain the kidney beans and add them to the pan. Simmer for a further 10 minutes before serving.

4 servings
Preparation time
10 minutes
Cooking time
20 minutes
Ingredients
6 small leeks, finely chopped
8 eggs
85g (3oz) raclette cheese, cut into
  8 slices
Salt and black pepper

Eggs cocotte on a bed of leeks topped with cheese

Œufs cocotte à la fondue de poireau et raclette

■ **CONSOLIDATION EXCEPT FOR PP THURSDAYS**
■ **STABILIZATION EXCEPT FOR PP THURSDAYS**

Preheat the oven to 230°C/450°F/Gas 8.

Cook the leeks in a non-stick frying pan with 4 tablespoons water over a medium heat for 12 minutes.

Spoon a layer of leeks into the bottom of four ramekin dishes, break 2 eggs into each, season with salt and black pepper and cover with 2 slices of raclette cheese.

Place the ramekin dishes in a bain-marie and cook in the oven for about 8 minutes or until the egg whites are set. Serve straightaway.

4 servings
Preparation time
20 minutes
Cooking time
25 minutes
Ingredients
16 portobello mushrooms
2 red onions, finely chopped
100g (3½oz) sliced wholemeal bread
2 teaspoons chopped parsley
150g (5½oz) low-fat feta cheese,
    crumbled
2 garlic cloves, finely chopped
Salt and black pepper

Crispy stuffed mushrooms

Champignons farcis croustillants

▪ **CONSOLIDATION EXCEPT FOR PP THURSDAYS**
▪ **STABILIZATION EXCEPT FOR PP THURSDAYS**

Preheat the oven to 200°C/400°F/Gas 6.

Peel the mushrooms. Cut off and finely chop the stalks. Oil a non-stick frying pan with 3 drops of oil and wipe off immediately with kitchen paper. Heat the pan and fry the red onions. Then add the chopped mushroom stalks.

Toast the wholemeal bread and crumble the slices into a large bowl. Add the parsley, feta, garlic, salt and black pepper. Stir in the chopped mushroom mixture.

Fill the mushroom tops with the stuffing mixture and bake in the oven for 15 minutes. Serve straightaway.

4 servings
Preparation time
10 minutes
Cooking time
12 minutes
Ingredients
60g (2¼oz) rocket leaves
2 small courgettes
Salt and black pepper
2 garlic cloves
300g (10½oz) wholewheat penne
  (uncooked weight)
Drizzle of balsamic vinegar
A little grated Parmesan cheese

Courgette and rocket penne

Penne à la roquette et aux courgettes

■ **CONSOLIDATION EXCEPT FOR PP THURSDAYS**
■ **STABILIZATION EXCEPT FOR PP THURSDAYS**

Wash and dry the rocket and place in a large bowl. Wash the courgettes, grate very finely using a mandoline cutter and add them to the rocket.

Bring 3 litres (5¼ pints) water to the boil in a large pan. Add a little salt and the garlic cloves. As soon as the water has come to the boil, add the penne and cook according to the instructions on the packet. Drain and immediately add to the bowl containing the courgettes and rocket.

Season with salt and black pepper, stir all the ingredients together and drizzle over some balsamic vinegar. Serve straightaway with a little Parmesan on top.

4 servings
Make a day in advance
Preparation time
20 minutes
Refrigeration time
Overnight
Cooking time
30 minutes
Ingredients
400g (14oz) sea bream fillets
Juice of 4 limes
2 red onions, finely chopped
2 tablespoons finely chopped
  mint
6 tablespoons finely chopped
  coriander
Pinch of chilli powder
Salt and black pepper
2 tablespoons olive oil
280g (10oz) green lentils
1 carrot, diced
2 tablespoons chopped fresh ginger
2 tablespoons soy sauce

Brazilian sea bream ceviche with lentils

Ceviche brésilien de dorade
aux lentilles

■ **CONSOLIDATION EXCEPT FOR PP THURSDAYS**
■ **STABILIZATION EXCEPT FOR PP THURSDAYS**

Cut the sea bream fillets into very thin slices and place them in a large dish. Pour over the lime juice and place in the fridge for 1 hour to allow the fish to 'cook'.

Add the red onions, mint, half the coriander, the chilli powder, salt, black pepper and the oil. Refrigerate overnight.

The following day, cook the lentils in water equivalent to five times their volume for 30 minutes. Drain and transfer to a large bowl.

Add the carrot to the lentils along with the ginger, the rest of the coriander and the soy sauce. Check the seasoning and adjust if necessary.

To serve the cerviche, arrange the marinated sea bream slices on top of the lentils, allowing no more than 225g (8oz) lentils (cooked weight) per person.

4 servings
Preparation time
20 minutes
Cooking time
25 minutes
Ingredients
1 large onion, finely chopped
2 garlic cloves, finely chopped
175g (6oz) Arborio rice
800ml (28fl oz) low-salt chicken
  stock, fat skimmed off
150g (5½oz) virtually fat-free quark
400g (14oz) chicken livers
Dash of raspberry vinegar
Black pepper

Chicken liver and quark risotto

Risotto aux carrés frais et aux foies de volaille

■ **CONSOLIDATION EXCEPT FOR PP THURSDAYS**
■ **STABILIZATION EXCEPT FOR PP THURSDAYS**

Fry the onion and garlic in a high-sided non-stick frying pan over a medium heat. Add the rice and toast for 1 minute, stirring well. Gradually add the hot chicken stock, a ladleful at a time, waiting for each ladleful to be absorbed before adding the next. The rice should be cooked but still slightly firm. Once it is ready, turn off the heat and stir in the quark.

Cut the chicken livers into fairly thick strip and fry them in a non-stick frying pan without any fat for 4–5 minutes over a high heat. Take the pan off the heat and pour over a good dash of raspberry vinegar, then add some black pepper.

To serve, arrange the chicken livers around the risotto, allowing a maximum of 150g (5½oz) cooked rice per person.

4 servings
Preparation time
20 minutes
Cooking time
20 minutes
Refrigeration time
2 hours minimum
Ingredients
150g (5½oz) quinoa
300ml (10fl oz) low-salt chicken
   stock, fat skimmed off
150g (5½oz) virtually fat-free quark,
   with garlic and herbs
1 teaspoon sherry vinegar
Black pepper
8 thin slices bresaola, cut into
   thin strips
2 tomatoes, deseeded and diced
Rocket leaves, to serve

Quinoa, quark and bresaola timbales

Timbales de quinoa aux carrés frais et à la viande des Grisons

■ **CONSOLIDATION EXCEPT FOR PP THURSDAYS**
■ **STABILIZATION EXCEPT FOR PP THURSDAYS**

Rinse the quinoa under cold running water, then place it in a pan. Add the chicken stock and bring to the boil. Cover the pan as soon as the stock starts to boil. Cook for about 20 minutes over a low heat. Take the pan off the heat and leave to cool down.

Stir the quark into the quinoa, then add the sherry vinegar and some black pepper. Mix in the bresaola and tomatoes and combine carefully. Divide between four ramekin dishes lined with clingfilm and press the mixture down slightly. Refrigerate for at least 2 hours.

When ready to serve, carefully turn the timbales out of their moulds and serve with a rocket salad.

4 servings
Preparation time
15 minutes
Cooking time
45 minutes
Ingredients
12 tablespoons oat bran
4 tablespoons cornflour
150g (5½oz) raclette cheese
4 eggs
½ teaspoon baking powder
200ml (7fl oz) skimmed milk
Salt and black pepper
100g (3½oz) bresaola

Contains 1 tolerated food portion
per person

Mountain cheese and bresaola loaf

Cake des alpages à la raclette

■ **CONSOLIDATION EXCEPT FOR PP THURSDAYS**
■ **STABILIZATION EXCEPT FOR PP THURSDAYS**

Preheat the oven to 180°C/350°F/Gas 4.

In a dish, mix together the oat bran and the cornflour. Chop the raclette cheese into small cubes and coat them with the oat bran and cornflour mixture. Put to one side.

In a large bowl, beat the eggs together until creamy, then add what remains of the oat bran and cornflour mixture along with the baking powder. Pour in the milk. Add black pepper to taste but use only a little salt as the bresaola is very salty.

Chop the bresaola into small pieces and add to the dough along with the cubes of raclette cheese. Carefully stir all the ingredients together and spoon the mixture into a silicone loaf tin.

Bake in the oven for 45 minutes, keeping a careful eye on the loaf. Once it is cooked, leave the loaf to cool down before turning it out of the tin. Cut into slices to serve.

4 servings
Preparation time
25 minutes
Freezing time
5 minutes
Refrigeration time
2 hours minimum
Ingredients
1 very ripe melon
8 teaspoons low-fat cream (3% fat)
1 teaspoon ground ginger
2 eggs, separated
2 teaspoons crystallized stevia
2 gelatine leaves

Contains 2 tolerated food portions
per person

Melon mousse

Mousse au melon

■ **CONSOLIDATION EXCEPT FOR PP THURSDAYS**
■ **STABILIZATION EXCEPT FOR PP THURSDAYS**

Halve the melon, scoop out the seeds and remove all the flesh.
Blend the melon flesh with the cream and ground ginger.

Place the egg yolks and sweetener in a heatproof bowl and set
it over a pan of simmering water. Beat until the eggs are thick
enough to coat a spoon. Pour into a large bowl and very gradually
add the puréed melon, stirring continuously with a wooden spoon.

Soak the gelatine in a small bowl of cold water. Then dissolve the
gelatine in 2 tablespoons hot water and mix it into a little of the
melon mixture. Next stir this gelatine into the rest of the puréed
melon. Place the bowl of puréed melon in the freezer for 5 minutes.

Beat the egg whites until stiff and then gently fold them into the
melon mixture. Cover the bowl and leave the mousse to set in the
fridge for at least 2 hours before serving.

Strawberries and creamy topping

Fraises en nappage lacté

4 servings
Make a day in advance
Preparation time
15 minutes
Refrigeration time
24 hours
Ingredients
600g (1lb 5oz) creamy fat-free
   natural yoghurt
2 egg yolks
2 teaspoons crystallized stevia
1 teaspoon vanilla flavouring
500g (1lb 2oz) strawberries, hulled

▨ **CONSOLIDATION EXCEPT FOR PP THURSDAYS**
■ **STABILIZATION EXCEPT FOR PP THURSDAYS**

Strain the yoghurt through a fine-meshed sieve, placed over a bowl, and refrigerate for 24 hours.

The following day take the yoghurt out of the fridge and prepare the topping. In a large bowl, beat the egg yolks with the sweetener and vanilla flavouring until frothy. Then add the strained yoghurt and stir together thoroughly.

Cut up the strawberries and divide them between four individual sundae dishes. When ready to serve, pour the creamy topping over the fruit.

4 servings
Preparation time
10 minutes
Cooking time
6 minutes
Ingredients
250ml (9fl oz) skimmed milk
2 eggs
Pinch of salt
1 teaspoon ground cinnamon
8 Canderel vanilla sticks
4 large slices stale wholemeal bread
½ teaspoon maple syrup flavouring

Dukan French toast

Pain perdu Dukan

- CONSOLIDATION EXCEPT FOR PP THURSDAYS
- STABILIZATION EXCEPT FOR PP THURSDAYS

In a large bowl, beat together the milk, eggs, salt, cinnamon and 4 of the vanilla sticks.

Dip the slices of bread into this milky mixture, making sure both sides are coated. Then gently fry them in a non-stick frying pan for 2–3 minutes on each side.

Mix together 3 tablespoons warm water with the maple syrup flavouring and the 4 remaining vanilla sticks.

To serve, pour this sauce over the fried bread slices.

Plaited wholemeal 'shabbat challah' bread

Pain complet et tressé façon 'hallot de chabbat'

Makes 4 loaves or 12 rolls

Preparation time
20 minutes

Resting time
45 minutes

Cooking time
30 minutes

Ingredients
1 x 8g sachet dried yeast
1 egg plus, 1 egg yolk
1 tablespoon salt
1kg (2lb 4oz) wholemeal flour
8 tablespoons powdered sweetener (or granules)
4 tablespoons orange flower water

- **CONSOLIDATION EXCEPT FOR PP THURSDAYS**
- **STABILIZATION EXCEPT FOR PP THURSDAYS**

In a large bowl, dissolve the yeast in 370ml (12fl oz) warm water. Leave to rest for 15 minutes.

Stir the whole egg and salt into the yeast mixture. Then add the flour and stir in the sweetener and orange flower water. Knead for 10 minutes to expel any air. Pull the dough into 12 pieces and either form these into 4 plaited loaves or make 12 small round rolls.

Brush the loaves or rolls with the beaten egg yolk (this will ensure the bread is golden) and leave to rest for at least 30 minutes, covered with a clean tea towel, on a baking tray lined with greseproof paper.

Preheat the oven to 200°C/400°F/Gas 6.

Bake the bread in the oven for 25–30 minutes, checking carefully to see when it is cooked.

4 servings
Preparation time
10 minutes
Cooking time
25 minutes
Ingredients
1 large pineapple
4 teaspoons white rum flavouring
½ teaspoon ground cinnamon
Pinch of ground allspice
6 pinches ground ginger

Spit-roast pineapple

Ananas à la broche

■ **CONSOLIDATION EXCEPT FOR PP THURSDAYS**
■ **STABILIZATION EXCEPT FOR PP THURSDAYS**

Preheat the oven to 180°C/350°F/Gas 4.

Place the pineapple on to a rotisserie and attach it firmly with the spit forks. Cook in the oven until the skin begins to crack.

Remove the pineapple, place in a dish and leave to rest so that the heat reaches right inside. Then cut the pineapple lengthways and remove the fibrous core. Take off the skin and cut the pineapple into slices.

Collect any juice and pour into a small pan. Add the juices from the pineapple, the white rum flavouring and spices and bring to the boil.

Serve the pineapple slices accompanied by the spicy sauce.

4 servings
Preparation time
15 minutes
Refrigeration time
35 minutes
Ingredients
200g (7oz) frozen red berries
Zest of 1 unwaxed lemon, finely
  chopped
400g (14oz) fat-free fromage frais
1 teaspoon crystallized stevia
1 teaspoon vanilla flavouring
4 egg whites

Fromage frais mousse with red berries

Mousse de fromage blanc aux fruits rouges

■ **CONSOLIDATION EXCEPT FOR PP THURSDAYS**
■ **STABILIZATION EXCEPT FOR PP THURSDAYS**

Leave the fruit to thaw for 1 hour. Purée the fruit and add the lemon zest.

Whisk the fromage frais with the sweetener and vanilla flavouring. Stir in the puréed fruit.

Whisk the egg whites until stiff, then fold them into the puréed fruit mixture.

Pour the mousse into individual sundae dishes and serve well chilled.

4 servings
Preparation time
10 minutes
Cooking time
5 minutes
Refrigeration time
1 hour
Ingredients
2 mint tea bags
2 tablespoons cornflour
2 teaspoons Hermesetas liquid
  sweetener
A few drops of green food colouring
  (optional)
4 small oranges, peeled and segmented

*Contains ½ tolerated food portion
per person*

Mint tea sundae

Coupe fruitée parfumée au thé

■ **CONSOLIDATION EXCEPT FOR PP THURSDAYS**
■ **STABILIZATION EXCEPT FOR PP THURSDAYS**

Pour 500ml (18fl oz) boiling water over the tea bags and leave to infuse. Use 4 tablespoons of the tea to dissolve the cornflour, then pour this back into the tea infusion. Heat the tea in a pan until it thickens and then add the sweetener and colouring (if using).

Pour the tea into individual dishes and chill for 1 hour.

When ready to serve, arrange the orange segments on top, fanned out in a rosette shape.

Spicy apple compote

Compote de pomme aux épices

2 servings
Preparation time
15 minutes
Cooking time
15 minutes
Ingredients
2 large Golden Delicious apples
4 tablespoons vanilla flavouring
2 pinches grated nutmeg
4 tablespoons skimmed milk
Pinch of grated fresh ginger
4 cloves
Pinch of ground cinnamon

■ **CONSOLIDATION EXCEPT FOR PP THURSDAYS**
■ **STABILIZATION EXCEPT FOR PP THURSDAYS**

Peel and core the apples and cut them into pieces. Place in a pan with 3 tablespoons water and cook, covered, over a gentle heat. Add the vanilla flavouring and nutmeg.

Once the apples have started to soften, stir in the milk along with the grated ginger and cloves. Sprinkle with cinnamon and serve.

4 servings
Preparation time
15 minutes
Cooking time
10 minutes
Refrigeration time
8 hours
Ingredients
4 gelatine leaves
2 vanilla pods
500ml (18fl oz) skimmed milk
4 egg yolks
4 tablespoons Canderel granules
200ml (7fl oz) low-fat cream
   (3% fat)
A little balsamic vinegar
20 fresh raspberries

Vanilla panna cotta, with balsamic syrup and raspberries

Panna cotta vanille, sirop balsamique et petites framboises

■ **CONSOLIDATION EXCEPT FOR PP THURSDAYS**
■ **STABILIZATION EXCEPT FOR PP THURSDAYS**

Soften the gelatine for 5 minutes in a little cold water. Split the vanilla pods, scrape out the seeds and place in a pan with the milk. Bring to the boil.

In a bowl, beat the egg yolks with half the sweetener. Remove the vanilla pods and pour the milk over the egg yolks, stirring all the time. Return the milk to the pan and warm over a low heat, stirring continuously with a wooden spatula, until it is thick enough to coat a spoon.

Remove the pan from the heat and stir in the gelatine. Leave the mixture to cool down to room temperature.

In a large bowl, whisk the single cream with the remaining sweetener. Add the gelatine mixture to the cream and stir thoroughly. Pour into individual non-stick moulds and leave to rest at room temperature before refrigerating for 8 hours.

Turn the panna cottas out of their moulds on to dessert plates and serve drizzled with a little balsamic vinegar and decorated with the raspberries.

6–8 servings
Preparation time
15 minutes
Cooking time
1½ minutes
Ingredients
8 mint leaves
8 tablespoons goji berries
880g (1lb 15oz) cooked couscous
2 teaspoons ground cinnamon
2 tablespoons crystallized stevia
600g (1lb 5oz) creamy fat-free
    yoghurt

*Contains 1 tolerated food portion
per person*

Yoghurt and goji berry couscous pudding

Semoule de couscous au yaourt et aux baies de goji

■ **CONSOLIDATION EXCEPT FOR PP THURSDAYS**
■ **STABILIZATION EXCEPT FOR PP THURSDAYS**

Wash the mint leaves. Leave the goji berries to swell for about 10 minutes in a small bowl of hot water.

In a microwavable dish, mix together the couscous, cinnamon, goji berries and 1 tablespoon of the sweetener. Cook in the microwave for 1½ minutes on maximum.

Add the yoghurt to the couscous and stir it in very thoroughly.

Divide the mixture between four bowls. Top each bowl with 2 mint leaves and sprinkle over the remaining sweetener before serving.

2 servings
Preparation time
10 minutes
Refrigeration time
3 hours
Ingredients
2 peaches
100g (3½oz) fat-free fromage frais
2 teaspoons crystallized stevia
2 egg whites

Peach mousse

Mousse à la pêche

■ **CONSOLIDATION EXCEPT FOR PP THURSDAYS**
■ **STABILIZATION EXCEPT FOR PP THURSDAYS**

Purée the peaches with the fromage frais and sweetener.

Beat the egg whites until stiff and gently fold them into the peach purée.

Refrigerate for 3 hours and serve the mousse well chilled.

INDEX